JUST DOING
MY JOB

STORIES OF SERVICE FROM WORLD WAR II

SANTA
MONICA
PRESS

JUST DOING MY JOB

STORIES OF SERVICE FROM WORLD WAR II

JONNA DOOLITTLE HOPPES
AUTHOR OF *CALCULATED RISK*

Published by:

Santa Monica Press LLC
P.O. Box 1076
Santa Monica, CA 90406-1076
1-800-784-9553
www.santamonicapress.com
books@santamonicapress.com

Printed in the United States

Santa Monica Press books are available at special quantity discounts when purchased in bulk by corporations, organizations, or groups. Please call our Special Sales department at 1-800-784-9553.

ISBN-13 978-1-59580-042-8
ISBN-10 1-59580-042-5

Just doing my job : stories of service from World War II / [compiled] by Jonna Doolittle Hoppes ; foreword by Arthur J. Lichte.
    p. cm.
 ISBN 978-1-59580-042-8
1. World War, 1939-1945—Personal narratives, American. 2. World War, 1939-1945—Biography. I. Hoppes, Jonna Doolittle, 1950-
D736.J865 2009
940.54'8173—dc22
                        2009002307

Cover and interior design and production by Future Studio

940.5481
J

Mixed Sources
Product group from well-managed forests and other controlled sources
www.fsc.org Cert no. SW-COC-002283
© 1996 Forest Stewardship Council

For my dad,

John P. Doolittle

CONTENTS

ACKNOWLEDGMENTS

In many ways this book is truly a collaborative effort. It could not have been written without the support of so many wonderful people. Cindy Woods, my right hand, kept me on track. She read, re-read and then read the whole manuscript again. Sue and John Paul opened the files of the Warhawk Air Museum in Nampa, Idaho, arranged amazing interviews and kept me off the streets while in their beautiful city. Jack Hammett not only shared his story of Pearl Harbor, but also introduced me to members of the Freedom Committee of Orange County, a group of veterans who visit schools and talk about our history with the children. Tom Macia answered endless questions on guns and tanks and bullets and all those details. He was amazingly patient with a novice. Uncle Bob Nightingale kept me flying. I'm sure he's glad it was only on paper, although I still have that gizmo that will earn a real flight in his T-28. Bob Lindsay, as always, provided professional advice and guidance. I don't know what I would do if I couldn't call him every time I had a question. Karen and Steve Hinton, Ed Maloney and the Planes of Fame Air Museum have given the book and me a home away from home. Larry Fuller spent hours reading the manuscript and offering endless encouragement and helpful suggestions. Thank you, Joseph "Ford" Murray, for those wonderful history lessons! You are simply the best! Ginny Stevenson found my opening quote by Goethe. Marie Moramarco sat with me and shared Nick's story. I can only imagine how hard that must have been having so recently lost him. Lt Col Kevin Webb acted as a technical advisor and helped clear the way for General Lichte's foreword. My parents, always supportive, read the manuscript with their red pens in hand—still correcting my grammar and punctuation after all these years! My daughter Shawna took a turn at each story—proofing my work the way I used to proof her homework! Stacy, my technical support on the computer, helped me collect and preserve the photographs. I'm sure she is convinced that her mother is incapable of learning the correct use of our scanner! Steve showed great patience with my constant disappearances—both physical and mental. And thank you to Bonnie Hearn Hill for your rule of 12.

I need to mention here how fortunate I am that my publisher, Jeffrey Goldman of Santa Monica Press, took a risk on a new author when he published my first book. I am indebted to him for his faith, insight and judgment. I also owe a debt of gratitude to Brittany Yudkowsky for her professionalism and skill in editing this book. If she keeps on me, she might even bring me up to speed.

A special thank you goes to the wonderful individuals who shared their stories with us. I stand in awe of their perseverance, loyalty, and contributions to our country. I am so grateful for these new friends.

FOREWORD

by Arthur J. Lichte
General, USAF

President Roosevelt often suggested that the efforts of civilians on the home front, supporting the war through personal sacrifice, were just as critical to winning the war as the efforts of the servicemen themselves. For most during this time period, sacrifice was a daily part of life. Countless people, from all walks of life, contributed to the war effort without ever donning a uniform. The role of women during this period is well documented and symbolized by the likes of Rosie the Riveter. Additionally, this was the era when the Civil Air Patrol and Coast Guard Auxiliary were established. It took a wide range of military personnel and civilians to win the war, and that's what this book is really about.

As an Airman, I'm extremely honored to pay tribute in a small way to all who sacrificed, including some very brave and dedicated Airmen and their families. Our former USAF Chief of Staff often used the phrase "Heritage to Horizons." It's the idea that Airmen have a proud heritage we can call upon as we move toward unlimited horizons. Heroes like the Doolittle Raiders are not only a part of our Air Force heritage—they are our legends. They're our MacArthurs and Pattons, our Nimitzes and Kimmels. It's impossible to overstate their positive effect on the modern Air Force as we continue to support contingency and humanitarian operations around the world. The incredible story of the Doolittle Raiders is one every Airman knows. When pilots Doolittle, Hoover, Gray, Holstrom, Jones, Hallmark, Lawson, York, Watson, Joyce,

Greening, Bower, McElroy, Hilger, Smith, Farrow and the other Raiders flew from the deck of the USS *Hornet* more than 60 years ago, they risked their lives to turn the tide in the Pacific theater—and they were successful. Their mission was the first attack on the Japanese mainland in the war. Not only did they deliver combat power, they boosted American morale. Remember, their mission occurred only four months after Pearl Harbor. The eventual triumph of the Allies was far from certain, but the Raiders certainly set us on the right flight path.

Today, our young Airmen remain inspired by the innovation and courage of their forefathers, dedicated warriors like the Raiders. We are grateful for the freedoms and liberties for which they risked their lives to provide us, and we pledge to preserve the heritage we inherited from them while continuing to protect our nation. We pledge to continue to seek the unlimited horizons ahead of us. Their legacy will continue to inspire not only the Airmen of today but also the Airmen of tomorrow. To all those whose shoulders we stand on—veterans, family members and other civilians who just might be next-door neighbors—we say, "Thank you for your service." Without doubt, the WWII generation possesses great character and honor. This generation stands en masse among great people of character in our history who have answered the call to defend our liberty and freedom. However, character is not just passed on in the genes; it must be taught, studied, nurtured and encouraged.

Accordingly, it is important to not only capture the stories of veterans, but also those who contributed during WWII but didn't serve in the military. Through them, we better understand the sacrifices made by all who have served and continue to serve today. They save us from oppression, push back terrible evils that threaten us and give us the promise of a peaceful tomorrow. The remarkable people mentioned in this book clearly gave to our nation by "just doing their jobs," but they truly gave much more.

Winston Churchill once said, "You make a living by what you get but you make a life by what you give." Giving is a part of the strong character of America and is especially evident in the selfless service of its military. Traditionally, service members have voluntarily given their time, talents, energies, and even their lives to answer our nation's call.

America owes a special thanks to those who were willing to make the ultimate sacrifice for our country. Our entire nation also owes them a debt of gratitude for their inspiration and contributions to the greatest military and finest country in the world.

INTRODUCTION

"Happy is the man who recalls with pride his ancestors, who treasures the story of their greatness, tells the heroic tales of their lives, and, with joy too full for speech, realizes that fate has linked him with a race of goodly men."

—Johann Wolfgang von Goethe

Working on this book has been a great honor, but these are not my stories. I am simply the scribe, bringing to the reader wonderful tales of courage, love, sacrifice and honor. In doing so, my life has been enriched beyond measure. What a privilege to sit with these heroes, to listen to their words and watch their faces as they remember events that ultimately contributed to the Allied victory in World War II and to the people they became.

The stories you are about to read are firsthand accounts of the war years and may differ from what you've heard or read in the past. However, these are the people who were there, members of what we call the "Greatest Generation."

Now I must warn you. Do not call them heroes. They won't let you. Over and over again I heard the phrase, "I was just doing my job." They can get a little testy when you insist.

I will never forget finishing Bob Coates's story of the sea battle off Guadalcanal and waiting for his response. Much to my dismay, he was a little uncomfortable with what I wrote.

"You made me sound like a hero," he explained.

"Bob," I asked, "did I get any of the facts wrong?"

"No."

"Did I capture the battle?"

"Yes."

"And did you stand at your post and perform your assigned duty even though the ship was under direct attack?"

"Yes."

"And is this chapter pretty representative of what your fellow sailors did that night?"

"Yes."

"Well, Bob," I said, "your story represents all the men in that battle. And if the guys in the story sound like heroes, then maybe you were."

And each story was like that. Beginning with an interview and ending with the manuscript bouncing back and forth until the chapter accurately represented personal memories. Images evolved of heroes doing their jobs.

My goal in writing this book is twofold. First, I wanted to introduce the reader to a handful of the Americans who pulled together for the common good. These are the people who sacrificed for the freedom we enjoy today. Some were born in the United States and have always been Americans. Others chose to come here for freedom, love and to pursue the American Dream.

My second goal, and of equal importance, was to preserve a little piece of history—to capture and pass on to our grandchildren's grandchildren the stories of our heritage. So many of the stories have already been lost. If we do not make the effort, more stories will be lost forever. Our World War II veterans are leaving us at an alarming rate and taking their stories with them. How will future generations understand what it means to be Americans? How will those authors writing books and screenplays ever get it right if the stories aren't there for them to use as research? Already two of the people in this book are gone: Nick Moramarco and Bob Johnson.

That brings me to a confession. The writing credit for Bob Johnson's story belongs to Cindy Johnson Woods. When I sent her my draft of his story for editing, she kept it for weeks. What she returned was a beautiful tribute from a daughter to her late father. I wouldn't consider touching a word of Cindy's story for her dad.

In closing I would like to make a request of each and every reader of this book. Please take the time to record your own story. You can visit a museum and participate in the Oral History Project, where DVDs are sent to the Library of Congress. You can write your own book, even if distribution is limited to family members. You can even sit down and pen a letter to your children or grandchildren. Each of our stories is an important part of our heritage.

JACK HAMMETT

―― ∞ ――

NAVY CORPSMAN
IN PEARL HARBOR

The rumble of distant maneuvers woke me, but the sharp knocking on the bedroom door pulled me from my bed. Padding barefoot, clad only in my skivvies, I rubbed the remnants of sleep from my eyes before cracking open the door and peeking around it to view the early morning visitor.

"Rent day."

I mutely translated the landlord's heavily Chinese-accented pidgin into English before turning to my wife for the rent. Thirty-five dollars a month seemed steep for a single room without cooking privileges in the small house shared by two other couples, but it was the going rate in the island paradise of Oahu, and I felt lucky to have it.

Mary Jo retrieved the money from her stash, then ducked back under the covers. Still sleepy from the previous night's music and dancing, she snuggled under the top sheet and thin blanket.

Again, I cracked the door just wide enough to pass the

cash into the landlord's eager hand. But the man's casual re-mark stopped me from closing the door.

"The Japs are bombing Pearl Harbor," he said, much the way one would comment on impending rain.

"What?" I stammered, attempting to process the words. With five short strides, I crossed the foyer and stepped onto the lanai.

Sure enough, all hell had broken loose just 10 miles down the hill.

"Mary Jo, turn on the radio," I called as I surveyed the billowing towers of smoke that clung to the coastline.

"THIS IS NOT A DRILL! THIS IS NOT A DRILL! PEARL HARBOR IS BEING BOMBED BY THE JAPANESE! ALL MILI-TARY PERSONNEL ARE ORDERED TO THEIR COMMANDS IMMEDIATELY!"

Ashen-faced, Mary Jo joined me on the lanai. Within seconds, another explosion sent a ball of fire and smoke hundreds of feet into the air.

Three Japanese fighters, sporting the easily recogniz-able "red meatball" on the underside of their wings, wheeled over the house, skimmed the top of Diamond Head, and then headed back toward the harbor. I watched them with growing alarm.

Two naval destroyers, bow waves washing their iron sides, zigzagged just off shore, dodging geysers of seawater and rocking with the near misses of Japanese bombs.

"What's happening?" asked Frenchy, a fellow sailor stationed at the Sub Base and housemate, as he crossed the foyer from the room he shared with his wife.

"Take a look!" I called back. "Listen to the radio!"

"THIS IS NOT A DRILL! THIS IS NOT A DRILL!"

The announcer's voice trembled with excitement, but I had trouble processing the words. No one thought about be-ing attacked with Japan 4,000 miles away. Surely, the only viable threat to America's neutrality came from Europe, on the other side of the world.

"PEARL HARBOR IS BEING BOMBED BY THE JAPANESE! ALL MILITARY PERSONNEL ARE ORDERED TO RETURN TO THEIR DUTY STATIONS!"

Neither Frenchy nor I wasted another moment. We both threw on the crisp white uniforms of the US Navy, kissed our wives and headed, full speed, out the door.

"Be safe, Jack," Mary Jo called. Later, she would tell people, "I kissed him goodbye and sent him down into a war."

Frenchy and I, running down the stairs and into the street, flagged down a passing pickup truck and piled into the cab.

"Take us to the Army-Navy YMCA," I ordered the Japanese driver as we slammed the door shut. The truck careened down the hill, skidding around corners and sliding through stop signs. Chaos reigned at the taxi stop where Frenchy and I jumped out. Taxis that usually held six passengers and charged 25 cents per person, filled every available space, loading eight or more anxious servicemen before tearing off toward the Hawaiian bases, forgoing their usual fare.

"Where are you going?" I yelled as I darted toward the first cab.

"Hickam!" the driver shouted back.

I passed it by, inquiring of the next driver, "Where are you going?"

"Schofield."

Fighting our way through the chaos, Frenchy and I approached a third cab.

"Where are you going?"

"Pearl Harbor! Pile in!"

The taxi peeled away from the curb and flew through the narrow streets of Honolulu before racing down the two-lane highway that bisected the cane fields stretched between

Waikiki and Pearl Harbor. A second wave of Japanese planes cast shadows across the landscape, strafing anything that moved and dropping ordnance on the crippled ships listing dockside in Battleship Row.

Skidding to a stop at the main gate, Frenchy and I jumped out of the cab. Confusion dominated this scene as well. Dozens of sailors milled around the gate in a state of stunned bewilderment. Heavy gasoline-fueled black smoke filled the air, blotting the sun from the sky.

With a quick wave, I turned left and headed up the road toward the Naval Hospital. Frenchy turned right toward the Submarine Base. Neither of us knew if we would ever meet again. Just as we started off, a Japanese fighter flew low over the field. Tiny, intense dots of scarlet fire erupted from the leading edge of its wings as the pilot strafed the milling crowd. I dove for the ground, still damp from the previous night's rain, and covered my head with my arms. As quickly as the barrage of bullets started, the strafing stopped. Wiping the red Hawaiian mud from my pants, I was amazed to see that no one had been hit. Then I ran like hell.

The hospital resembled a scene from Dante's *Inferno*. Chaos reigned here just as it had in the city and at the gate . . . only here it had turned to carnage. The wards were already overfilled with the injured sailors. The wounded continued to flow in, some walked under their own steam, others supported by friends, and many were carried on stretchers, their bodies mangled.

"Report to the nurses' old quarters," I was told when I reported for duty.

The sights and sounds in the makeshift hospital ward stunned me. The sheer number of casualities that demanded immediate attention refused to penetrate the fog that protected my brain. I stood still, surveying the scene. Everywhere I looked I saw broken bodies—the dead, the dying, some just barely hanging on, others merely stunned . . . all mixed together in a jumble.

The smell of blood, vomit, human excrement, burned skin and singed hair assaulted my nostrils. A cacophony of sounds—the wounded crying out in pain, the soft sobbing of fear, the sharp bark of orders, the moans of dying men—battered my ears. Without equipment, just my hands and the skills I'd developed over the past year, I plunged into the mêlée.

"Keep as many men at as many guns for as many days as possible."

The motto of the Hospital Corps, like a mantra, wove through my befuddled brain. I knelt beside my first patient.

"How you doing, Mac?" I asked.

Feeling for a pulse, I studied the young sailor. Flash burns from the fuel-fed explosions covered the young man's torso and legs, melting scraps of uniform into his once fair skin. Leaning closer, I repeated my question, a little louder this time.

"How you doing, Mac?"

"Leave him alone, Hammett, he's dead." The sharp order penetrated the protective layers of insulation in my head. "Find something to do."

It took a few seconds for me to process the words and realize that there was no pulse beating beneath my fingers. Then, like a machine on autopilot, I started to move throughout the room.

To those in pain, but with sufficient chance of survival, I administered a ½ grain morphine tartrate syrette, and with the patient's own blood, marked an "M" on his forehead. For those in pain, but wounded beyond any viable hope of survival, I administered the morphine and left the forehead unmarked. With great care, I helped move the dying to the lanai, away from the turmoil of triage.

Decisions became automatic for the living casualities. If we thought a sailor could make it, we would administer first aid and put him in the queue for surgery. If we knew the man was going to die, we would move him to the lanai and make him as comfortable as possible.

The train of bodies entering the collection center was endless, and I moved from one patient to another, checking breathing, stopping hemorrhages, treating shock, immobilizing fractures, performing triage for further care and sending them on to surgery or orthopedics or burn wards.

But the cries of the dying touched my soul. "Don't put me in there!" one sailor cried as we moved him to the lanai. The cries of the dying men would echo in my head forever.

After four hours of triage came four hours of identifying the dead.

Form N, the pink Navy death certificate required the name, date of birth, religion, cause of death, circumstances of injury and fingerprints for each decedent. I stared at the form . . . the bodies were maimed and torn apart. Some had no hands, let alone fingers. A few had dog tags; many did not. Name tags clinging to the remnants of uniforms—some borrowed from bunkmates—were an utterly unreliable source of identification.

I filled in what I could, leaving most of the form empty. I covered each card with as many fingerprints as possible—oftentimes only the thumb. Then I stuck the form on the dead man's clothing and carried the body down the narrow flight of stairs into the basement.

The basement became a temporary underground morgue and filled rapidly. Bodies lined the room, heads against the walls, feet edging the narrow aisles. Soon, rows of bodies filled the center of the room, head to head. As the cellar filled and the surface of the floor left no room for more rows, we began to stack the new bodies like cords of wood, layer crossed upon layer crossed upon layer.

The walls of the room absorbed the stench of death and echoed the silence. Soon the fading light from the sun would retreat from the single window and abandon the dead to the engulfing darkness.

There was no time to eat . . . and had I thought about food, it was unlikely I could have eaten. My once white uniform was stained with blood, vomit and human excrement and saturated with my own sweat.

As the December sun slid around the edge of the earth, casting the muted tones of dusk over the island, I left the triage center for the first time since entering that morning and walked the 200 yards to the harbor.

Oil-saturated ash drifted like damp black snowflakes and clung to every visible surface. Standing there, I surveyed the devastation. The USS *Nevada* lay directly across from Hospital Point, her stern in the sugarcane fields and her bow nearly awash in the harbor. Beached by her crew in a final, unselfish act of service, she left the harbor's channel open.

To the right, just off Ford Island, the remnants of the Pacific Fleet's Battleship Row lay smoldering in total ruin. The USS *Oklahoma*, belly up like a beached whale, echoed with the desperate calls of trapped sailors. The Hawaiian sunset, marred by billowing clouds of black smoke, reflected off a restless sea coated with oil and splotched with lingering patches of fuel-fed fires. Motor launches, like colonies of industrious ants, swarmed the channel pulling casualties and bodies from the oily water.

I stood in silent company with doctors, nurses, corpsmen, sailors and civilians, united by the day's events, surveying the devastation. Tears streamed down our weary faces. In a period of one hour and fifty minutes of combat, the world had changed forever. Complete and utter destruction, perpetrated by the nation of Japan on the once believed invincible

Pacific Fleet, had shifted America's heart from isolationism to war. Nothing would ever be the same again.

Heart-heavy but my spirit unbroken, I trudged back to the nurses' old quarters and the triage center. The stream of victims continued to flow in, filling every nook and cranny. Triage duty followed identification of the dead in successive four-hour shifts—a pattern that would continue for the next 72 hours.

Just as the sun surrendered to night's darkness, the sudden staccato echoing of anti-aircraft fire shook the hospital. The rumble of aircraft sounded overhead—and everyone who could dove for cover. With a pounding heart, I ran down the narrow steps into the basement and ducked under the window. From my position, I watched as tracer fire of anti-aircraft guns lit up the sky.

Just as suddenly as it started, the firing stopped.

The silence that followed was complete. Awareness of my circumstances dawned slowly. Believe it or not, I discovered that you can smell death. Alone in the pitch blackness of the basement, I realized that my companions, stacked so carefully in the deteriorating aisles, were all dead. Fear, the companion unrecognized during the endless hours of triage and body identification, made its presence known. And I fled, tripping as I scrambled over the bodies, clawing my way to the narrow staircase and up into the chaos of the triage center. Upstairs, in the light, I had difficulty orienting myself and even breathing. My terror turned into profound sadness when the pilot of a downed plane arrived on a stretcher in the collection room.

"Why did you shoot at me?" he asked as the corpsmen carried him into surgery. His flight suit soaked up the American blood that slowly drained away with his young life.

"Why did you shoot at me?"

The words echoed through the wards and halls and

across the hospital grounds as the first American casualty downed by friendly fire died.

At Pearl, the dead filled the underground morgue and overflowed onto the tennis courts behind the hospital. Navy corpsmen were pulled from triage and reassigned to grave duty. I was one of the first given the new assignment. In the still of night, I helped load 35 bodies onto a five-ton stake truck for delivery to the Nuuanu Cemetery in downtown Honolulu.

Rumors abounded, but there were none we could trust. It was commonly believed that the Japanese had landed somewhere on the island. Blackout rules were strictly enforced and, as I drove through the city of Honolulu, I was unable to see any of the damage or destruction. I worried about Mary Jo. Could she protect herself if the Japanese attacked her? At 17, would she know what to do? Would she be safe?

The truck bounced over the pitted road and into the cemetery. A long trench, dug into the damp earth, waited for the downed Americans. One by one, we gently lowered the men into their common grave.

The bodies were wrapped that night, but not placed in coffins. The sheer number of dead overwhelmed the system. In the following days, privilege followed the officers into death and, whenever possible, their remains were buried in caskets. But the enlisted men received plain wooden boxes built for Hawaii's Japanese population. These boxes were too small for the American sailors, but those on grave duty did what they had to do to make the dead fit into them.

The search for casualties over the next few days turned up fewer and fewer survivors. Soon, efforts focused on the gathering of the dead. Navy corpsmen, on loan from the hospital wards, assisted in the efforts to retrieve floaters: bodies of sailors drowned in the attack, some only recently surfacing from the salty depths. The stench of these bodies was so

extreme, gas masks were required. Many of these bodies were forced into the miniature coffins.

After 72 hours, married men were given a short liberty to check on their wives. With four hours off, I hitched a ride home. Fear mingled with fatigue. In three days so much had happened. I worried about Mary Jo. I hadn't heard anything about or from her. Now, I would see for myself.

The car barely stopped before I jumped out and flew up the front steps. My once white uniform was a mess. Mary Jo insisted I strip and then shooed me into the ancient shower. She stared at my stained uniform before carting it off to the trash. When I climbed out of the shower, she sent me to bed for a couple hours of sleep. I slept soundly for the first time in three days. There was no time for conversation.

Later, I learned about the butcher knife brigade, the wives in our group who had armed themselves with butcher knives for protection against the impending Japanese invasion, and all the other things the women did to protect themselves and their country.

December 7, 1941, pulled Americans together. I would meet professional ladies of the night who volunteered as nurses' aides at the Naval Hospital, working side by side with Navy nurses and corpsmen in the burn wards. Carrying bedpans, helping to debride burn wounds and remove damaged flesh, they performed many unpleasant, but necessary, tasks. Their efforts were selfless and valuable.

I would hear how my wife threatened to report the Japanese grocer to the military police when he closed his store, cutting off the only food supply, but continued to sell goods to his Japanese customers from the back door. The store re-opened.

That afternoon, after far too little rest, I kissed Mary Jo goodbye, thankful for what little time we had to share.

"Be safe," she called after me as I returned to my duties. "I'm proud of you."

"Thanks, honey," I called back. "I'll see you later."

Jack served 23 years in the Navy on active duty. Upon retirement, he moved to Costa Mesa, California, and helped
build Bristol Park Medical, a group practice for physicians.
He also served two terms as mayor of Costa Mesa. Jack
and Mary Jo have four children and six grandchildren.

Decorations and Awards: Navy Commendation with star,
Navy Good Conduct with four stars, Navy Unit Commendation with star, American Defense Service Medal with
star, American Campaign Medal with star, WWII Victory
Medal, Korean Defense Service Medal, National Defense
and Pearl Harbor Survivor's Medal

ELMER "DICK" D. TROXCIL

MARINE ABOARD THE USS *NEVADA*

My name is Elmer Dawe Troxcil. My parents actually gave it to me, but they didn't much approve of it, so they nicknamed me Dick when I was just a baby. And that nickname stuck.

I was born in Omaha, Nebraska, in the rolling hills of the Dissected Till Plains on the edge of the Great Plains where the sky goes on forever. I grew up on a farm in a state landlocked by landlocked states. I didn't see an ocean until I enlisted in the service.

At 18, I decided to join the Navy. My dad took me into Omaha, and when I went to sign up, the Navy doctor checked me out, then asked, "Why are you going into the Navy?"

"Because it's there," I answered.

"Have you ever heard of the Marines?"

"No, sir."

He showed me a picture of a marine in his blues and I fell in love with that uniform.

"That's exactly what I want," I said, and signed up.

My call came in about four days later. It was October 1940. Seven of us from five different states met in Des Moines, Iowa. It took three days to get to California by train. This was before Camp Pendleton. We trained at Camp Elliott, just east of San Diego. After boot camp and basic training, all seven of us signed up for Sea School.

In the end, we were all assigned to sea duty on the USS *Nevada*, a 27,500-ton battleship built in Quincy, Massachusetts, and commissioned in March 1916. A veteran of World War I, the *Nevada* was up in Bremerton, Washington, for repairs. They sent us up on *Nitro*, an old ammunition ship. That in itself was quite a trip. You see, they didn't have a place for us to bunk, so we wrapped ourselves up in blankets and slept on hatch covers, making the best of things. The old ship stopped at every port, taking on ammo or delivering it. The trip took us 18 days. We were aboard for so long that they started issuing us liberty passes so we could get off the ship and explore some of the coastal towns.

The USS *Nevada*'s home port was San Pedro, California. About three weeks after I came aboard, she finished up her business in Washington and steamed down the West Coast to San Pedro. It didn't take long to establish a routine. We would anchor in port on the weekends and head out to sea for patrol or maneuvers during the week.

Eventually, someone decided that the Pacific Fleet would be safer in a single location, so we weighed anchor and headed for Pearl Harbor. We settled into much of the same routine in Pearl. We went out during the week on maneuvers, then headed in on Friday to spend our weekends in port.

The Pacific Fleet battleships rotated duty. Half of the ships were under command of Vice Adm William S. Pye and the other half were under Vice Adm William Halsey Jr. Early in December, Vice Admiral Halsey dashed off with his aircraft carriers to reinforce Wake Island's Marine detachment. The

slower battleships stayed at Pearl. The Navy believed the saf-
est place for our fleet was the harbor, so for the first time since
July 4, 1941, all of our battleships were in port the weekend
of December 6, 1941.

The Marines shared sea duty with the Navy. The way it
works aboard the ship, the Marines have two separate crews,
port and starboard. One crew is on duty while the other is
off. On December 6, 1941, most of the starboard crew went
ashore. I was on port duty, working four to eights. That's four
to eight in the morning and four in the afternoon to eight at
night. My duty station was down in the brig, where a couple
of sailors were locked up. I was relieved around 0745 and went
up to the fantail of the ship to "make colors," the raising of
our flag.

It was one of those perfect Hawaiian mornings. The
sun rose over the harbor, white clouds drifted lazily across
a crystal blue sky and palm fronds rustled in the breeze. All
seven marines on port duty stood in a row, identically dressed
in blue trousers and khaki shirts, field scarves tied loosely
around our necks and white hats on our heads. We stood at
attention, presenting arms, our guns held in front of us perpendicular to the deck. The ship's band played the national
anthem as the Stars and Stripes rose above the fantail of the
USS *Nevada*.

At 0750, the first Kate, the Japanese navy's standard
torpedo bomber, passed over our ship, strafing the deck about
six or eight inches from our feet. Bullets ripped into the teak
and splinters hit our legs. We were trained to remain motionless during the national anthem and we stood at attention
for those last few seconds until the final note. Then we broke
ranks and ran. Our rifles clattered to the wooden deck as we
scrambled for our assigned positions on the big guns.

My general quarters, or assigned battle station, was a
machine gun on the main mast. I climbed up the ladder in-

side the tripod, a tube about three feet in diameter that runs up alongside of the mast, and out onto the birdbath, the platform where my machine gun was housed. I could hear the bullets from the Japanese planes hit the cowling around my gun. We opened fire at about 0802.

We didn't have time to think. Thinking would come later as we tried to account for the missing. Instinct and training took over. Each man did what he was trained to do when our reality was only a simulated attack. This training saved many of our lives.

The *Nevada* was the last in line at Battleship Row, moored at quay F-8, just aft of the USS *Arizona*. At 0806, an armor-piercing bomb hit the *Arizona*. It ignited the forward ammunition compartment. The massive explosion blew the ship apart. A blast of fire-fueled heat swept through the harbor, scorching the perch on the main mast. The shock from the explosion sent the *Nevada*'s bow 10 or 15 feet out of the water. At first, everything seemed to stop, our ship almost perpendicular to the water. I wondered if she would roll over, but she didn't. The *Arizona*, on the other hand, sank in a matter of minutes. She disappeared with Rear Adm Isaac C. Kidd and 1,177 of her sailors on board.

At 0810, a Japanese torpedo exploded against the *Nevada,* ripping into our port side about 14 feet above the keel. I got the Kate that dropped it. Shot her out of the sky. She crashed down about a hundred yards off our port side. Got another one, too. I'm pretty sure it was the one that hit the *Oklahoma*.

Moments later, a second bomb hit the *Nevada*, striking next to the #7 casement that shielded the big guns. The explosion blew into the galley and cut through our water lines. Without them, my water-cooled machine gun would not fire. After a couple of minutes of trying to restart my gun, I climbed back into the tripod, down the ladder and reported to the #7 broadside battery.

The bomb that severed the water line hit #7. Four of the five men manning the five-inch guns were blown off the ship. Only First Sergeant Inks was left. At first, I tried to help the first sergeant man the gun, but the damage made firing impossible. I climbed out through the casement onto the catwalk and began helping pass wounded sailors and bodies from the catwalk and deck back into the ship. There was this one fellow, he was just destroyed. But we got him inside and the corpsmen saved his life.

In port, there is always a battleship designated as a standby and ready to move out in a hurry. The *Nevada* was on standby that morning with her boilers running at half power. I doubt there was a crew in Pearl that didn't fantasize about firing up and shoving off. But the *Nevada* was the only battleship to make a run for it. The quartermaster called for the crew to break loose from our mooring. At 0840, we got underway. She backed clear of her berth without help from the tugs and began to steam down the channel.

The second wave of Japanese planes was mostly high-altitude bombers wheeling above Pearl. Spotting our run for open waters, they made us their primary target. If they hit us just right, we'd sink and block the harbor. Like a cork in a bottle, we would trap the rest of the fleet.

The Japanese must have dropped somewhere between 50 to 75 bombs on us that morning. Waterspouts rose up on both sides of the ship like geysers as she steamed through the harbor. It's a funny thing what you record in your mind when faced with such a dire situation. We took seven bombs in a row. I counted each one.

Some caused more damage than others. The port director's platform took a direct hit. The bomb exploded at the base of the stack on the upper deck. The #1 turret was hit, blowing large holes in the upper and main decks. Two bombs hit the forecastle. One exploded near the gasoline tank. Leaks and fumes fueled the fires. The bombs kept falling.

The damage mounted, and our run for it came to an end. Fires burned on the decks. Water leaked into the hull. Our junior officers were young and they still hoped to stay in the fight. They steered her toward the shore and the soft bottom on the west side of Ford Island.

But fearing that the ship would settle too far into the soft sand, she was ordered to reverse. Two tugs, the *Hoga* and *Avocet*, came alongside and guided her to the peninsula. We ran her aground, stern first, the bow eventually settling in the shallow water off Hospital Point.

The Japanese kept bombing for another 15 or 20 minutes. Since we were beached, we were no longer a target. We swarmed the deck to help our injured crewmates and we moved the bodies below. Fumes filled my lungs and burned my eyes. Standing on the deck with my khaki shirt stuck to my body, I noticed clouds of black oil-fed smoke billow into the sky, blotting out the sun. The perfect Hawaiian day had indeed turned dark.

We fought fires from bow to stern. I could smell the burnt paint, and it took us until noon to put them out. Devastation lay in every direction. We lost 60 men from the *Nevada* and 109 more were wounded.

The *Arizona*, *California*, *West Virginia* and *Oglala* sank at their berths. The *Oklahoma* and *Utah* capsized with members of their crews trapped inside. The *Maryland*, *Pennsylvania*, *Tennessee*, *Shaw*, *Cassin* and *Downes* were badly damaged. Everywhere I turned there were fires. Even the surface of the water burned. In all, 2,350 men were killed and 1,178 were injured.

They transferred the Navy, leaving only a skeleton crew aboard the *Nevada*. The surviving marines stayed aboard. We spent our days cleaning the decks and salvaging what we could. I don't remember where the food came from, but we did eat. Sometimes sandwiches, sometimes bowls of beans. And I don't remember where we slept, someplace on the deck. It was quiet and lonely. But we stayed with the old girl.

In March, the Navy decided to salvage the *Nevada*. They made a huge steel patch and tacked it onto the gaping hole in the port bow. In order to raise her, the stagnant water in her holds needed to be pumped out. Three of us volunteered to go down and keep the pumps clear. The water was rancid, oil-slicked and filled with stuff: items from the lockers, bits of clothing and decaying body parts. We had to dive down and keep the crud from clogging the pumps.

The salvage officer treated us really well during this time. At the end of each day, he took us over to the Navy barracks and let us take hot showers. They fed us a hot meal, then delivered us to the Royal Hawaiian Hotel. We spent our nights at the hotel, waking up to a hot breakfast before returning to the dark holds of the ship.

It took about a week to clean her up. After they raised her, she was hauled over to dry dock. Her engines needed cleaning, but otherwise they were functional. It wasn't long before we left, under our own steam, for Bremerton, Washington. The crossing was uneventful, the weather pleasant.

They completely rebuilt her in Bremerton, took everything down to the main deck. Her dual masts were replaced with a single mast and she was entirely restructured. They took off all the old guns. We had never had any 20 mm guns or anything like that, but the rebuilt *Nevada* had 20s, 30s, and the new anti-aircraft guns. They even replaced the balls on the 16-inch guns. It took eight or nine months to do and we marines stayed with her.

We got to know the Olympic Peninsula during our time in Washington. My buddy, Johnny Bagly, was dating Mary Jane, a local girl. They figured I might like her friend

Ethelyn—Ethelyn "Tooty" Illene.

"You've got to meet Tooty," Johnny told me.

I agreed to meet up with Johnny, Mary Jane and Tooty at the Craven Center, a ballroom and bar that catered to the troops during the war.

Well, after two or three dances, it was clear that Tooty and I weren't hitting it off. I wasn't much of a talker and I didn't dance all that well. Couldn't see much reason in staying around.

A group of marines decided to take off for the Blue Moon, a bar where some of our friends had been badly beaten the week before by some local boys. We started a brawl and it wasn't long before the shore patrol picked us up. I knew most of the guys on duty that night and the captain was a friend of mine. About the time they were loading us up for the trip back to town, Johnny and the girls showed up.

"Can they ride back to town with us?" I asked the captain. He agreed to let them.

I'm not sure what changed on that trip, but from that point on, Tooty and I were inseparable. Her family was Coast Guard. When I asked her father, a captain in the Coast Guard, for her hand in marriage, he tried to discourage us.

"You're infatuated now," he said, "but you don't know how you'll feel in two years."

He'd had a less-than-happy wartime first marriage and he didn't want to see the same thing happen to his daughter. Tooty and I discussed it, but both of us felt the same way. I knew my time in Washington was growing short. The USS *Nevada* would soon return to duty. And my sea duty was almost up, so I would soon be assigned to a ground unit in the Marine Corps. Pearl Harbor underscored our mortality. We wanted whatever happiness we could grab.

Thirty days after we first met, Tooty's father took us down to the courthouse and witnessed our vows. He then took us out to dinner. I couldn't have asked for better in-laws. And my folks loved Tooty.

Time slipped away, and the *Nevada* was soon ready for her sea trial. The shakedown cruise found a few problems and they added three weeks to our stay in Washington. But eventually, she was seaworthy and we shoved off for San Pedro.

We hit a storm on the way down. Almost like a typhoon, waves swept the decks, forcing everyone to stay below. Somebody had to be on buoy watch and I drew the short straw. They tied me to the top turret and handed me a bullhorn. My job was to tell anyone who ventured out on deck to "get the hell back inside."

By the time we made it back to San Pedro, my two-year sea duty was up. I spent some time at Camp Elliott as a drill sergeant before I was shipped off to the Pacific. I went through all the islands: Nouméa, New Caledonia; Banika, Russell Islands; Guadalcanal; Kwajalein; Eniwetok; and Guam. I've never liked talking about my experiences on the beaches of the Pacific. Maybe someday I'll tell those stories, but not today.

We were scheduled to be part of that first invasion of Japan. We had everything loaded and were waiting when they dropped that first atom bomb on Hiroshima. I was in the first wave. We assumed we would lose at least two waves before securing a foothold on the islands of Japan. They projected losses on both sides into the millions. Can't say I'm sorry we dropped those bombs.

Having gone into the Navy before the war started, and having spent as much time overseas as I had, gave me all the points in the world.[1] But I was one of the last to come home. I

---

1 The Advanced Service Rating Score was a system that awarded points to servicemen based on their length of service, number of months spent overseas, awards, and number of children (up to three). The total score was used to determine when a serviceman would be sent home.

had four years in just before we hit Guam and I thought "This war is going on for ages." So I extended for two years. About six or eight months later, the war was over. When I got back to the States, I still had a year to go, so they sent me to the San Diego recruit depot as a drill instructor.

The USS *Nevada* continued to see service during WWII. They sent her to Norfolk Naval Shipyard for further modernization, and then assigned her to convoys in the Atlantic. She saw duty in the Normandy invasion and in Operation Dragoon in the south of France.

They sent her to New York for repairs, then she made her way to the Pacific, where she supported our troops in Iwo Jima and Okinawa.

After the war, the *Nevada* became the target ship for the first Bikini atomic experiments. She was designated ground zero. Both "Able" and "Baker" missed her, but they left her damaged and extremely radioactive. On August 29, 1946, she was decommissioned.

Her final sortie came on July 31, 1948. Used as a gunnery target for three Navy ships, the USS *Nevada* was finally sunk by a US aerial torpedo. She rests 65 miles southwest of Pearl Harbor.

I loved the Marine Corps and would have stayed in. But I was a bit of a hothead as a kid. I made corporal three times and sergeant once. It would have taken four years to make another rank. But I was married now.

And it was a good marriage. Despite her father's concerns, Tooty and I were married for 54 years. I still love the Marines and, in my heart, I'll always be one.

After leaving the service, Dick drove a truck for Safeway Stores, Inc., for 32 years. He retired in 1978 and moved to Kingman, Arizona. He returned to California in 1990. Dick and Tooty have three children and eight grandchildren.

Decorations and Awards: Commendation, Appreciation of Service Medal presented by Brigadier General L.C. Shepherd

ROBERT "BOBBY" L. HITE

————✦————

DOOLITTLE RAIDER
AND JAPANESE POW

There are some days when Lady Luck smiles on you and others when she turns her back and abandons you to your fate. Sometimes, it's only through that peculiar perspective of hindsight that you can determine the difference.

My B-25 needed spark plugs. By the time I landed in Alameda, California, Lt Col Jimmy Doolittle was loading the last of 16 bombers onto the aircraft carrier USS *Hornet*. My plane would not make it on board. My crew would go as surplus crew members.

I think we all had some idea of the mission, but when they announced it over the *Hornet*'s loudspeakers—THIS TASK FORCE IS BOUND FOR TOKYO— I didn't completely share in the jubilation. After all, I wouldn't be one of the 80 men who bombed Tokyo in retaliation for the Japanese attack on Pearl Harbor.

I couldn't believe my luck when Bill Farrow approached me on April 16, 1942. He had a falling out with his copilot and had a proposition for me.

"Bobby, will you go with me?"

"Well yes, if you ask me to go, I will," I said, my heart jumping at the possibility. "I'll go as your gunner, your engineer, anything!"

"I need a copilot," Bill said.

Two days later, an urgent announcement rang out over the USS *Hornet*'s loudspeakers.

"ARMY PILOTS—MAN YOUR PLANES!"

We scrambled for the B-25s lashed to the bucking decks of America's newest aircraft carrier. Our task force had been spotted 250 miles farther off the coast of Japan than the scheduled launch. We would take off a day early with a critical shortage of fuel.

I climbed into the copilot's seat next to Bill. We ran through the checklist while our navigator, Lt George Barr, rechecked the flight plan. Sergeant Harold Spatz loaded our gear. Our plane, the *Bat Out of Hell*, had her tail stuck out over the keel of the ship.

"Do you know how to row a boat?" Farrow yelled out the window to Cpl Jacob "Jake" DeShazer as the bombardier completed a last minute check on the four incendiary bombs loaded into the *Bat*'s belly. There was a very good chance that none of the planes would make the coast of China but no one was saying it out loud.

I watched the first plane, piloted by Doolittle, lift off the carrier deck with room to spare. Just barely four months after the Japanese attack on Pearl Harbor, a joint Army-Navy strike force would drop bombs on major military targets in Japan, forever dispelling the Japanese myth of divine protection.

One hundred and fifty dollars richer than when I boarded the *Hornet* just over two weeks earlier, I hoped to live long enough to enjoy the rewards of a few well-played hands of poker. The Navy boys, at first unhappy about what they believed was a mission to ferry Army planes to Hawaii, rejoiced with the announcement of the imminent attack on Japan— but still played a mean hand of poker.

Waves crashed over the bow of the *Hornet* and swept the deck with sheets of icy water. Navy deckhands fought to keep their footing while they manually maneuvered the planes into position. With the nose wheel lined up on the center line, the B-25s had six feet of clearance between the right wing tip and the carrier's island and six feet between the outer edge of the left wheel and the drop-off edge of the flight deck.

I looked back from the cockpit into the fuselage. Our B-25s were stripped down to minimize their weight, but they carried two rubber bladders filled with gasoline, four 500-pound bombs and five crew members. At take-off, the *Bat* was 31,000 pounds of bombs, gasoline and men rolling down the plunging deck on the downward pitch then lifting into stormy skies with the upswing of the bow.

I ran another check of the instruments as the planes continued one successful take-off after another. A particularly savage burst of wind lifted the nose of the *Bat* off the deck, dipping her tail toward the water. Sailors, slipping on the wet decks and fighting the wind, swarmed around our plane, every available man grabbing a handhold on the nose and front wheel and, with sheer determination, held her steady as Farrow revved then idled the engines. I marveled at the agility and tenacity of the Navy men then recoiled in horror as the blast from Doc Watson's engines blew Robert W. Hall into the *Bat's* propeller. Within seconds the blade chewed into the young sailor's arm then spit him into a bloody heap on the deck. The image and uncertainty of his fate haunted me as the *Bat* took position and lifted skyward on the run to Japan.

Flying low over the Pacific, I contemplated Doolittle's final lecture.

"You are to bomb military targets only and, whatever you do, stay away from the Imperial Palace."

The crews drew straws to decide which plane would have the honor of targeting the emperor's home, but Doolittle remained adamant.

"Bombing military targets is an act of strategic warfare, but hitting the 'Temple of Heaven' or other non-military targets such as hospitals or schools would be interpreted as an inexcusable barbarian act. It could mean your life if captured."

"Besides," Doolittle told us," It isn't worth a plane factory, a shipyard, or an oil refinery, so leave it alone!"

We flew low, barely skimming the water's surface a mere 100 feet off the deck. We were tempted by the sight of a lone Japanese aircraft carrier but resisted the urge to sink it and flew on to our targets in Nagoya. The last of 16 planes, I knew everyone on the island would be looking for us. Every member of our crew searched the skies for enemy aircraft. As we approached Nagoya, George Barr spotted three fighters above and to the right. Farrow, knowing the B25 could not outrun the fighters, pulled up into the scattered clouds to avoid detection.

The horizon was speckled with flak and anti-aircraft fire exploded around us as we approached Nagoya. Within a short time our first target, a battery of oil storage tanks, came into view. Farrow pulled up over the target and Jake DeShazer let the first bomb fly. A successful hit!

We flew on to our primary target. With three direct hits on the aircraft factory, we headed across the bay. Men, women and children waved as we hedgehopped over the picturesque valley that led to Osaka. When we reached the city, Farrow changed headings to a more southerly direction and flew toward the southern tip of Kyushu. Just as we passed through the narrow straits by Kyushu, George Barr spotted two of our planes.

"Must be Hilger and Smith," George said, pointing out the two American bombers.

The planes, skimming low over the water, roared toward the China Sea where one promptly peeled off in a northerly direction and the other turned south. George decided to split the difference and chose a route up the center. The hours dragged on and we shivered with the constant cold. The increasing storm stirred the sea and strong winds buffeted the plane. The *Bat*'s prop struck a wave top and Farrow fought to maintain control. Flying required the pilot's full attention and we passed the controls between us. Midway over the China Sea, the weather worsened, water spouts sprang from the surface of the water, forcing the plane to seek the relative safety of a higher altitude. With growing concern, we checked the dwindling fuel supply.

George presented the alternatives. We could continue at this speed and reach landfall after dark and then proceed on dead reckoning toward Chuchow, or speed up, burning our precious fuel but allowing for a visual fix when we crossed the coastline. Both options deserved consideration, but Farrow and I decided to continue at our present speed and take our chances with the encroaching darkness. We made landfall as night fell and climbed to 11,000 feet, above the turbulent weather, to clear the mountains. The gages indicated another 40 gallons of gasoline remained. George urged us to change course and fly west for 15 minutes then alter our heading to a southerly direction in hopes of avoiding Japanese patrols. But the lure of a possible safe landing and a pilot's natural instinct to protect his crew and plane enticed Bill and me. We decided to continue in a southwesterly direction.

Favorable tail winds blew the *Bat* well past the Chinese coast and into the interior. Still flying above the storm, we searched for a hole in the cloud cover. My heart sank when George spotted Nanchang. The gasoline supplies exhausted, we would bail out in Japanese-occupied territory.

Fuel-starved engines coughed and sputtered. One by one, starting with Spatz and quickly followed by DeShazer and Barr, we jumped into the unknown. Bill and I were the last to bail out.

Ebony skies surrounded me as I lowered myself through the hatch in the navigator's compartment. "One, two, three," I counted, and then on to ten before pulling the ripcord. The parachute filled with air, jerking my body upward before allowing it to sway in the harness. Away from the constant drone of the B25's engines, I listened to the absolute lack of sound. Even with the raging storm silence engulfed me.

"It's so quiet," I thought. "You can hear a mouse piss on a cotton ball!" I smiled at the irreverent image.

I continued to drift, floating in darkness so thick that judging a landing proved impossible. My contact with the ground, although expected, seemed sudden, jarring my entire body. One foot landed on a levee, viciously twisting my ankle, the other sank into a rice paddy. The water, saturated with "night soil," crept up my thigh and soaked through to my skin. Remembering Doc White's lectures on the Japanese use of human excrement as fertilizer, I cringed and tentatively sniffed the air. At least the smell wasn't overpowering . . . yet.

With great effort, I pulled my foot free from the muck and, limping on my injured ankle, hobbled across the levee to the road. Rain pelted my flight jacket and my shoes, manure soaked and squishy, rubbed my socks against the cold skin of my feet.

The storm clouds, spitting rain, covered the stars, leaving the uneven road nearly impossible to navigate. Stiff winds, pregnant with raindrops, battered my hunched form and crept under my flight jacket, saturating my uniform all the way down to my skin. Dry clothes, hot coffee and a warm bed sounded really good.

Shivering from cold, I searched for shelter. Graves in a cemetery offered the only possibility, so I tucked myself flat against a mound, on the down side of the wind, and attempted to close my eyes. My wet clothes clung to my shivering body. I forced my icy fingers into sodden pockets. Sleep, greatly needed, eluded me.

The hours ticked by slowly and the day broke cold but dry. Stiff from the long night, I found my way back to the road. A farmhouse stood alone in the middle of rice paddies. Three young children played in the yard. Counting on the fact that the Japanese troops occupying China would not bring their children and on the hatred that the Chinese must feel toward their oppressors, I approached the youngsters.

"*Lushu hoo megwa fugi!*" I called out. "I am an American!"

Reaching into my knee pocket, I pulled out three coins and passed one to each child. "*Lushu hoo megwa fugi!*" I repeated the phrase all the Raiders learned aboard the USS *Hornet*, hoping the children understood. I followed my peace offering with chocolate. The children chattered among themselves, their voices soft and lilting.

Within minutes the farmer and his wife joined us. I reached into my knee pocket again, this time pulling out a pack of Lucky Strikes. "*Lushu hoo megwa fugi!*" I said with a slight nod and a tentative smile.

"American," I said pointing to my chest. "I need to go to Chochung."

With a slight bow, the farmer accepted the cigarettes then motioned for me to follow. Puddles from the night's rain pooled in the uneven road. Clothes, still damp from the storm, chafed as I followed the farmer. Eventually, we stopped in front of a small house with a soldier standing in the yard. I didn't recognize the uniform, and with the naiveté of a young man, I trusted the Chinese farmer.

I couldn't understand the rapid, soft-spoken exchange between the soldier and the farmer. My only hope was that they would help me find my crew and then help us escape. I stood quietly and waited. With curt gestures, the soldier told me to follow him. He led me down a path toward a small building.

The soldier wordlessly indicated for me to wait there, then disappeared.

The wait wasn't long. I saw them come from behind the building, but it took time for my fatigued mind to process. A dozen soldiers with rifles surrounded me. Twelve bayonets pointed directly at my chest. Hope fled and my spirits sank. These were not friendly Chinese. With odds of twelve to one, escape was impossible. Lt Robert L. Hite was now a prisoner of war. And, I soon learned, so were the rest of my crew.

The interrogations began almost immediately. Handcuffed with four guards stationed outside my solitary cell, I waited for my turn in the large, almost bare room. It came soon enough. I faced a dozen officers and an interpreter. Name. Rank. Serial number. The only information required under the Geneva Convention, this mirrored the information offered by the other crew members from the *Bat Out of Hell*. This infuriated our Japanese captors.

The random nature of questions reassured me. Obviously the Japanese knew nothing of our raid on Tokyo. I wondered how long before the news would spread from Japan to occupied China, and what the Japanese would do if they figured out that we were five of the airmen flying those bombers.

Threatened with dire warnings of instant death if any of us tried to escape, we were blindfolded and handcuffed, and then led to a 1938 Ford truck. The truck bounced along the rutted roads, jostling the occupants. I could see under the edge of my blindfold, so I peeked out. I spotted a plane that closely resembled an American DC-3. Two rows of seats lined one side of the aircraft while a single row lined the other. Handcuffed to seats, four guards assigned to each of us, there was little chance that we could take over the plane and fly to safety . . . although I knew the thought passed through each crew member's mind.

The ancient city of Shanghai lay like a tarnished gem overrun with Japanese soldiers on the eastern coast of China. Five four-door 1938 Ford sedans waited on the edge of the airstrip. One prisoner per car, they sandwiched us in the back seats between two guards, another two guards in the front seat of each car. We sped through the deeply rutted streets. Again I peeked out from under my blindfold. I saw children and dogs scamper out of the path of our speeding car. The incessant blowing of horns added to the air of confusion.

Conditions worsened for us in Shanghai. Placed again in solitary confinement, I sat cross-legged in the center of my cell. My ankle throbbed and the mingled odors from the now pungent "night soil" and my own sweat assaulted my nostrils. My stomach growled with hunger and I pushed thoughts of food away. Weary from lack of sleep, my eyes grew heavy and my head began to slump forward.

I immediately awoke to shouting. The boisterous Japanese guard rattled the cell door, his face against the barred window. The foreign words escaped me, but not their meaning. We would not be allowed to sleep. I shivered in spite of the heavy flight jacket. Cold and hungry, my only companion was fear.

The evening grew dark outside, but a single bulb burned brightly in the center of my cell. A Japanese guard brought a cheese sandwich and a cup of tea. Famished, I gobbled it down. I couldn't remember the last time something tasted so good. Sensing a change in the treatment, I curled up into a ball, cradled my head on my arm and fell into a deep but temporary sleep.

Startled by the slamming of the door against the wall, I awoke to find four guards standing over me. Without warning, they jerked to my feet and hustled me out of the cell. In the deep quiet of the middle of the night, armed guards half dragged, half pushed me across an open courtyard and up three flights of stairs in a large building.

By the time I stood in front of the Japanese interrogators, all hope of concealing my participation in the raid on Tokyo evaporated. The officer in charge held a complete list of airmen from the 16 crews. They asked about Jimmy Doolittle. They asked about the *Hornet*. I gave them my name, rank and serial number, then, in a streak of genius, and unknowingly corroborating similar claims by my crewmates, told them the planes had come from the Aleutians. For once, the Japanese seemed satisfied. I returned to the cold, lonely cell.

The next morning we were on the move again. Blindfolded and handcuffed, we climbed back on the plane and, within a short time, were airborne. Even though conversation was forbidden, I found solace in the company of my crewmates. We faced the unknown, but we faced it together. When the plane began its descent, I peeked under my blindfold. The sprawling city of Tokyo awaited our return, this time as prisoners of war.

There is an international code dealing with the etiquette of combat, and I fully expected the Japanese to respect the global laws of warfare. But history is riddled with man's inhumanity to man. Innocence was a casualty of war that dark night in Tokyo and our belief in justice died a slow, painful death over the next few months.

The *Kempei Tai* perfected the science of torture. Starved, blindfolded, handcuffed, stripped and beaten, we continued to resist our captors. But in the hands of the *Kempei Tai* sadism evolved into an art form. Interrogations took place around the clock, every two to three hours. Deprived of sleep, subjected to finger torture where sharp sticks were jammed between our fingers and our bound hands were squeezed together by one guard while another slid the sticks back and forth—dislodging our knuckles and splitting skin— and forced to kneel with a bamboo pole placed behind our knees while a guard jumped on our thighs, painfully pulling our knees apart, the mistreatment wore us down.

I fought the urge to talk; the one thing I knew would stop the torture. But my tormentors refused to give up. Pinned to the ground with my hands bound behind my back, I continued to resist. Undeterred, one guard sat on my legs and another on my stomach, while a third, sitting on the ground, pinned my head between strong thighs. They placed a towel over my face, and formed a cup-like pocket over my mouth and nose. I tried to hold my breath when the bucket of water hit my face and pooled in the towel cup. Sputtering, I held out as long as possible before losing consciousness, drowning in the onslaught of water, I gave into the darkness . . . only to be revived by the guard applying pressure to my lungs and abdomen. As soon as my breathing returned to normal, the process started over again, and again.

The questions never stopped. It became clear that the Japanese had most of the answers and were simply looking for confirmation. Weak from lack of sleep, dysentery and starvation, and consumed with a burning anger, I tried to give them logical, false answers that led to dead ends. Any answer unacceptable to my captors resulted in kicks to my shins and blows to my head and body. Certain that I couldn't withstand much more, I spent endless hours between interrogations in my solitary cell worrying about my mother and sister and wondering about the welfare of my crewmates, the fate of the hapless sailor who fell into the *Bat's* prop, and the whereabouts of Doolittle and the other Raiders.

We were not alone. Three other Doolittle Raiders, Lt Dean Hallmark, Lt Robert Meder and Lt Chase Nielson, had been captured and shared the weeks of interrogation and torture. Around the clock we were questioned about the raid, our training, and the United States in general, and then suddenly the weeks of solitary confinement ended. I shared a cell with George Barr and even though we had not been allowed to change, bathe or shave in over 60 days, and the sour odor from our unwashed bodies, long matted hair and beards was overpowering, just being together lifted my spirits and reaffirmed my resolve. George and I huddled together in the dark, airless cell comparing notes on our treatment, discussing the red herrings offered to our interrogators and simply appreciating the company of another human being.

Fed nothing more than six slices of bread and hot tea each day, we suffered from malnutrition and dysentery. The *benjo*, an open hole cut in the floor for the toilet, stank and attracted a number of flying insects and scurrying rodents. But for the first time since our capture, we were allowed to sleep at night, although the interrogations continued throughout the day.

In early June, they led me to the interrogation room and told me to sit at a table. The interpreter pushed a stack of papers in front of me and handed me a pen.

I stared at the paper. The pages were filled with Japanese characters. I couldn't understand a single word. It was obvious that the Japanese expected me to sign.

"What is it?" I asked.

"A confession," the interpreter replied. "If you refuse to sign, you will be executed in the morning."

Believing it to be a transcript of my answers to the long hours of questioning, I signed. When the last of the eight captured Raiders signed what turned out to be a confession to acts of unprovoked and untrue brutal war crimes, all interrogations ceased.

On July 15, 1942, the guards returned my shoes and socks. Pulling them on, I joined the others in the prison courtyard. The Japanese took a series of photographs, then placed blindfolds on our eyes and cuffs on our arms and legs, and loaded us into a Chevrolet and three Fords. We were driven to the railway station and hustled onto a train.

The return trip to Shanghai took the better part of a week. We traveled by train, ferry and freighter. We spent our time locked in small, hot, airless, stinking cells and with guards posted outside our cell at all times.

The accommodations in Shanghai were horrific. The prison was located in the Bridge House, a former British hotel. Our cell was a 10x15-foot room that we shared with about 30 other people. A Chinese man, dying from dysentery, was the only person with room to lie down. Three women huddled in the corner. I noticed that the other prisoners wore rags and most were covered with open sores or weeping scabs.

The *benjo* overflowed, adding its peculiar stench to that of unwashed bodies and putrid infection. At least I found comfort in being with the other Raiders.

Meals consisted of bowls of yellow, watery rice mixed with pebbles, worms, maggots and dirt. At first we turned the food down, passing it into the eager hands of the Chinese prisoners.

"We'll die if we don't eat anything," Chase said one morning. "I don't know about you guys, but I intend to stay alive and someday tell the world what the Japs have done to us!"

"At least they have a little fat on them," I said, inspecting a wriggling maggot before popping it into my mouth. The others agreed and grudgingly ate the meager fare.

After three days, the other prisoners were removed from the cell, and, at last, we could stretch out on the floor.

It was impossible to ignore the lice that bred in our body hair. Relentless scratching reopened wounds. But the bugs were the least of our problems. Armies of rats moved about the cell during the night. We all took turns standing guard while the others slept.

The time together was a healing tonic. Although the guards would shout and bang on the door when they caught us talking, not one of them seemed brave enough to enter the cell. Bolstered by the fear exhibited by the guards, we freely exchanged stories.

George Barr had been orphaned as a young child and grew up in a home for boys. He wanted to teach high school after the war.

Jake DeShazer had grown up on a farm and loved hunting and fishing. His father was a lay minister and wanted Jake to study the Bible. But Jake wasn't interested.

Bill Farrow talked about his fiancée and his plans to marry her as soon as he got back to South Carolina. Thoughts of her kept him going.

Dean Hallmark came from Texas, just like I did. He loved flying and planned to stay in the service.

Bob Meder was the intellect of the group. He shared stories of his home in Ohio and kept us going when times got tough.

Chase Nielson wanted to stay in the service, but even more, he wanted to punish the Japanese for their cruel treatment. I think his anger kept him going.

And Harold Spatz, who was the youngest of the group, worked as hard as he played.

I looked around at the men who shared my fate and wondered if any of us would survive imprisonment. Insufficient food and sleep took its toll. My temper grew short. I was impatient with my cellmates and even more impatient with the guards.

"*Kurah!*" the guard yelled through the barred slot near the top of the locked door. "No talking!"

"Blow it out your barrack bag!" I yelled back, smashing my fist against the small window.

Almost instantly the door flew open and a Japanese officer rushed into the cell brandishing his sword. Swinging wildly, he slashed me with the scabbard.

Blood ran down the side of my head onto my face. Almost four months of torture and confinement sent me into a blind rage. Impulsively, I grabbed the scabbard and wrenched it away from the officer.

The bare blade of the sword glistened in the dim light, the point inches from my belly. Everyone held their breath as my eyes met and held the guard's. I'd finally had enough.

Time stood still as an unspoken agreement swept through the room. The Japanese officer might take me out, but not without a fight. Bill Farrow stepped forward next to me. Slouching like collegiate wrestlers, we faced the Japanese officer.

Sensing the danger, he lowered his sword and backed away. The tentative truce held and a newfound respect for the American prisoners swept through Bridge House. Our meals, for a limited period of time, improved. When it returned to watery rice and tea, I decided to take my winnings from the poker games on the USS *Hornet* and see if we could bribe the guards.

"We want good food, baths and haircuts," I told the guard as I passed him the roll of bills. Our wish list was granted.

I couldn't believe the velvety feel of the water or the soap against my bare skin. Already the tub had been drained and refilled. Still a layer of scum, black with lice, coated the water. I was halfway through my second cake of soap when I reluctantly climbed out of the tub. Dressed in new clothes, my hair shaved and beard clipped, I felt like a new man.

My mouth watered as I eyed the steak, fresh vegetables, strawberry jam and French bread. It almost rivaled my mother's Texas cooking. I knew the money wouldn't last, but I planned to enjoy every bite of good food while it did.

Within hours of the feast, Dean Hallmark developed a stomachache. Leaning over the *benjo*, he vomited until only bile was left. His temperature shot up and his muscles grew too weak to support his body.

We took turns helping him to the *benjo*. We gathered our jackets into a pallet bed. I supported Dean's head in my lap.

"Sing 'Stardust,'" Dean asked.

"And now the purple dust of twilight time," I sang softly, "steals across the meadows of my heart."

"Sing it again," Dean requested when the last fragile note faded.

"Sometimes I wonder why I spend the lonely nights dreaming of a song. The melody haunts my reverie and I'm once again with you."

I knew if something didn't change soon, that Dean would not live to see the end of the war. My fellow Texan had wasted away, his 200 pounds melted down to a mere 140 at the most. I looked around the cell. The faces that looked back at me were gaunt. Clothes hung loose on emaciated bodies. Secretly I wondered if any of us would see our families again. Although the torture stopped and we shared a cell, the meager rations could not sustain life for much longer. But the worst was yet to come.

There was no law on the books that allowed the Japanese to charge the American airmen as war criminals. So they enacted one and applied it ex post facto to the Raiders.

On August 28, 1942, we stood before five Japanese officers. Dean Hallmark lay on a stretcher on the floor, flies buzzing around his prostrate body. The *judges* sat behind a long table on a raised platform. The chief judge, a bald-headed man in his fifties sat in the center, surrounded by four younger men decked out in ridiculous black wigs.

The *trial* was conducted entirely in Japanese, the verdict a forgone conclusion. George Barr, too weak to stand, collapsed and was given a chair. An interpreter ordered us to give a brief history of our lives, beginning with high school.

I mumbled my story, carefully avoided any discussion of the raid. No one took notes. I was fairly certain that no one was even listening.

When the last Raider spoke, the judge read the verdict and sentence in Japanese. No one bothered to translate it into English. When he was finished, seven of us were led into an adjoining building and locked away in solitary cells. Hallmark was transported back to Bridge House.

On October 14, 1942, five of us were marched into a small room jammed with officers. Farrow, Hallmark and Spatz were missing. The same five judges sat behind their table on the raised dais.

We were, an interpreter said, "convicted of war crimes punishable by death."

All of us, except Chase Nielsen, stood at attention, nothing registering on our faces.

Sweating profusely, the interpreter continued, "But, through the graciousness of His Majesty, the Emperor, your sentences are hereby commuted to life imprisonment . . . with special treatment."

The *special treatment* was solitary confinement. If the United States won the war, the five of us would be shot.

We were transported back to Nanking. I didn't know that Farrow, Hallmark and Spatz had been executed by firing squad. I hoped they were being held as insurance against defiance on our part. I thought maybe Meder, Nielsen, DeShazer,

Barr and I were insurance against an escape attempt by Farrow and the others. At least, I wanted to believe that.

On December 1, 1943, a year and eight months after being taken prisoner, Robert J. Meder died of beriberi and malnutrition. His death was a personal blow.

The hours of solitary confinement wore away at each man differently. My health declined and my spirit suffered. I wrote a letter to the prison governor requesting a Bible. The words in the Bible saved my life.

By August 1944, I was so weak that I could no longer stand up. I weighed about 80 pounds. Fearing the loss of yet another Raider, the Japanese moved me to a cell with a screen door. I could hear Chase talking to Jake.

"Ole Hite won't be here tomorrow," Chase said. "In his condition, I don't think he can make it."

I tried to reassure Chase, but I couldn't make myself heard. So I prayed, asked the Lord to either heal me or give me peace. I was unafraid and welcomed the release. I closed my eyes.

Then I thought about my mother and my sister and my brother. I didn't want them to suffer.

"If they still need me Lord," I prayed, "then please heal me and give me strength."

That night my fever broke. I ate rice boiled to a starchy consistency. Within a week I could stand. They moved me back to my original cell. I knew the Lord had performed a miracle of healing and had used the Japanese to perform it. I promised to dig deep in my heart and search for forgiveness.

On June 15, 1945, three years and two months after being taken prisoner, the Japanese moved us to Peking. With our hands and legs cuffed and tied together in pairs, with two guards assigned to each Raider, there was no possible chance for escape.

Placed again in solitary confinement, I found solace

in my daily conversations with Jake DeShazer. Each day, we would retreat to the back of our cells and speak through the *benjo*.

"Shave and a haircut . . . " I knocked out on the adjoining wall, and then waited patiently for Jake's affirmative response. But no knock answered. I waited about a half an hour, and knocked again. Still no response.

I started to worry. Jake always answered. A short time later, the guards gathered at Jake's door, talking among themselves. I leaned against my cell door, trying to hear anything that would indicate what had happened to Jake.

I heard Jake's door open. The doctor went in and, after a short time, he left. I worried that Jake had fallen ill. I couldn't stand the thought of losing my friend. I wasn't sure how much more I could take. We were down to four Raiders out of the original eight captured. By the end of the day, would we be down to three?

I waited all day, the hours long and slow in their procession. Then suddenly, as the afternoon began to wane, I heard Jake knocking on the wall.

"Shave and a haircut . . . "

I answered the knock then flew back to the *benjo*.

"What happened? Are you alright?" My words came out in a rush.

"The war is over. We're going home." Jake said.

"What? How do you know?"

"When I woke up this morning the Lord told me to pray for peace. I've been praying all day." Jake said. "Then, just a few minutes ago, he told me that I didn't need to pray anymore. The victory is won."

It was August 9, 1945, the day Maj Charles W. Sweeney dropped the second atomic bomb on Nagasaki.

We were released from prison on August 20, 1945. Three years and four months after being captured by the Japanese, our ordeal was over. We were going home.

I often wondered if Lady Luck walked with me during those years of confinement. Sixteen Raiders lost their lives during the war. Some died on the Doolittle Raid, some died flying the Hump,[1] and others were killed in Europe. If I hadn't flown with Bill, I might have been on one of those planes that went down. I'll never know. But I do know the Lord was there.

Bobby retired from the Air Force as a lieutenant colonel. He served on active duty in the Korean War. Bobby worked in the hotel industry in Camden, Arkansas. Bobby and Porsche have two children, five grandchildren, and five great-grandchildren. Porsche passed away in 1999. On November 11, 2000, Bobby married Dorothy "Dottie" Fitzhugh, widow of close friend and fellow Doolittle Raider, William "Bill" Fitzhugh. Bobby and Dottie live in Nashville, Tennessee.

★ ★ ★ ★

Decorations and Awards: **Distinguished Flying Cross, Purple Heart with one Oak Leaf Cluster, Chinese Breast Order of Pao Ting**

---

1 When the Japanese cut off the Burma Road, Allied pilots began flying from India to China over the eastern end of the Himalayan Mountains, an area they called the Hump, to resupply the Flying Tigers and the Chinese government of Chiang Kai-shek.

ROSE BEAL

———⟨⟩———

ESCAPE FROM NAZI TERROR

Don't think of me as an old lady. Try to think of me as young, because I was a girl when it all happened. I was just 11 years old when Hitler came into power. And of course, it didn't mean anything to me. I didn't understand it. But I remember that day because my grandmother, who lived with us, was crying all day long. And I remember my mother trying to calm her down.

"Look," my mother said, "this isn't going to last very long. No chancellor after World War I lasted more than six months. And besides, the German people are much too smart to pay attention to this ignorant Austrian."

Well, no matter how hard my mother tried, my grandmother just kept on crying. She knew all about Hitler. She knew he hated the Jews. She was terribly worried about her children. She cried for six weeks. And then, very suddenly, she died.

She was spared the knowledge that, indeed, four of her children, their spouses, six grandchildren and one great-grandchild were all murdered during the Holocaust.

Two weeks after she died, we experienced Boycott Day. On April 1, 1933, the Nazis enacted the first boycott of Jewish stores. They put storm troopers in front of department stores and regular shops like ours. They posted signs that read,

"DON'T BUY FROM THE JEWS"

"YOU'RE A TRAITOR IF YOU BUY FROM THE JEWS"

"WE'RE GOING TO PHOTOGRAPH YOU IF YOU BUY FROM THE JEWS"

About a month or so later, they collected all the books by Jewish writers, scientists, musicians and artists. They picked them up from the libraries and from the schools and from the universities, and in my city, in Frankfurt, they put them in front of city hall and they started a big bonfire. It became a crime to have a book by a Jewish author in a private home.

Everything happened very quickly. My life changed. The streets were not safe anymore. We were ambushed by other kids and these were the very kids we played with just a few months before.

The most frightening thing for me was when storm troopers, masses of them, marched in long columns through the streets of Frankfurt, their boots making a lot of racket on the cobblestone. And they were singing. Germans always sing when they march. And the songs they sang were very frightening. I still remember the melodies. I still remember the words.

"When Jewish blood is spurting from our knives, things are going well."

And . . .

"Heads are rolling and Jews are howling but we'll march on."

So you can imagine, it was very frightening for an 11-year-old. Whenever I heard them come, I hid in the nearest house and I didn't come out until they were long gone.

Our teachers and our parents told us not to hang out on the streets, or go to the park, or play on the playgrounds. It had become too dangerous for us kids in the streets, particularly for the boys. They were beaten up . . . severely.

And yet, with all of this happening, people in the Jewish community, including my mother, still believed that somehow Hitler would magically disappear. We didn't want to leave Germany. This was our home.

That changed about two and a half years after Hitler came into power. In 1935, the Nuremberg Laws were passed by the National Socialist German Workers Party. These new laws stripped us of all civil rights—and all human rights. No Jew could hold a government position. Judges and lawyers were banned from the courtrooms. Jewish doctors could only treat Jewish patients. All Jewish professors and teachers from the universities and public schools lost their jobs. And all Jewish children were expelled from the public school system. We couldn't fraternize with non-Jews. Marriage between Aryans and non-Aryans was banned. If you were caught violating one of these laws, you were punished.

They gave the Jews mandatory middle names, Israel for males, Sarah for females—it was on all identity papers—so if you were stuck or anything, you always had to have those ID papers. Everyone knew who was Jewish.

Signs were posted in many of the stores, cafes and theaters.

"JEWS NOT ALLOWED!"

"JEWS NOT WANTED HERE!"

And in the playgrounds, parks and municipal pools, which we always used, the signs read: "JEWS AND DOGS NOT ALLOWED!"

It was at that time that my mother, a single parent with two sons and a daughter, decided if we wanted to live, we needed to get out of Germany. And we needed to get out in a hurry. She wrote to our relatives in America, asking them to send us the necessary papers. At first they didn't understand.

"You have three young children and a good business. Why would you want to leave?" they asked.

My mother explained that we were no longer safe in our home and if we wanted to live, we would have to leave.

They graciously sent us the necessary documents. Papers that in reality were an affidavit guaranteeing that we would not become a public charge in America—that we would not go on welfare.

When all the papers were at the American Consulate, we were informed that the documents were in order but—a big but—we wouldn't get a visa to immigrate to America for approximately three and a half years.

America had a very serious immigration quota, and we were at the bottom of the list. It would take that long to move up to the top. It was very disappointing for us but there was nothing we could do. We just hoped that nothing bad would happen to us during those years of waiting.

But that was not to be.

My parents were born in Poland and, even though my brothers and I were born in Germany, we were considered Polish citizens. On October 6, 1938, Poland announced that any Polish citizen living in a foreign country for more than five years would no longer hold a valid passport.

In the middle of a cold October night, a loud banging on our apartment door woke us from our sleep. Three men came into our home. Two of them were policemen, the third, a Gestapo agent, a member of the much feared secret state police. They told us to get dressed and come with them. We had no idea what it was all about, we just knew that we were being arrested.

I didn't want to get dressed in front of these guys so

my mother asked them to leave the room and they explained to us that they couldn't do that because some of the Jews had the audacity to try to commit suicide by jumping out of the window—and they weren't going to let that happen on their watch. So we got dressed—one of the guys kind of turned around—and they did tell us that we would never come back to our home again and we could take as much clothing as we could carry on our body. It was the 28th of October and it was already cold—winter starts early in Europe.

When we got down to the street, we realized that we were not the only ones. There were people coming from all directions—each with the three officers accompanying them— and they led us through the streets of Frankfurt. Slowly it became daylight and we went to a gathering point where we were loaded onto big trucks. We were driven to the main railroad station. At the end of all of the tracks was an old dirty train with wooden benches and we were loaded onto that train. By that time we knew that we were being deported to Poland. The Polish border is quite a ways from Frankfurt. We were on that train, guarded by policemen who pretty much left us alone. We were there all night and for the better part of two days. There was no food and there was nothing to drink. We finally arrived at the Polish border and that's where all hell broke loose.

In Beuthen, the policemen didn't even get off the train. We were turned over to storm troopers. They were terrible. They greeted us with revolvers drawn, shooting bullets into the air. They carried rubber nightsticks and, if somebody didn't move fast enough, they beat them on the legs, particularly the older people who couldn't get off the train after sitting for so many hours. They beat them up. They yelled obscenities and all kinds of dirty names. They called us Pig Jews and told us to get a move on. We were herded into a tunnel.

There were more than 3,000 people with suitcases

packed into that tunnel. Some of the people were sick, evacuated from hospitals and taken directly to the border. There were children with measles and scarlet fever, and old people, barely able to stand.

Our family was one of the last to come down the stairs. The air was a little better at the entry end of the tunnel, so we stayed there for as long as we could. Eventually we had to move forward. It got tighter and tighter and tighter. There were people fainting, and a couple of people near us died. But they couldn't fall down because we were that close, that tight.

Drunken East Prussian SS men, their hands resting on holstered guns, amused themselves by walking through the crowd. They shouted orders for the dirty Jews to make a path.

"Get out of our way!" they yelled. "Don't you Pig Jews touch us!"

And of course, if someone tripped or got in their way, the storm troopers beat them, again and again and again. I'm convinced they were just looking for an excuse to use their guns.

A group of men were praying. They were told to stop, but they didn't stop. They were savagely beaten.

Kids were crying. There was no food. There were no toilet facilities. Just a tunnel filled with thousands of people, so you can imagine the stench—the smell in that place.

Ice-cold water dripped from the roof of the tunnel. I think now it was probably the condensation of our own breath. We were very, very hot—we had all these layers of clothes on and we couldn't take them off—there was no room to take them off.

We moved slowly, only a few steps each hour. Occasionally, a family made it through the door at the Polish end of the tunnel. Luckily, we never made it though that door.

There was a lot of noise, a lot of confusion—and we didn't know if they were going to shoot us . . . we heard gunshots outside. After some hours of that, I kind of lost it. I started screaming and I started crying. It was the wrong thing to do because you really shouldn't attract attention—only nobody, nobody I'm sure heard me and I screamed at the praying men to stop praying.

"There is no God!" I said.

I told the children to be quiet.

And worst of all, I called the storm troopers names.

My family was very worried that they would hear me. My brother stood behind me and tried to keep me quiet.

"Look," he said to me, "we are going to get out of here alive and we are going to go to America. And one day, I am going to come back and be a very important man. And I am going to tell the world what happened to us. And I'm going to make them pay."

We stayed in that tunnel for 14 long hours. We had not slept or eaten in over 30 hours. All we wanted was to cross through that door into Poland.

We were still in the tunnel, moving forward very slowly. We were right at the end of the tunnel and could see daylight. I just wanted to get out. I didn't care what would happen to us. I just wanted to breathe in the fresh air—I couldn't stand the stench anymore. We were just at the gate and could see the barrier of the border.

Then the door opened and a big man, dressed in an elegant SS uniform, weighted down with numerous decorations, stepped into the tunnel.

"Quiet!" he yelled.

And the voices in the tunnel died down.

"Through the kindness of our führer, Adolph Hitler, you have permission to go home."

Only it wasn't really a kindness. The Poles had closed

the borders. We were overcome, but still glad of the news.

The tunnel emptied quickly. Totally exhausted, we returned to the train station. We took all of the extra layers of clothes off and made a pillow out of them. Then we lay down and waited for the train.

Many years later, I read the statistics of this transport. There were 17,000 of us. Six thousand made it across the border and ended up in a ghetto.

They were relatively safe until Hitler invaded Poland at the start of World War II, and all of them were killed, many of them in Auschwitz.

Nine thousand unfortunates were trapped in a strip of land called No Man's Land, between Germany and Poland. There were no facilities. There were some old horse stables left from World War I, and those 9,000 all perished. They died of starvation. They died of the cold. They died of disease. There was a typhus epidemic that wiped them all out.

Of the 2,000, with us among them, who were allowed to return home, it is estimated that only about 200 made it out of Germany before the start of the war. The rest of them were gassed in gas chambers. We were among the 200 obviously, or I wouldn't be here. So, out of 17,000, there were 200 survivors.

On November 7, 1938, 17-year-old Herschel Grynszpan, a Polish-German Jew whose parents were on the Poland Transport, walked into the German Embassy in Paris and shot Nazi Foreign Service Officer Ernst Vom Rath twice in the abdomen. Vom Rath died two days later. Hitler, incensed by the assassination of one of his men, gave Joseph Goebbels the order to punish the Jews. Goebbels and Reinhard Heydrich set up the so-called *Reichskristallnacht*, Crystal Night, the infamous Night of Broken Glass.

We had been home only a few days when we were awakened in the early morning hours of November 10, 1938.

There was a lot of noise, a lot of screaming, and the unmistakable sound of breaking glass.

We looked down on the street and there were groups of civilian men with iron bars and long sticks. They shattered all the windows and broke into the houses. They threw furniture out of the broken windows and smashed the remnants into small pieces when they hit the ground.

We could hear them chanting.

"Today the Jews will get what they deserve. We're going to kill them all!"

The most frightening part was, we knew that they meant it.

More and more windows were broken, the looters got into the houses, climbing up to the upper floors. Furniture flew out the windows.

"We're going to kill all of the Jews! We're going to kill all of the Jews!"

If a Jew left his home and ventured out onto the street, he was beaten. Our neighbor, an old lady living with her adult son on the first floor of our building, was beaten to death while the mob held her son back.

We got away from the window and we sat all day long around the dining table and held hands. My mother kept saying, "At least we're all together." What she really meant was, if we got killed, then all of us would get killed.

It went on all day. And then finally we heard them come into the first floor of our building, breaking things up. They came up to the second floor and the noise of broken furniture and glass penetrated the walls of our apartment. We were on the third floor.

And then it stopped. Just as suddenly as it started, it stopped. There was an eerie stillness.

Our doorbell rang and an SS officer came in. *Sturmbannführer* Hoffman-Horn asked us if we were hiding any men. We didn't know what he meant by that—of course we didn't—so he searched the apartment. And then he pulled us children aside. We shared a last name, so he told us kids that we should keep an eye on our mother. And if she said or did anything against the Führer, we should turn her in. He told us that he would have respect for us if we did this. Then he asked my two brothers to come down on the street and help clean up the mess. So my brothers and a lot of other teenage boys went on the street and did the best they could with all the broken glass and the broken wood and the broken furniture.

A short time later the trucks came. And those trucks came all night long. We heard crying and screaming and shouting. Needless to say we didn't even get undressed and didn't think of sleeping. And by next morning—all through Germany—every Jewish man between the ages of 16 and 60 was arrested and sent to a concentration camp.

All the synagogues and temples were burned to the ground on Crystal Night. All the Jewish businesses, big department stores and small shops were destroyed, totally destroyed.

My mother's business was in the old section of Frankfurt, a section known as *Frankfurt Altstadt*. My mother asked me to go down to our store with her and see if it had survived the looting and destruction. We didn't dare let the boys out of the apartment; we were worried something would happen to them. So they stayed home while my mother and I went to our store.

We passed by the burned-out synagogue. A lot of Germans were standing around, only this time they weren't cheering. They were very somber. I guess seeing a house of God destroyed didn't sit too well with many of them.

When we got to our store the showcase windows were all broken, the fixtures and the furniture were smashed, and there was no merchandise left. It was a clothing store, totally looted. So there was our livelihood, such as it was. Not many people went into Jewish stores, but enough did so we could still eke out a living there. Now there was nothing left.

On top of this, the government confiscated all Jewish bank accounts. The damage from Crystal Night was assessed very quickly throughout Germany. It went into the billions. And Hermann Goering, who was the number two guy next to Hitler, decided since all of the damage was the fault of the Jews, the Jews had to pay for it. So they just attached all of our bank accounts.

It was just about three and a half years since we had applied for the American visa. My mother asked me to go to the American Consulate, which was in a different city—about a three-and-a-half-hour train ride from Frankfurt—and find out just what the status of our immigration visa was. She had to stay behind; she had to somehow get some money. She had to take care of what was left of the business.

So there I was, 16 years old, and I was sent on this errand.

"If it isn't there," my mother said to me, "just beg them. We need to get away."

So I arrived and there were a lot of people milling around the American Consulate. They were all looking for asylum, for refuge. It didn't do any good. They wouldn't be let in. I got in because we had pending papers. And I got to see a young man. He pulled our file.

"I've got good news for you," he said. "You've been approved for immigration to the United States."

It was good news. The bad news was that this was the middle of November 1938 and the quota for that year had been used up. We had to wait until the next year. That was a terrible blow. They had already arrested the men; we were waiting to be arrested. It was just terrible. And much later I got very angry about it. This was the day after Crystal Night. What if they had just borrowed some quota numbers from the following year?

Anyway, I got back and my mother decided we would go to Berlin. We would leave the city and go where nobody knew us and we were not on any list. The Germans did not arrest randomly. They all had lists—long lists. We would be safer in Berlin. We had a big family in Berlin and it would give us an opportunity to say goodbye to them before going to America. So off we went to Berlin and we stayed there until after the first of the year, and we said goodbye to our relatives. That was our last goodbye. Each and every one—they were just killed. These were my uncles, my aunts, my cousins, my friends. We never saw them again.

We went back home to wait for a call from the American Consulate. Then, in March, we were called to come to Stuttgart to get our American immigration visa.

My mother's passport had expired in November 1938, and the US Consulate refused to put the visa stamp in an invalid passport.

We went to the police station to plead our case. My mother was almost arrested as a stateless person.

We explained everything to the man in charge and he took pity on us. He called a friend at the Polish consulate and asked him to extend my mother's passport.

"I want to get rid of these Jews," he told his friend.

The request was granted and her passport was extended for two months.

Our American visas were finally ready.

As we sat in the waiting room of the American Consulate, the radio came on. Hitler had just marched into Czechoslovakia. Well, everybody knew that war was imminent. Hitler made a pact with England, with Prime Minister Neville Chamberlain, and he broke it when he invaded Czechoslovakia.

When we got in to see the vice consul, he advised us to be sure to book passage on an American ship. During times of war, he explained, ships get returned to their country of origin. If we sailed on a German ship, and war broke out while we were at sea, our ship would return to Germany. That was good advice.

He issued our American visas. Now I don't know what I imagined or what I thought. I knew it was the most important piece of paper in my life—and I thought it would be some scroll or some document or something substantial. But it was only a little two-by-two stamp in my passport. I often wondered how a little bit of ink and a little bit of paper can save your life. But it did.

We got our American visas and prepared to leave Germany. It still took another month because the Germans put a lot of obstacles in our way. There were taxes to pay, including a special tax for emigration. In mid-April, we closed the door to our apartment as though we were coming back and we took the train to France.

One last miracle saved us at the French border. Before we crossed the border, an SS officer noticed that my mother's passport had expired in November. She had illegally lived in Germany for four months. At the last moment, just as the train began to pull out of the station in Kehl, he relented.

"Well, OK," he said. "Get on that train now!"

We jumped on the moving train, knowing that our lives had been saved one last time.

The American ship we booked passage on was the USS *President Harding* and it was anchored in Le Havre, which is on the coast of Normandy in France. The very coast where our soldiers entered five years later to liberate Europe.

Boarding that American ship was quite an experience. It was my first contact with the American people. I was amazed at how nice they were. They took our suitcases from us and showed us into our cabin. They took us to the dining room and served us meals. There were no sign anywhere saying "Jews not wanted."

They just treated us like human beings. Extraordinary! Awesome! We hadn't been treated that way for many years. It was overwhelming.

We were on that ship for 12 days. It was an old ship, and she took her time crossing the Atlantic. We saw the *Queen Mary* coming and going. And then on Saturday, May 6, 1939, we pulled into New York harbor. The magnificent skyline of New York framed my first view of America. Pretty soon, Lady Liberty rose up from the harbor. We were all on deck and we were hugging and we were crying and we were laughing. And we were free. Finally, we were truly free.

We each had a suitcase for clothes and, between the four of us, we had $2.50. The rest the Nazis kept. But we didn't care. We were looking forward to a new life and to freedom in this country.

I ended up as the cashier at Melody Lane, a restaurant at the corner of Hollywood and Vine. I couldn't have left that job even if I had wanted to. You see, I was in something called an "essential job"—a necessary job vacated by women when they flooded the factories to fill higher-paying positions. But I didn't want to leave. A lot of our soldiers frequented Melody Lane. I remember four marines in particular. They would come into town for the weekend. Afraid they might be rolled, each of them would hand me the money from his paycheck on Friday afternoon. I put each marine's money into an envelope and tucked it away in the restaurant's safe. On Sunday, before they returned to duty, I'd give each man his envelope, his money safe.

One Saturday, my boss opened the safe and found four envelopes of cash.

"What's this?" he asked.

I explained. He just looked at me and shook his head.

I'll never forget the Friday when only one of the marines came into the restaurant with his cash. When I asked him where the others were, he told me they had all been killed. I was so sad.

I was married at the time. My husband was an actor who had escaped from Austria early in the war and immigrated to the United States. He was serving in the American Army and fought in the Battle of the Bulge.

In fact, the three most important men in my life were all in the service. My brother Sol fought in the Pacific. And my brother Bernard kept the promise he made to me in the tunnel on the Polish border. He returned to Germany with the American Army and, at the end of the war, was part of the Counter Intelligence Corps. His job was to hunt down Nazi war criminals and bring them to justice. He had promised to return as an important man and make them pay. And he made them pay. He loved his job.

I am an older woman now. I want to tell you, to share with you, that this country never disappointed me. I've had a very good life here. We all had a very good life here. We truly lived the American Dream.

Rose became an American citizen on May 11, 1945. She worked as a buyer for Bullock's department stores and retired after 32 years. Rose was instrumental in the building of the Holocaust Memorial in Palm Desert, California. She lives in Boise, Idaho, and volunteers as a docent at the Idaho Human Rights Education Center. Dedicated to bearing witness to the Holocaust, Rose makes regular appearances as a speaker. She has two children and six grandchildren.

ROBERT "BOB" COATES

NAVAL BATTLE
OF GUADALCANAL

On December 5, after two weeks of very intense war maneuvers, the USS *Nevada* sailed into Pearl Harbor. I'd been on board just over three months and was ready to see the world.

"Take any shore liberty you can," our division officer advised us after quarters, or roll call, and before entering port that morning, "because the Japs are throwing their weight around in the Pacific and we're going to have to rein them in. It may be a long time," he added, "before you get another chance."

He didn't have to tell me twice. After securing the *Nevada* in the last berth on Battleship Row, just astern of the flagship, USS *Arizona*, I headed for Honolulu to do some Christmas shopping for my mother.

I wandered down the winding streets of Honolulu taking in the sights, sounds and smells of the island culture. I ate fresh pineapple and had a banana split. Before the day was over, I found a Hawaiian tablecloth and wood tray for my mother and had them shipped home in time for Christmas.

I'd worked real hard to pass the test for seaman first class, which earned the right to an overnight liberty. Our sailing team, of which I was a member, sponsored an all-night beach party on December 6th, so I headed down to Nanakuli to join in the festivities.

There is nothing quite like Hawaii in December. Warm breezes ruffle the palm fronds and turquoise waves roll over the sand with a cadence all their own. Music filled the air that night and the native women entertained us with traditional hula dances and songs of romance.

The next morning I strolled down the beach with some others to an open-air shop. As I walked along the water's edge, a plane roared overhead, flying right down on the deck.

"They're pretty serious about making these war games realistic," I said to the sailor walking next to me. "They've even painted the Rising Sun on some of the Army's planes."

Reality hit as soon as we reached the coffee shop.

A radio blared with breaking bulletins. The proprietor, voice cracking, seemed unable to process the news: the Japanese were bombing Pearl Harbor. The United States of America was under attack.

When I arrived back at Pearl, the USS *Nevada* was in the process of getting underway. I boarded a wooden "liberty boat" filled with about 40 returning sailors and sped toward the battleship. But when we pulled alongside, the crew waved us off. What a terrible feeling. I believe I understood why horses try to get back inside a burning barn. I should have been aboard that ship. It was my home.

Next we came alongside a destroyer, and most of the other sailors boarded to help get her underway. Two of us were turned away with orders to keep the liberty boat in operation.

Bullets ricocheted off the destroyer's rigging and

pelted the water as Japanese planes strafed the harbor and everything in it. I revved the liberty's single engine and headed toward the relative safety of the dock where we could take cover.

When the strafing stopped, I ventured out, running the liberty boat to ships. That night two other sailors and I were issued rifles with fixed bayonets. We were detailed to round up some Japanese who were reportedly hiding out in the lumberyard, intending to set it on fire as a beacon for the Japanese fleet. We rounded them up without any trouble, but I was really scared that one of our sailors would accidentally shoot me. I knew they had live rounds in those guns with the safety off.

Rumors ran wild: The water was poisoned. The food was poisoned. The Japanese were landing at different locations around Oahu. We didn't know what to believe.

I continued to coxswain a liberty boat for the next two days. We ferried workers to the sunken battleships, rescuing survivors and pulling bodies from the debris-strewn harbor. Most of them were cooked by the burning oil floating on the water.

On the night of December 9th, I finally laid down on the dock to get some sleep. I awoke with every inch of my exposed skin covered with mosquito bites, to a loud speaker announcing, "All survivors of the *Cassin* and *Downes*, report in."

I went aboard the *Nevada* on the 10th. The crew had run her aground, to keep her from blocking the channel, and she sat with just a few inches of freeboard above the waterline on her main deck.

The captain personally handed out the orders to each and every sailor. With tears streaming down his cheeks, he handed me orders to report to the USS *San Francisco*. "Give them bastards hell, son," he said.

"Yes, sir!" I assured him. "That's exactly what I'll do."

This was the first time I'd ever seen a grown man cry.

Commissioned in 1934, the *San Francisco*,[1] a flagship, was configured to carry the flag officer. Armed with nine 8″ main battery guns in three turrets, eight 5″ dual purpose anti-aircraft guns mounted in tubs, and a number of 1.1″ British pompoms and 20 mm guns, she had the fire power to back up her cruising radius of 14,000 miles. She carried a wartime complement of about 1,100 men.

There was a large contingent of "Battleship Sailors" newly assigned to the *San Francisco*. Those of us without ratings were ordered to one of the deck divisions. Although trained as a radioman, my new duty was with the First Division.

My battle station was on the shell deck of turret number one. I helped load the 8″ shells into a hydraulic hoist, which conveyed them to the gun deck above. My anti-aircraft station was "pointer" on one of the 5″ guns and I liked to think that several Japanese planes, as well as other targets, bit the dust as a direct result of my marksmanship.

During this time, I slept at my general quarters station on the shell deck of turret number one. I became quite adept at sleeping curled around the hoist, lying in the oil on the deck, and always making sure that none of my extremities got in the crack between the rotating center column and the barbette, where they would have been pinched off if the turret was "trained on" unexpectedly.

We spent the next few months patrolling the Pacific, often unescorted. We got down to eating hominy grits three times a day. I'm sure they were quite high in protein, judging

---

1 The USS *San Francisco* was a 10,000-ton "treaty" cruiser built after the second London Naval Treaty in April 1930, which attempted to get countries to limit the size of their battleships to no more than 8,000 tons. When Japan refused to sign the treaty and began building super ships, the treaty became moot.

by the number of worms nestled in the mush.

Capt Daniel Judson Callaghan, former naval aide to President Roosevelt, was the skipper of the USS *San Francisco* when I came aboard. Scuttlebutt had it that Callaghan drew that duty because of his impatience with the Commander-in-Chief, US Pacific Command (CINC-PAC) for failing to be more aggressive.

Callaghan, the epitome of a naval captain, was well liked by his men. An aggressive and intelligent warrior, he found it difficult to command his men to retreat from a battle. When the commander of the task force ordered the *San Francisco* to withdraw from her mission to relieve the forces at Wake Island, Captain Callaghan couldn't stomach telling his men that they were turning tail.

"We are now making an offensive sweep to the eastward," he told the crew.

We were there to fight a war and none of us wanted to turn tail and run. We appreciated his dedication and leadership. We knew he understood.

Callaghan was promoted to rear admiral in April of 1942 and replaced by Capt Charles H. McMorris in early May. A "tin can," or destroyer, sailor at one time, McMorris could really con[2] a ship. He handled the 588-foot *Frisco* like a good coxswain would handle a whaleboat. Aggressive and fair, McMorris easily earned the respect of his crew.

Shortly after McMorris took command, I was transferred from the First Division to the Communication Division as a radioman. My new battle station was located in the aft superstructure. That would be my home for the next three years.

With the loss of so many battleships, the heavy cruisers of the Pacific Fleet performed double duty during this

2   Navy term for controlling a ship.

phase of the war, and the USS *San Francisco* participated in her share of air raids, escort duty and sea battles.

On August 7, 1941, the First Division of Marines landed on Guadalcanal. On August 10th, a Japanese counterattack sank three of the *San Francisco*'s sister ships and the Australian HMAS *Canberra*. The USS *Chicago* was badly damaged in the battle. Although not actively involved and under strict radio silence, those of us on the *San Francisco* observed the gun flashes and wondered about the action off Guadalcanal.

We stood "watch-on, watch-off," reporting for duty every other four hours throughout the night, and turned to[3] during the day. It was pure luck if anyone got more than three and a half hours sleep in any 24-hour period. The oppressive heat and endless hours spent at general quarters left us all a little rummy.

The only respite from this routine came during assignments to the carrier task force, which thwarted the Japanese carrier groups' major thrust. We were operating with the aircraft carriers when the USS *Wasp* was sunk, and witnessed many of our capital ships being sunk or sustain heavy damage.

Throughout August and September, our warships would cruise into the coastal waters and shell the Japanese position. The Japanese sent planes down to strike our ships and shell our Marines on a daily basis. Dogfights dominated the skies as our pilots challenged the enemy in one-on-one combat, holding their own against the more agile Zero.[4] Our little task force was severely outnumbered by the Japanese fleet.

The strategic advantage of Henderson Field contributed to the US control of the waters surrounding Guadalcanal

---

3 Reported to your regular duty station.
4 The Mitsubishi lightweight fighter aircraft operated by the Imperial Japanese Navy Air Service.

during the daylight hours. But the night waters belonged to the Japanese.

Commander South Pacific (COMSOPAC) refused to commit us to a night battle, so we retreated to the open waters after dark, while the Japs made nightly raids on our Marines, shelling them unmercifully.

On the night of October 11, 1942, we challenged a large Japanese task force for the first time. Rear Admiral Scott, who used the *San Francisco* as his flagship, had spent two weeks drilling our task force in night battle tactics.

We faced a Japanese fleet that held a decisive edge, having proved itself adept at this type of fighting and equipped with deadly torpedoes and flash-less powder. But the Battle of Cape Esperance gave us our first sea victory in a night battle.

Our cruisers *Boise* and *Salt Lake City* were badly damaged, and the destroyer *Duncan* was sunk, but the USS *San Francisco* gave a good account of herself. We put several salvoes into two Japanese cruisers and lit up a Japanese destroyer without any damage to our ship.

We led so many forays into the waters around Guadalcanal and were continually losing ships, that we were likened to an old mother cat, always going out and losing one of her kittens.

We continued night patrols off Guadalcanal, each of us learning to catch a minute or two of sleep standing up. I would have given my paycheck just to be able to get one good night's sleep with my clothes off.

In late October 1942, we were attacked by Japanese subs. The klaxon's electronic siren split the air, sounding general quarters, and I scrambled up the ladder outside Radio Two, taking the shortcut to the emergency radio located below decks under Radio One.

Either our violent evasive maneuvering to avoid a torpedo or the concussion from a hit dislodged the armored hatch cover just as I scooted through the manhole. The hatch cover fell, hitting me on the head. The weight of the impact split my head open and nearly severed the two middle fingers on my left hand.

When I came to, I wrapped my right hand around my injured fingers in an attempt to stem the bleeding. Still unsteady from the blow to my head, I made my way down to sickbay. I wanted to get back to my duty station as quickly as possible, and told the doctor that when I showed him my bloody hand. But he refused to stitch my fingers until the attack ended. I looked around the sickbay. The doctor had everyone lying down in case we took a direct hit. The Japanese torpedoes were so strong, that anyone standing near a direct hit risked broken legs from the concussion.

The only positive that came from my injury was a change in battle stations. With my arm in a sling, it was too difficult to open and dog-down[5] hatches. This suited me fine. A person could develop a phobia way down below decks if the ship was hit by a torpedo. I vividly remembered some of those poor souls we helped out of the capsized *Oklahoma* at Pearl. It may sound cruel, but I believe some would have suffered less if we'd left them behind.

By early November, it became obvious that the Japanese were preparing for the *Big One*, an all-out offensive against Guadalcanal.

Vice Adm Robert Ghormley had been replaced as Commander of the Southern Pacific by Vice Adm William "Bull" Halsey. Our old skipper, Rear Adm Daniel J. Callaghan, formerly Ghormley's chief of staff, returned to sea duty. Since he was senior to Rear Admiral Scott, Callaghan took over command of the task force, requisitioning the *San Francisco* as his

---

5   Close and secure the hatches, making them watertight.

flagship. Rear Adm Norman Scott moved to the USS *Atlanta*, an anti-aircraft light cruiser.

Our skipper, Capt Charles H. McMorris, received notification of his promotion to rear admiral and relinquished command of the *San Francisco* to Capt Cassin Young, who, up until a few days before, had been captain of a repair ship.

Everyone knew at the time that we were heading for a showdown with the Japanese, yet the new commander of the task force, who had not been to sea in months, relieved a commander who had spent weeks honing the ships for this particular encounter. To make matters worse, the Navy replaced a battle-wise skipper with an officer who had no combat experience. All the while, McMorris sat in New Caledonia waiting for orders while the battle took place.

We left Espiritu Santo on November 10th, with orders to cover the unloading of supplies and reinforcements for the Marines on Guadalcanal. Two days later, our task force was attacked by approximately 30 Japanese twin-engine light bombers.

Our anti-aircraft batteries managed to shoot them all down. The final Japanese Betty, rather than crash into the ocean, turned toward the *San Francisco* and, kamikaze style, took out the after structure.

The impact, which sounded like a high-speed car crash, shook the entire ship. The plane hit directly above my duty station, with only the thin ceiling above my head protecting me from the burning debris. The explosion wiped out Control Aft, killing or injuring almost everyone above us, including the executive officer. I stayed at my post, doing my best to keep the radio equipment and radar working.

A radioman is privy to intelligence not widely distributed throughout the ship. I was in a unique position as the radioman because I had access to radio transmissions and could read and decipher messages flashed between ships.

That evening, after transferring our wounded to a troop ship, we escorted the transport ships to safe waters. As we turned back toward Guadalcanal, COMSOPAC alerted us that a large Japanese task force, consisting of battleships, cruisers, destroyers and aircraft carriers, was heading for Guadalcanal with an estimated time of arrival around midnight. Our heavy ships were in New Caledonia, without a chance of returning in time for the battle. That meant we were "it."

COMSOPAC's message ended with three words: "Go get 'em."

As dusk fell, I joined some good friends on the fantail, the one place on the ship where we could relax a little and get a breath of fresh air.

"What's the latest scoop?" someone asked as soon as we settled in.

Without releasing any confidential information, I told them as much as I could about the Japanese task force heading our way.

No one seemed particularly concerned about the size or composition of the enemy fleet; we all believed that we would make them pay dearly. After all, we had "Es" on our main turrets, and these anti-aircraft machine guns held the world record for rapid and accurate fire.

"Tomorrow's Friday the 13th," someone remarked, and the thought sobered us.

"Let's hope we engage them before midnight," another sailor added and we all nodded our heads.

I'd never been a superstitious man, but I couldn't help but agree.

"And we have 13 ships in our task force."

A quiet descended on the fantail as each of us, lost in our own thoughts, mulled over this fact. Our only hope was surprise and each of us offered up a silent prayer.

Rain squalls washed the decks and visibility dropped

to zero as we steamed back into the waters around Guadalcanal. Since we were facing an enemy who outgunned us, we used the darkness as cover and entered the restricted waters in a single file formation.

As night fell, I found myself in the bridge making sure the remote equipment functioned properly. Intelligence reports suggested that the Japanese had three different task forces in the area. We had no idea which task force or combination of ships we would face. Directional radar, the type the *San Francisco* carried, could only detect ships when pointed directly at them, making it impossible to get an accurate count of the enemy's strength.

Our orders were to intercept the enemy.

Standing on the bridge, I overheard the conversation between the ship's officers.

"How about the battleships?" the flag officer asked Callaghan.

"It really doesn't make a difference if it's a battleship or a destroyer," Callaghan answered, "We will follow orders."

I was pretty sure Callaghan didn't care what they were because he believed we would whip them anyway. It felt good to have a man like Callaghan as our leader.

The destroyers—*Cushing, Laffey, Sterett* and *O'Bannon,* in that order—led the column. They were followed by the cruisers—*Atlanta, San Francisco, Portland, Helena,* and *Juneau.* Four more destroyers—*Aaron Ward, Barton, Monsen* and *Fletcher*—brought up the rear.

At 0130 on the morning of Friday, November 13, 1942, the *Helena* picked up targets at about 27,000 yards and we changed course to head directly for them. We knew our only chance was to get as close as possible and fire first. If we stood off, their battleships would blow us all out of the water at their leisure.

I stood at my battle station and held my breath. The

black night surrounded each ship and heavy rain pelted the deck. I could feel the enemy, but I could barely make out the *Atlanta* up ahead or the *Portland* at our stern.

Two columns of Japanese ships, each led by a destroyer, headed our way. The plan was to cross their T when we reached striking distance.

As we began to execute a column turn to starboard, the *Cushing* made a sudden turn to port. The *San Francisco* was just in the knuckle of her turn to starboard, when the captain ordered a sharp turn to port in order to avoid ramming the *Atlanta*.

"What are you doing?" Callaghan challenged the *Atlanta*.

"Avoiding our own ships!" the *Atlanta* responded.

Within minutes all hell broke loose. Confusion reigned as ships attempted to avoid ramming each other.

It seemed to me like an eternity before Callaghan regained a semblance of order in our battle line. But the damage was done. The element of surprise, so crucial to our success, was lost.

The Japanese turned on their searchlights, flooding our decks with bright light.

Shells started raining down on the *San Francisco*. Like a rag clenched in the mouth of a terrier, the old ship shuddered with each hit.

Chief Warrant Officer Keesey looked over at me, his eyes growing bigger and bigger with each explosion.

"My God!" he exclaimed, "They're hitting us!"

"Get the big ones first!" Callaghan ordered. "Odd ships fire starboard, even to port."

I don't know how many ships obeyed that command. The *San Francisco* did not. We acquired a target to starboard and immediately set it on fire.

After two nine-gun salvos, we shifted fire to a cruiser

drifting near the destroyer we had just lit. We fired two nine-gun salvos into her, and then again shifted fire, this time to the battleship *Hiei* as she appeared at our bow.

"Cease fire!!" Callahan's orders rose above the din of battle. "Firing on our own ship!"

We obeyed the admiral's order. In the chaos, the *Hiei* also ceased firing and began to signal us with her blinker.

It took a few minutes for me to realize that the cruiser we had taken under fire was the *Atlanta*. In the disorder and darkness, as she swung out of column to avoid running into our own destroyer, she got tangled up with the Japanese fleet.

With our aft superstructure destroyed by the Betty, we were fighting half-blind. I couldn't help but believe, had we been undamaged, we would never have turned our guns on our own ship. My heart sank as I thought about the men on the *Atlanta*.

We eventually took the *Hiei* under fire again. But by this time, the battleship *Kirishima*, a cruiser, and several destroyers trained their guns on the *San Francisco*. We continued to fire on the flagship, *Hiei*, putting several nine-gun salvos into her. But we took a terrible beating.

The *San Francisco* shuddered and shook as 15 one-ton projectiles hit the ship. The ricocheting shrapnel sounded like buckets of rocks thrown against the ship's decks. She took around 70 hits from the enemy's five- and six-inch guns and dozens of smaller caliber hits.

All but one of our five-inch guns were shot clear off the ship. The one left was badly damaged. We no longer had gun crews to man the guns. Admiral Callaghan and his staff were killed. Our captain and all senior officers were killed, except for the unconscious navigator who was blown off the bridge and was as good as dead.

The surviving senior officer was Lt Cdr Bruce McCandless, the communications officer.

Fires broke out from stem to stern, and we were in serious danger of capsizing from the water we'd taken on. Only the skillful pumping of flooded compartments into unflooded compartments kept us afloat. We lost our steering twice, but lucked out and recovered by steering from control aft using telephone lines.

Just at the end of the action, a Japanese destroyer made a run down our port side. I braced myself for the torpedo hit, knowing we were sitting defenseless in the water. But the explosion never came.

I surveyed the damage as well as I could in the dark. Most of the ladders had been destroyed or shot away. It was difficult to walk around, especially near the superstructures.

Our casualties were heavy, with over 200 dead. Almost all damage sustained was topside, with the heaviest concentration in key areas. Turrets one and two were both put out of commission, and number three could only be fired by local controls. It was a miracle, with all the damage to both the fore and aft superstructures, that Radio One and Radio Two were spared. We used them as first-aid stations.

The battle lasted less than 30 minutes.

As we limped away, both task forces licking their wounds, we came upon the *Helena*. She challenged us.

McCandless couldn't remember the response. In a panic, we watched as the *Helena* prepared to fire on us. Then McCandless sent a message using a flashlight. "CA38 . . . CA38"—the *San Francisco*'s cruiser number.

The crew of the *Helena* was apprised of our situation and their captain took command of the *San Francisco*.

A short time later, the badly damaged *Juneau* joined us. She was down by the head[6] from a torpedo hit. Three of

---

6   The bow was not floating properly.

our destroyers caught up as we headed for Espiritu Santo. We left the *Atlanta* behind. Rear Admiral Scott had been killed during the battle. Just before she sank, her officers observed green dye markings at some of the shell holes—the green dye used by the *San Francisco*.

US losses were heavy. In addition to the *Atlanta*, four of our destroyers were sunk in the melee and the *Portland*, badly damaged by a Japanese torpedo, lost her steering.

As the sun rose that Friday the 13th, I found myself busy repairing antennas and damaged equipment. The radio buzzed with blow-by-blow communications between Henderson Field and our Marine and Navy pilots engaged in combat with the Japanese ships still floundering in the waters off Guadalcanal.

The *Hiei*, having sustained some 85 shell hits, mostly from the USS *San Francisco*, was unmanageable. Although dead in the water, she still managed to respond with very intense small caliber anti-aircraft fire. Our planes went through hell attempting to sink her.

It was sad to hear the flak exploding around them as they fought their way into firing range, then not hear an explosion from their torpedoes. I wasn't sure if we'd dropped that fatal torpedo or if the Japanese felt sorry for the poor performance of our torpedoes and scuttled the *Hiei* themselves.

Our casualties were heavy and we requisitioned a doctor and three pharmacist mates from the *Juneau* to help with our wounded. I could tell that they were reluctant to come aboard. Although most of the fires were now out, the *San Francisco* still smoldered and there was some concern that we would not be able to outrun an enemy attack or to make it to port.

Standing in the forecastle, I bent over the equipment necessary to install an emergency antenna for Radio One. We were steaming three cruisers abreast, the *San Francisco* in the center with the *Helena* about 1,200 yards to our port beam and the *Juneau* the same distance off starboard.

The crew scurried about the decks repairing damage wherever they could, the smell of battle hung in the air, embedded deep within the pores of the ship.

Checking the position of the crippled fleet, I noticed the *Helena*, her signal light flashing like crazy. I looked down into the water and spotted a Japanese torpedo coming toward us. It looked like it would hit our bow.

Instinct took over and I put as much distance as possible between my body and the bow of the *San Francisco*. I started running aft, waving my arms and shouting to the officers gathered on the bridge. I wasn't sure if I got their attention, but didn't slow my flight. As I reached the ladder to go up the aft superstructure, the air was shattered by a massive explosion.

I looked to starboard and a fireball rose from the sea where the *Juneau* once sat. Debris showered our ship, and when the smoke blew away in the stiff breeze, absolutely nothing was left. Just as if a magician had waved his handkerchief over the cruiser—poof—the *Juneau* disappeared into thin air, taking with her over 700 sailors, including the five Sullivan brothers.[7]

I continued to search the area where the *Juneau* went down for as long as I could. But the fine new ship was gone. Eventually we steamed out of the area toward a safe port.

One of our destroyers went back to search for survivors. When she caught up with us, she sent a blinker message

---

7 The Sullivan brothers were five siblings killed in action when the USS *Juneau* sank in the sea battle off Guadalcanal. Their deaths, which wiped out nearly an entire generation of the Sullivan family, were the basis for a change in military policy. From that point on, siblings were banned from serving together in combat.

to the *Helena.*

"Negative. Negative. No survivors."

We continued on to Espiritu Santo, staying busy burying our dead and caring for our wounded. Our galley was shot up and our evaporator so badly damaged that we had only the small amount of fresh water left in pots to drink.

When we arrived at Espiritu Santo on November 14, 1942, the *Helena* tied up next to us and their band put on a performance in honor of our fallen officers and our service in battle. A *Helena* sailor, draped in a mattress cover, danced to the "Sheik of Araby." Although relieved to find ourselves in a safe port, we couldn't begin to forget those no longer with us.

After being outfitted with enough replacements to sail safely, we went on to Nouméa. While in Nouméa, Vice Admiral Halsey came aboard to inspect the damage. He ordered us back to San Francisco for repairs.

Halsey was promoted to four-star admiral after that fateful battle on Friday the 13th. We stopped the Japanese in his all out effort to retake Guadalcanal, but the cost in American lives and ships was great. It is generally not recommended policy for cruisers to tangle with battleships, but you have to do what you have to do. It did make the Japanese rethink their strategy. They were now on the defensive and we planned to keep them there.

We received a Presidential Unit Citation for our service in the first major sea battle of Guadalcanal. And when we arrived in San Francisco, we were given a key to the city and a ticker-tape parade up Market Street.

The governor of California, Culbert Olson, hosted a reception in our honor. I saw a few familiar faces from back home, and it felt really good to see someone from my hometown.

Of course, much of our reception was for propaganda purposes and the press extolled our bravery, making it appear that we were the only ship in the fracas. The papers published, erroneously, that we each received 30 days leave for our bravery. We actually got 10, but the rest of the Navy believed the headlines. It caused some resentment.

I don't think anyone can have a feel for what that first year of the war was like, unless you were in the Pacific on a warship. We were outgunned, outmanned, out everything-ed. We ran out of food, spent most of our days at sea and got very little sleep.

I spent the rest of the war in the Pacific, and was actively engaged in every major campaign until the war ended. While none of it was a picnic, it all seemed anti-climatic after Guadalcanal.

I believe that any sailor aboard a warship in those close-in battles off Guadalcanal used up a good percentage of his nine lives. There were quite a few who used them all up.

By the end of that first year, we knew that, no matter what, we would eventually win. But it was far from being a sure thing that first year.

It was years before I learned that there were survivors from the *Juneau*. Even today, I don't know what to say. They were my brothers and my heart aches to think about them. "War is hell" may be a cliché, but it's still true.

Bob spent six years on active duty in the Navy, and then went to work for the Navy as a civilian in the San Francisco Bay Area. He purchased a ranch in Idaho shortly before the birth of his first child. He accepted a position as a research engineer with EGG, and worked on a number of projects for the Atomic Energy Commission. Bob retired in 1982. Bob and his wife, Esther, have two children, four grandchildren, and one great-grandchild. He lost Esther just one week short of their sixtieth wedding anniversary. Bob lives in Nampa, Idaho, and volunteers at the Warhawk Air Museum.

Decorations and Awards: Presidential Unit Citation, Asiatic-Pacific Ribbon with 17 Battle Stars, American Defense Ribbon with star

BILLIE REEG

———⟡———

ENGLISH WAR BRIDE

Air-raid sirens screamed dire warnings as German planes took command of the night sky above London. It was September 7, 1943, and I was thankful for the Anderson shelter, covered with a fresh planting of fall flowers, in my backyard. I huddled close to my mother and grandmother. We'd heard the sirens before, but this time they were punctuated with the sharp explosions of incendiary bombs that sent shock waves through the thick layers of concrete-lined earth and shook us as we hugged each other.

When the trembling stopped and the shrill warning ceased, I climbed out of the shelter. I could hear my neighbors leaving their own shelters, glass crunching under someone's boot, children crying, and the soft, soothing voices of concerned mothers. Smoke laced with the thick dust of pulverized cement assaulted my nostrils. My childhood home, flattened by a German bomb, laid crumbled, a pile of debris on a newly vacant lot.

The houses in Bromley-by-Bow were surrounded with

four-foot stone fences. The three of us climbed over the back fence. Picking our way across remnants of broken bricks, stone and roofing material, we entered an unoccupied house and stretched out in the hallway.

"Mum," I said. "Look up!"

"Oh my goodness!" she said.

The roof, blown clear off the house from the concussion of bombs, opened up a window onto the fall sky. We lay there on our backs watching clouds of dark smoke drift across the English night, shadowing the moon and blotting out the stars.

My poor dad worked for the post office on the graveyard shift. He returned home the next morning and found the remains of our home. Believing that Mum and I had perished in the blast, he was desolate. It took a couple of days before we were reunited.

Homeless after the Blitz, I moved with my workmates from the British Oil and Cake Mills into a boardinghouse in Bromley, Kent. We all wanted to do our part, so I signed up as an air raid warden. I wandered the streets with my best friend, Doreen Crawford, carrying a pail of sand and searching for unexploded incendiary bombs.

In the evenings, we watched Londoners pull thick blackout curtains over their windows, leaving the streets shrouded in a cloak of darkness. At night, we carried flashlights, probing the bushes for wayward bombs and scanning the sky for the telltale signs of enemy bombers.

I couldn't tell the sound of a friendly plane from an enemy bomber. One evening, around dusk, Doreen and I spotted a plane in the distance. Thinking it was one of ours, we stood in the middle of the road and waved to the pilot. When the plane started strafing the street, bullets bouncing off the pavement and into the store fronts, we dove into a hedge . . . hopefully out of sight and range.

In England, every woman between 18 and 42 was expected to serve her country either in the Army, Navy, Air Corps, ammunitions factories, or Women's Land Army. We either volunteered or were conscripted. I've always been fond of animals, so I decided to sign up with the Women's Land Army. Land Girls worked the farms, filling in for the men drafted into the armed services. I spent a month studying at an agricultural college in Sussex, where I learned the basics of farming, specialising in dairy cattle. With the training under my belt, I was issued a uniform—blouse, pants, socks, shoes, sweater and greatcoat—and my first assignment.

I reported to a dairy farm near Ongar, Essex, where I met my new friend Dot. To say the farmer wasn't a very nice man was an understatement. He made a point of sending us to opposite sides of the farm so he could isolate Dot.

"Billie, promise you won't let him separate us," Dot begged as she pulled on my shirt sleeve. "I don't want to be alone with him."

"Don't worry," I promised. "We're in this together."

We rose every morning at 4:30 AM, rain or shine, to bring the cows in from the fields for milking. We'd chase them around, waving our arms, driving them into the barn. Fingers freezing, we broke through the layer of ice on the buckets of water, and washed each cow's teats before milking them.

The barnyard cats huddled close in hopes of a free drink, and frequently Dot or I would send a stream of milk into one of the open mouths. Long, hard days followed the milking. We performed all the jobs once done by men. In addition to milking, we mucked the stalls, harvested the root vegetables, repaired fences, cleared fields and any other job that the farmer declared necessary.

We worked seven days before getting our first day off, but eventually the work weeks settled into a routine of six days on, one day off. Food was in short supply and we rarely had enough to eat. We probably would have made the best of it, but the old farmer just wouldn't leave Dot alone.

We tolerated him for as long as we could, but finally it got out of hand. We notified the Land Office of our decision to quit. They found us new positions at another farm, a co-op dairy farm near Willingale in Essex.

Our new farm produced Grade A milk, mostly for hospitals, so we really felt like we were directly helping our boys.

We lived in half of an old house with a farmer and his wife. The head cowman and his family lived in the other half. We stayed in the attic, right above his quarters. He woke us in the morning by banging on his ceiling with a broomstick.

"I'd like to take that bloody broom away from him!" I mumbled as I pushed the blanket back and lowered my bare feet to the cold floor.

There was no heating in the little attic room, and a pane was missing from the only window. We didn't drag our feet getting dressed in the morning, it was simply too cold!

Our landlady was an evacuee from London and seemed incapable of boiling water, much less cooking a meal, so the cooking duties fell to me. She had a small child and paid him very little attention. I felt sorry for the little fellow.

We had to watch out for the head cowman. He liked to chase us around the barn while trying to undo the straps of our overalls. He was harmless, just a bit of a nuisance.

Willingale was a quaint little village with two churches, a pub, several homes and a community hall. The American Army Air Corps built an airbase nearby. Most of our boys were in France, so it was quite a treat to have the Americans around.

The two churches shared a community center and they let us use it for dances. There weren't many girls in Willingale, so the Army Air Corps sent busses to the larger towns in the area to bring girls in as dance partners.

Dot and I would walk across the fields to the village for the dances and to sing songs at the local pub. Proud to be in service, we almost always wore our uniforms.

One evening, Dot and I decided to attend the dance after work and walked to the community center from the farm.

"Who are you going to dance with?" Dot asked when we arrived.

I looked around the dance floor.

"There's a fellow over there who's a good dancer," I said. "I bet I can make him come over here and ask me to dance."

"You can't!" Dot said, eyeing the airman.

"I can."

"How are you going to do that?"

"Why," I said, smiling, "I'm going to make eyes at him."

"You wouldn't!" Dot challenged.

"Just watch me!"

PFC Roy O. Reeg made his way across the room and asked me to dance. We spent the rest of the evening on the dance floor, swinging to the "Boogie Woogie Bugle Boy" and slow dancing to the soft vocals of the Andrews Sisters.

At the end of the evening Roy walked us back to the farm. I offered to let him ride my bicycle back to the base. I knew Roy would make a point of returning it.

Dating in war-battered England presented challenges. On the rare days that we both had off, we traveled to London to view the sights and eat in restaurants. Sometimes we even went to a movie. The bombs continued to drop; I just hoped one wouldn't hit the theater while we were in it.

Several dates and dances later, Roy asked me to marry him. After completing reams of paperwork seeking permission from his commander, my parents, his parents, and anyone else with an interest in our lives, we set the date for December 27, 1943. Dot and I went to London to buy a wedding dress and I was fortunate to find one, especially with the shortages and rationing.

There were no caterers in Willingale, especially during the Christmas holiday and, even if there were, I couldn't afford one. So early on the morning of our wedding, I hitched up the farmer's horse and cart and drove across the village to the hall to prepare a wedding feast. Neither my family nor my London friends were able to attend the wedding. Transportation was difficult and limited. Willingale was quite a distance from my family's home in Pitsea, which is in the southern area of Essex. They would have had to travel by train through London, which was heavily bombed and still under attack.

When I finished setting up the refreshments, I drove the cart back to the farm. I didn't have time to heat water, so I took a cold bath, dressed in my white gown and drove the cart to the church. I'm pretty sure our wedding day was the first time Roy was ever on time for anything. I was 22 minutes late.

I think every girl remembers her wedding day. We exited the church through an arch of sabers. Most of the airmen from the base and an assortment of villagers from Willingale attended our reception. Although there were a number of airmen assigned to assist me in the kitchen, I still bustled around with a tray of food, fussing over our guests.

"This is a swell party," an officer said to me as I offered him a bite to eat. "Who's the bride?"

After a brief honeymoon in Bournemouth, Roy and I fell back into our routine. I worked on the farm and Roy flew sorties as a B-17 tail gunner over France and Germany. I had a permanent base pass and frequently visited Roy on base.

When I became pregnant, Roy insisted I see an American doctor.

"Isn't it great to look at a woman for a change?" the doctor exclaimed to a medic after my examination.

Everything changed when the Americans began preparation for the invasion of France. The countdown to D-Day started. Security on the base tightened and I was no longer allowed near the flight line. They transferred Roy to southern England and I moved in with my family in Essex.

Diane was born on July 28, 1944. Roy was lucky; they allowed him a few hours' leave to see his daughter before shipping him across the Channel. That parting was bittersweet. I knew Roy, as a tail gunner, was in one of the most vulnerable positions in the plane.

On October 17, 1944, I took Diane to the American Embassy in London to register her as an American citizen.

"Would you like to go to the United States?" an official asked as I signed the paperwork

I knew Roy wanted to go home after the war. I wasn't in a hurry to leave my family or the country of my birth, but I would eventually need to immigrate to the United States. I figured I might as well go sooner than later. I passed the required physical and they sent me home to await instructions for passage to my new country.

Excitement jockeyed with apprehension. I had never strayed farther from London than Bournemouth, a seaside resort where Roy and I honeymooned and my family spent their summer holidays. Now, I was about to set out across the Atlantic Ocean in the middle of a war, with a five-month-old baby, to a country that I'd never seen, to stay with a family I'd never met. Roy, if he survived, would join us when the war ended.

On October 27th, the American Embassy issued my visa.

Sailing instructions arrived by telegram on December 31, 1944. I was to report to the American Embassy on the morning of January 2, 1945. With Diane bundled up in blankets and a small wooden trunk carrying all my worldly possessions, my parents, grandmother, sisters and I arrived at the Embassy. We were to say our goodbyes there.

A clerk passed me a sealed envelope for the station-master and reluctantly agreed to allow my sister Gladys to accompany me to the station. We arrived at London's Victoria Station around one o'clock. At five, my sister, with tears in her eyes, told us goodbye. The train that would take Diane and me to the ship that would deliver us to our new lives didn't load until 8:00 PM that night. It seemed the British and Americans couldn't decide who was in charge of the transfer.

I had no idea where we were headed. The clickity-clack of the wheels on the track lulled Diane to sleep. The next morning, we arrived in Greenock, Scotland, and found ourselves deposited in an abandoned warehouse. My stomach growled with hunger. I hadn't eaten since noon the day before. My only nourishment had been a weak cup of tea on the train.

We waited in the warehouse all day. Around four in the afternoon on January 3rd, Diane and I boarded a small boat, which took us out to the *Aquitania*, a once-luxurious liner now outfitted to carry troops.

Once aboard the ship, the war brides and their little ones were escorted to our cabins. There were about 10 of us on board. The rest of the ship was filled with wounded American troops returning home. Many of the soldiers were lying in bunks stacked three high all around the decks, wherever space would allow.

Before sailing, we reported to the top deck for safety instructions and lifeboat assignment. The sailors passed out life jackets and life lights and ordered us to carry them with us everywhere. The RMS *Aquitania* traveled unescorted and zigzagged her way across the ocean in an attempt to avoid German U-boats lurking in the open sea.

Mealtime offered a feast of indulgence. I couldn't remember ever seeing that much food in one place.

Diane and I spent our free time visiting with the wounded soldiers. They loved holding Diane, passing her from bed to bed, tucking candy inside her blanket. They told me stories of their wives and children, often pulling pictures from their wallets. I enjoyed visiting with them, although it made me miss Roy even more. I wished he could hold Diane and wondered how he'd fare in the pending invasion of Normandy.

I tried not to dwell too much on my new family. I really didn't know very much about them, except that my new mother-in-law, Ivy, was born and raised in Trinidad, British West Indies. She met and married Roy Sr. in Panama, where he had served in the American Armed Forces during World War I. As a fellow war bride, I hoped she would make our transition to American life a little easier.

We sailed into New York Harbor on January 12th. A brass band onshore belted out "Twelfth Street Rag" as we passed under the benevolent gaze of Lady Liberty. We disembarked and were met by the Red Cross. Not all of the war brides were accepted into the United States. A few had gotten a little too cozy with the sailors on board the *Aquitania* and found themselves shipped back to England.

Diane and I were put up in a hotel for the night and boarded a train the next day for La Porte, Indiana, our new home. Again, curiosity about my new family ate away at my thoughts. Would I fit in?

American train stations differed in a number of ways from those in Europe. I held Diane in one arm and dragged my trunk with the other hand and stepped off the train into a snow bank. I didn't realize that you needed to move to the front of the train to disembark. As I struggled to free myself from the deep snow, a man standing on the end of the platform called out to me.

"I believe I am your father-in-law," he said.

What a first impression!

Roy's family was very nice to me, but I knew I had married momma's little darling. Roy was the oldest of three sons and enlisted in the Army Air Corps shortly after Roosevelt declared war. Both of his brothers served also, so his mother had a lot to worry about. I knew she accepted me when I heard her talking to a neighbor.

"Well, she can clean house."

Grace, my new sister-in-law, took me under her wing and made the difficult days of adjustment to my new life in a new country brighter. I was the first war bride to arrive in La Porte. As others began to arrive, we sought out one another and became fast friends. Eventually, we formed a club and called ourselves "The Fortnightly Club." We met every two weeks in each other's homes to share stories and support each other. Our members included girls from all over Britain and Europe.

It was 11 months before Roy arrived back in the United States aboard the *Queen Mary*. We settled down in La Porte off and on for a few years and then eventually moved to California. I applied for citizenship and on November 16, 1948, became a citizen of the United States of America. I grew to love my new country, although I made frequent trips "home" to England to see my family.

Billie and Roy moved to California in 1956. Billie worked in the accounting department for the City of Costa Mesa. During her tenure, she was a major influence in the establishment of employee benefits and the creation of the Costa Mesa Federal Credit Union. She retired in 1984, after 27 years with the city. Roy passed away in 1992, after nearly 49 years of marriage. Billie and Roy have four children, six grandchildren, and eight great-grandchildren. Billie lives in Prescott, Arizona.

WES COSS

——⚜——

ESCAPE THROUGH THE
FRENCH UNDERGROUND

The first enemy fighters came at us from the 11:30 position. Two ME-109s, in shallow dives, executed identical half-rolls, firing continuously. They passed under the *Stardust*, fully inverted with guns blazing.

Our navigator returned fire and the twin 50s in the upper turret hammered away, filling the cockpit with the deafening thunder of machine guns.

Oil pressure in the number two engine dropped.

"Feather number two," I called out to Bob Johnson, my copilot. He pushed the red "feather" button, shut off the fuel and turned off the ignition.

I held the B-17 in steady flight.

The prop on number two slowed, and then finally stopped as the feather button popped out, the number two prop now streamlined with the airflow.

I could see where a bullet tore through the rear section of the propeller blade, breaking it and leaving a gap that resembled an old-fashioned horizontal keyhole.

The *Stardust* fell out of position and pulled slightly to the left. I increased power to our three good engines and we climbed back into formation. Our scheduled mission was at the maximum range of our fuel endurance. If we avoided all problems, we would still sweat out the fuel on the return from our target, the airdrome at Salon-de-Provence in France. I was thankful that our course would take us back over Naples, where we could land and refuel. I had no desire to end up in the Mediterranean Sea, especially in the dead of winter.

The second attack started lower but followed the same path. I could see the red blasts from the guns of two FW-190 fighters as they made a shallow climb, rolled and passed just beneath us in inverted flight. I could hear the bullets rip into the *Stardust* and feel the jolting vibrations as the number one engine's rpm climbed higher and higher past the red line and caught fire.

Extensive damage made it impossible to feather the number one propeller. The spinning disc created by the propeller increased the drag on the B-17, pulling us more and more to the left. I tried to position the control surface trim tabs to help us fly straight and keep our wings level, but the tabs were already at their limit. Turning slowly to the left, we lost altitude and the protection of our squadron.

I decided to lighten our load and pulled the bomb salvo handle. The bomb bay doors opened and 12 500-pound bombs dropped off out of the bomb bay. Our rate of descent slowed, but the runaway propeller on the number one engine made it impossible to hold a straight course. I began to wonder if we would even make it to Corsica and the recently liberated airfield at Ajacio.

A single ME-109 came at us from one o'clock. Her bullets tore into the fuselage and the underside of our right wing.

"Waist to pilot," Sgt Joe Kinnane's voice crackled in my headset. "Number one is really burning."

"There is white smoke coming out of number three," Sgt Harold Rice, the ball turret gunner reported and I knew then that our underside had been hit.

"Roger," I acknowledged both of them. This definitely qualified as a "no win" situation.

Fire poured out of the number one engine and heavy vibration from the damage threatened to separate the left wing from the airplane. An emergency landing at Ajaccio, Corsica, evaporated as a viable option.

I rang the "bail out" bell and announced over the intercom system.

"Bail out—BAIL OUT!"

Bob and I fought to keep the airplane level. I reduced the power on number four and increased our descent. SSgt Edward Madigan, our flight engineer, tried to release the hatch pins from the escape hatch in the tunnel below the cockpit seats. They wouldn't budge.

"I'm going out the back of the airplane," Madigan said, before making his way toward the tail section, carrying his chute pack. I never saw him again. Ed never made it out of the plane.

It took both the navigator and bombardier to remove the pins and force the forward escape hatch open. Still fighting to control the plane, I looked down the tunnel. Walter Amundsen, our navigator, sat motionless on the edge of the opening. I unbuckled my seatbelt and made my way down into the tunnel. I placed my hands on his shoulders and pushed him out.

Returning to the cockpit, I reached to the left of the pilot's seat, grabbed my parachute pack and clipped it to my harness. I looked over at Bob Johnson. He motioned for me to jump, and indicated that he would follow.

A final German fighter attack raked the *Stardust* with bullets from the tip of her nose to the back edge of her tail.

Our cherished *Stardust* was going down.

I dropped through the escape hatch and floated on my back, the world slowly turning in a horizontal attitude. I could see the *Stardust*, burning brightly and spiraling down in a steep spin. Relieved to be out of the doomed bomber, I resisted the urge to pull my ripcord. I'd heard too many accounts of Allied airmen shot by Germans while drifting in their parachutes.

I looked at my watch. It was 12:26 on January 27, 1944. I was about to land in occupied France. I surveyed the ground beneath me and saw electrical transmission towers bisecting the barren and rocky hillside below. Knowing that I'd waited long enough, I pulled the handle on the ripcord. The chute flew out from the pack on my chest and cracked the air with the retort of a rifle shot as it opened above me. A strong wind pushed me toward the high-tension power lines and I envisioned myself entangled in the wires.

I made one last rotation before hitting hard on my back against the rocky ground. I saw the *Stardust* pass behind a hill and explode in a ball of fire, the brilliant flash followed by a loud thunderous clap. I checked my wristwatch. It was 12:29. The wreckage lay between me and the heavily fortified German-occupied coast of France.

I gathered my chute, removed my life jacket and throat mike. Stuffing them under a large bush, I covered the makeshift burial site with the few available rocks. An automobile passed on the bluff above me and I prayed that the occupants were more interested in the burning plane than in the white silk parachute that landed me safely on French soil.

Unsure of my precise location, I kept the smoke of the wreckage at my back and alternated running with rapid walking in an attempt to put as much distance as possible between me and the fallen *Stardust*. The barren, rocky terrain eventually gave way to a thick wooded area. I heard the sound of chopping and the guttural growl of what sounded to me like German. I made an exaggerated detour, avoiding the area and then continued in a north to northeast direction.

After hours of walking, I stumbled upon a stream that cut through the forest. I stopped to wash my face and hands and filled the small bladder from my escape kit with ice-cold water. Believing I needed to get as far away as possible from the downed plane, I continued picking my way through the woods.

A dog barked as I passed a small farm, causing my heart to race. Winter nights come early and the sky rapidly darkened around me. Silence reached out in every direction. I found myself alone, hungry and afraid. The seriousness of my situation slowly penetrated my overactive brain.

I didn't want to spend the rest of the war in a German POW camp. As a pilot assigned to the Fifteenth Air Force, I hadn't heard the stories told by members of the Eighth Air Force. I knew nothing about the Allied airmen routed out of France by members of the French Resistance.

On my own in an enemy-held country and unsure of my next move, I returned to the small farm and climbed into a haystack for the night. I offered a prayer of thanks for my safe delivery from the burning *Stardust* and asked for safe passage through occupied territory.

Restless sleep came in short stretches, punctuated by long, cold hours of worry. I feared the dog would hear me climb out of the haystack in the morning and desperately hoped no one would discover and follow my trail. I knew the Germans would find the wreckage of the *Stardust* and look for survivors. My spirits sank further as I contemplated the dismal future.

When the first reaches of dawn streaked the sky with pastel watercolors, I returned to the stream, washed my face and hands, refilled my water bladder and then followed its course through the woods. I crossed over the water at a small footbridge and took a path that led in a northeasterly direction, eventually climbing to the top of a hill partially covered with trees and shrubs. From the summit, I saw a valley filled with row after row of grapevines and divided by a simple lane that ended with a cluster of small homes.

Working my way down the hill, I sat in the shelter of a stand of trees and watched as a man labored in the vineyard nearest me. When he worked his way to the end of the row, I stood and crossed the short distance to the edge of the field.

Up close, I realized the worker was just a boy, somewhere around 15.

In the little French that I had picked up while based in North Africa, I blurted out, "I am an American. I am hungry and thirsty."

Without uttering a word, the boy dropped his tools and ran into the closest house.

I retreated back up the hill and watched.

Not more than 15 minutes later, a man and woman emerged from the house. He carried a French-English dictionary and, when they drew close, they both shook my hand. The man opened the book and pointed to the word *ami*, then to the French word for resistance, and then, with a smile, to the word safe. I breathed a grateful sigh of relief; I found myself among friends.

The wife carried a basket that contained a loaf of bread, cheese, a roll of hard sausage and two bottles of wine. She laid a tablecloth on the ground and spread out what, for me, after so many hours of not eating, truly was feast. I ate quickly while they watched.

Using the dictionary, the couple told me that someone would come for me after dark and take me to a safe place. I thanked them for their kindness and retreated a short distance up the hill where I would be sheltered from view. I finished the food, stretched out in the sun, dozing on and off throughout the afternoon. The tinkling of tiny bells awakened me and I found myself surrounded by a flock of grazing sheep. The sheep herder passed within 30 feet of my grassy bed, but, although I'm sure he saw me, paid no attention.

When darkness fell, the husband returned with his brother. He indicated that I was to follow them and they would lead me to a safer place. We stopped at the house and dropped off the empty basket. The wife brushed both of my cheeks with a light kiss and wished me Godspeed.

We emerged into the dark night and walked across the uneven ground through rows of dormant grapevines, their branches catching our pant legs as we passed by. We trudged through neighboring vineyards, up steep hills and across overgrown fields until we finally reached the main road.

"Wait here."

I crouched with the husband in the bushes and waited as his brother investigated.

Within minutes, we heard the soft whistle. Keeping low, we hurried across the road, ducking into another large vineyard. Finally, we came to an isolated lane that led to a large dark house that looked deserted from the outside. Two of us stayed back, hidden behind trees, waiting for the soft whistle.

Bright light flooded the interior. Seven or eight people sat around a table, lilting French conversation, melodious and flowing, filled the room. A few of the guests spoke English making it possible for me to explain that I was an American pilot and that my plane had been shot down while participating in a bombing raid on Salon-de-Provence airdrome.

I repeatedly asked if they had news of my crew, but no one admitted knowing anything other than the fact that six or seven parachutes had been spotted. That gave me reason to hope that most of my crew made it out of the plane alive.

Our hostess served a dinner of fried rabbit, oven-browned potatoes and a spinach casserole. My mouth watered and my stomach growled. The food tasted wonderful. I washed it down with numerous glasses of wine and finished the meal with hot cookies and crisp apples.

I learned that my new friends were members of the French Resistance, community members who went about their normal daily lives, but aided efforts to defeat the Germans whenever possible. They were crucial links in the underground chain that actively rescued Allied airmen.

The Resistance replaced my uniform with civilian clothes. They gave me a pair of dark trousers, a plain black belt, a long-sleeve shirt and a French navy-issue sweater. A heavy navy-type peacoat with ordinary buttons and a heavy black knit cap completed my disguise. The only things I kept were my long johns, socks, shoes, wristwatch and dog tags.

Exhausted after a sleepless night, I turned in around 10. I climbed into a feather bed with a thick feather comforter and plump feather pillows. I immediately drifted off and slept soundly through the night. Around eight the next morning, my hostess awakened me with a soft knock on the door.

I could smell the food before she brought the tray to the bed. I sopped up the yoke from a soft-boiled egg with several slices of bread coated in jam. The ersatz coffee tasted bitter and she apologized for its poor quality. I assured her it tasted fine.

The absurdity of awaking in the comfort of a feather bed with the warmth and smells of a hot breakfast served to me versus spending a cold and frightening night in a haystack was hard to comprehend.

Around 2:30 that afternoon, three men, driving a small covered van, picked me up. Two of us climbed into the back. I noticed my companion carried a small British-manufactured Sten submachine gun.

The van, powered by a strange charcoal burning engine, was not particularly powerful, and several times we climbed out and pushed the little vehicle up a hill.

At dusk, we pulled into a commercial garage that had

closed for the night. We made our way to the rear of the building, where four people waited for us in a small office. Greeted with handshakes, they invited me to sit in an unoccupied chair.

They passed around a small box of cookies. I helped myself to one. Fumbling, I dropped the cookie onto the very dirty floor. I picked it up and started to toss it into a wastebasket.

"*Non!*" one of the men barked. He reached over, took the cookie from my hand, brushed the dirt off, and handed it back to me.

I ate it. Lesson learned—we do not waste anything here.

One of the women in the group spoke excellent English.

"Are you the pilot?" she asked.

"Yes."

"What is your name?"

"Wes Coss."

"What is your squadron?"

"347th."

On and on she went, questioning me in detail about my fellow crew members, their hometowns, and our mission. I learned later that it was her job to establish my true identity as an American and not a German plant inserted to trap members of the Resistance. Had I not thoroughly convinced her, I would have been shot as soon as we left the area.

It wasn't until much later that I realized the grave risks taken by the French who assisted the Allied airmen. Discovery guaranteed either immediate transport to Nazi concentration camps, or, more likely, instant execution.

The night turned pitch black by the time we left the garage. We alternated driving and pushing the little vehicle for hours, eventually parking in front of a deserted house at the top of a steep hill. My escorts made sure the blinds were securely drawn before turning on any light. The house, a vacation home nestled on a creek in the mountains, served as a safe house for the Marquis, a collection of rural guerilla resistance fighters. They would play a significant role in Hitler's eventual defeat.

My new hosts pulled together some food for dinner. Not nearly as savory as our meal the prior night, at least it filled our bellies and I was grateful. Worn down with fatigue and anxiety, I checked the clock on the mantel. It was 10:30.

"Good night," I said, turning toward the couch.

A soft whistle sounded outside the window. One of my hosts opened the door and a man, obviously the boss, stepped into the room.

"Come with us," he said to me in English.

I climbed into the back of the van with one of the three Marquis fighters, all armed with Sten machine guns. We coasted down the hill, putted through the valley and stopped in a small village. The boss and one of the fellows who had ridden with me in the back, climbed out, with their guns. Minutes later they returned, carrying a box.

We retraced our route, pushing the van up the hills and coasting on the down slope. When we turned on to the main road, an automobile, driving very fast, came up on us. Their headlights bathed our little van in bright light. My companion peeked out through a small hole in the canvas.

"Gestapo."

He didn't need to say anything else. I knew the Marquis would not be taken alive. I doubted I would survive the shoot-out.

"*Passay! Passay!*" The driver yelled, waving his arm from the driver's-side window, signaling the big car to pass us.

Finally, the Gestapo sped by and disappeared into the night. I breathed a big sigh of relief.

We pushed the car up the hill to our hideout. The haul

that night was a box of ration coupons—food for the Resistance workers. Somewhat disgusted and pissed off by the risks taken on this dangerous raid, I bundled myself in blankets, curled up on the short couch and attempted some restless sleep. My companions slept with their machine guns.

A chunk of cheese, bread and jam made up our breakfast the next morning, along with ersatz coffee, a bitter combination of what tasted like oats, chicory and maybe a hint, just a small hint, of coffee beans.

At about 9:30 that Sunday morning, three days after bailing out of the *Stardust*, two men in a four-door automobile arrived to pick me up. I couldn't tell if we were driving east or northeast when we set off that morning, but we continued up through the rolling hills and into the mountains, eventually stopping at a farm nestled at the base of a sheer bluff.

The farmer took us behind the barn where we found two grossly overloaded donkeys tethered to the corral fence. Church bells rang in the distance as we began our trek along a steep, winding path up the bluff. It took over an hour of climbing to reach the top. When we stopped to catch our breath, my companions, Jean Juvenale and his friend Pierre, told me that some of my crew members would soon join us.

Finally, the terrain flattened out. A path led us through the brush and trees to a clearing where we paused to wait for the others. Eventually, Bob Johnson, Ernie Jenkins and Joe Kinnane joined us. I was overjoyed to be reunited with my co-pilot, bombardier and left waist gunner.

"We must keep you hidden until the Germans stop searching for survivors," our guide told us. "We anticipate your stay here will last about two weeks."

About a mile up the path, we stopped at a two-level stone building. The lower level housed sheep, the upper, which was even with the ground in the front, provided living quarters for the sheep herder, Marcel (pronounced Marseal).

The four of us shared the twelve-by-fifteen-foot room. One wall was dominated by a stone fireplace that provided the only source of heat. A small six-by-eight-foot kitchen and stone storeroom completed the farmhouse. A fire had destroyed the roof over the main room, so we put together a makeshift bed of straw and two old blankets, placing it as close as safely possible to the open fireplace. The kitchen, haphazardly covered with corrugated metal, overlooked the sheep's watering trough. Thick stone walls surrounded the three-sided sheep enclosure under the house. A bench of stone about two and a half feet wide and three feet high ran along one wall of the pen. Marcel, wrapped in his thick coat, slept on this bench.

The winter was brutally cold. Thin layers of ice formed on the watering trough during the night. We struggled, two per blanket, to keep warm while sleeping, moving our makeshift bed into the unheated kitchen on rainy nights.

Most meals consisted of mutton, beans and potatoes, although some days Marcel returned with wild rabbits tucked into the deep pockets of his ankle-length overcoat. We looked forward to those nights.

Marcel was about six feet tall, with long, shaggy, uncombed hair. Several of his front teeth were missing and he spoke almost no English. Taciturn and moody, we found it difficult to converse, until we discovered that Marcel had picked up some "bad" words from American soldiers during WWI. It got a little vulgar at times, but at least we could communicate.

Within a few days, we settled into a pretty good routine. We spent the mornings foraging for dead, dry wood and took turns fetching water from the only potable well, located about a quarter of a mile from the house. Sometimes in the afternoons, we would stretch out in the sun and watch the Germans take off and land at the auxiliary airfield in the valley below our hideout. However, one afternoon, a JU-88 came in very low over the trees where we were sitting. Afraid that the Germans had spotted us, we took off running for the house. After that, we took extra care to avoid discovery, always staying within sight of the safe house.

On the second Friday, visiting members from the French Resistance informed us that the Germans had given up the hunt and that we would soon move to the city. Certain that we had overstayed our welcome and that Marcel was anxious for us to depart, we all looked forward to the change.

A couple of days later, Jean Juvenale, Pierre Dudet, a local shoe manufacturer, and several other men picked us up. We made the trek back down to the farmhouse below the bluff, the same path we took about two weeks earlier. Ernie and Bob climbed into Pierre Dudet's car. They split us up, Ernie staying with Dudet and Bob hiding in the shoemaker's home. Joe and I rode with Jean Juvenale to Aix-en-Provence.

Our safe house was a two-bedroom, second-floor apartment, the home of Juvenale, his wife and their young daughter. We stayed in the daughter's room and shared her full-sized bed, a real treat after sharing a single blanket on our miserable straw pad.

For the first time in over two weeks, I climbed out of my long underwear and into a hot bath. I lowered myself into the steaming water and scrubbed with a bar of soap. I'd forgotten the luxury of being clean. When I climbed out, a black ring circled the tub. On my knees, I reached over and scrubbed it clean so that Joe wouldn't have to soak in my filth.

It took several days for Mrs. Juvenale to wash our clothes. Worried that the neighbors would notice and report an increase in laundry, she distributed the dirty clothes into several loads and dried them on wooden racks in her kitchen.

It was imperative that the Juvenales maintain their normal routine, so on the third day of our stay in Aix-en-Provence, Mrs. Juvenale entertained a small group of women. Hiding in the daughter's room, Joe sat quietly on the chair, while I sat on the bed. We could hear the women chatting and laughing. Suddenly, I had a strong urge to cough. I covered my face with a pillow and coughed lightly. That simply exacerbated the problem. The urge to cough grew stronger. Wearing slippers on my feet, I tiptoed across the room. Using two pillows to muffle the sound, I climbed into the closet and closed the door. I prayed, if one of the women heard me coughing, that she would believe it came from the neighboring apartment.

We needed some form of identification, so Jean arranged for a Resistance worker to take us to a shop where they provided counterfeit documents. The shopkeeper snapped my picture in a small curtained booth. My French identification papers read Rene Robert Costa and put me one step closer to making my way back to my squadron.

On Friday, Mrs. Juvenale hosted another women's club gathering and decided to move us out of the apartment for the day. They split us up. At around 8:00, a very pretty French woman knocked on our door. She couldn't have been more that 18 or 19. Taking my hand, we strolled across the city, like two lovers out on a beautiful, bright sunny morning.

She spoke fair English and seemed to delight in taunting the occasional German soldier as we passed. We ended up at her grandparents' house on the outskirts of the city. Her grandfather, "The General," was a retired general officer from WWI. Although he spoke only French, we chatted through his granddaughter.

A maid served a light lunch of sandwiches, fruit and wine.

"You must kick the *Boche*[1] out of France," he told me, glass held high in a toast.

I touched my glass to his in agreement then sipped the wine.

---

1 French slang term for the Germans.

We spent the afternoon looking at the General's scrapbooks and swapping war stories. It was with a touch of sadness that we parted later that afternoon.

"*Merci beaucoup*," I said, kissing her lightly on both cheeks. If only young love was allowed to blossom in such times. . . .

"*Au revoir!*" she said, almost skipping down the street. For a moment I stood struck, first by her beauty, demeanor and vivacious, bubbly personality, then by the risk she had taken by escorting me through the city. I had no doubt that she understood the danger.

The Resistance workers in Aix-en-Provence were a close-knit group and frequently shared meals at the Juvenale home. I was beginning to pick up some French and enjoyed practicing. I learned that they shared a deep hatred for the *Boche* and had devised their own justice system to punish anyone who collaborated with the Germans or turned someone in to the Gestapo. A one-armed Frenchman, who regularly dined in the Juvenale home, was the appointed assassin.

Jean believed that we should keep up our strength for the trek over the Pyrenees and frequently invited us on walks around the city. But each time we ventured out, we encountered German soldiers marching in the streets. Even with our French identification papers, these sightings made us nervous.

One Saturday morning, Jean invited me to join him on a bike ride through the city. Used to a bicycle with balloon tires, large fenders and back brakes, I was a little unstable on the French cycle, which had thin tires, hand brakes and a high, narrow seat the size of a banana. After a couple of tries, I mounted the bike and began pedaling.

Jean took off and I followed at the instructed 50 yards behind, struggling to keep him in sight on the narrow, winding streets. Black ice lurked in the shade. I watched Jean ride up a hill, then lost him as he descended the other side. This continued for some time. Finally, I crested a hill and spotted a line of German soldiers, stretched arm in arm across the road. They were singing and laughing, as if going to a soccer game. The hill was icy, and I used the brakes in an attempt to slow down. The bike began to teeter from side to side and I fought for control. My feet came off the pedals, which continued to turn, precariously hitting me in the ankles.

The Germans continued to block the road and panic took the place of reason. Out of control, I hurled toward the soldiers with visions of POW camps in my head. At the very last minute, they laughingly split apart and allowed me to pass, thoroughly enjoying my obvious discomfort. I have no idea how I avoided hitting one of them, or how I stayed upright on the bike.

When I caught up with Jean, he, too, was laughing so hard that he couldn't speak. Anger replaced fear, and I insisted we head straight home. I warned Joe, who refused any offers of bike tours through the city.

On February 22, around 10 days after taking shelter with the Juvenale family, Joe and I were taken by car to an apartment about 25 kilometers outside of Aix-en-Provence. Instructed to follow the driver alone, I got out of the car without Joe.

Our driver knocked on the door, and a Frenchwoman, probably in her mid-thirties let me in. Well-spoken, with a slight English accent, my new hostess was attached to the Free French Intelligence. Her job was to give me some intelligence information that I was to deliver to the British or the Americans.

"This will make me a spy," I argued when I discovered her mission. "They will execute me if I'm caught."

"What difference?" she asked. "You will be shot immediately if you are caught anyway."

She laid out French army maps marked with German

troop concentrations, gun emplacements and underground fuel supplies. She pointed out a hidden seaplane base and indicated the auxiliary airfields used by the Germans. She told me that someone had leaked information of our raid on Salon-de-Provence and that all flyable planes had been cleared from the field.

She imparted intelligence reports of German fortifications along the Mediterranean coast, and the reported Nazi practice of forcing all railroad passengers to work for 48 hours before being allowed to continue their journey. She drilled me over and over again on the information, promising to review it the next morning.

We shared the bed, but she was long asleep before I slipped between the covers. As I climbed into bed that night, I worried about my new status as a spy. Yesterday, I was just another airman, a regular POW if caught. Now, if captured, I would be shot as a spy. I decided not to share any of this information with Joe or anyone else. The last thing I wanted to do was compromise their safety.

She was up and dressed before I awoke the next morning. As soon as we completed breakfast, she continued drilling me on the intelligence information I was to carry to the Allies. She wanted to make sure that I could repeat it verbatim. When she was finally satisfied, she replaced my French ID with a Polish identification card. They used the same picture, only now my name was Josef, a 23-year-old worker. I couldn't even pronounce my last name.

"If a Frenchman stops you," she said, "just show him your ID and say nothing." She also gave me French papers indicating that Josef was required to travel from Marseilles to Perpignan, France. My journey to Spain had begun.

The knock came after an early dinner. I went into the bathroom to gather my toothbrush and razor.

"Go with this man. He will turn you over to a guide

who will purchase your train tickets. Follow your guide, but not too closely." She studied my face to make sure I was listening. "When your guide gets off the train, follow him. But do not sit near him and do not, under any circumstances, make any direct contact with him."

With that, she kissed me on both cheeks and bid me adieu.

I was happy to see Joe in the car and quickly filled him in on my evening with the mysterious Frenchwoman, carefully leaving out all of the intelligence briefings. The fun of letting him speculate if I'd "made out" or "struck out" diverted my attention from worrying about my probable execution, at least for a short time.

The trip to the train station in Marseilles seemed to last forever, but finally, we arrived. Our driver then took us into the station and located our guide. The guide wore a hat, rather than a tam and was easy to spot in his light tan overcoat. Joe and I carried our identification papers, and I'd cultivated a little blond fuzz mustache hopefully making me look closer to 23, but I knew if we needed to speak our cover would be blown.

We quickly shook hands with our new guide. He gave us tickets for Avignon and we followed him to the gate. Cautioned against any conversation, Joe and I silently found an empty compartment in the same coach as our guide, where we could see him, but not be spotted with him, and promptly faked sleep.

We were joined by a French couple, but were spared from conversation by our charade. The conductor made his way through the car, checked our tickets, punched them and moved on. We returned to our naps. At least Joe did, I faked it the entire time.

Our guide got off the train in Avignon and we followed him into the station. He stopped at one point, allowing us to catch up with him. He pointed to his watch, indicated one hour, he muttered, *"Merci."* I'm sure for the benefit of anyone who might be watching.

From that point on we kept our distance. After purchasing tickets to Perpignan, he slipped them to me while perusing the newsstand, then moved away. When the train was announced, we followed him to the boarding gate. Our guide was the first one though the gate.

The gate attendant looked at the guide's ticket.

"Merci," he said.

He continued to check tickets and with a polite *"merci"* would punch them.

When I came to the turnstile, the attendant checked my ticket.

"Thank you," he said, and punched it.

Joe followed me. Again the attendant said "thank you" in English before punching Joe's ticket.

Sweat popped out in little beads on my forehead. Dressed like the Frenchmen around us, I wondered how the attendant knew that we spoke English. Had our cover been blown? Fear struck us both.

Our guide settled near the front of the train car, we entered an empty compartment near the back. Although we couldn't see him, we knew he would signal us when the time came to get off the train.

Just as the train started to roll, three German soldiers entered our compartment. Overly alert, we feigned sleep. Neither Joe nor I spoke passable French. My papers listed me as Polish. I couldn't even read them.

Throughout the first half of the trip, blackout curtains covered the windows, and artificial lighting kept the interior bright. The shades were opened for the second half and a blue cove light was the only illumination in the compartment and in the aisle. I had a good view of the front of the car, and would sneak a peek whenever possible. Luckily, the Germans slept. I counted my blessings.

We stopped at towns throughout the night. The steady clickity-clack and rocking of the train kept me company. Sometime well after midnight, we stopped in a large town. The blackout curtains were drawn over the windows and the bright overhead lights were turned on. A German officer and French gendarme started at the front of the car and began checking identification papers. I nudged Joe. The German soldiers across from us began rummaging through their bags for their papers.

I kept my head against the wall by the door, watching for our guide. He stood and stepped into the aisle. Fumbling through his suit pockets, he made quite a show of searching for his papers. Not finding them on his person, he returned to his compartment and searched the pockets of his overcoat, finally producing the proper documents.

All the while, Joe and I tried to keep our breath even, praying that the Germans who shared our compartment wouldn't hear our hearts racing in our chests. Would we be questioned? Would our papers pass scrutiny? I was now officially a spy. Would I be shot?

We couldn't figure out why our guide drew such attention to himself. He was finally allowed to return to his compartment. When the inspectors were a mere two compartments away from us, the train began to roll. Both the gendarme and German officer bolted for the rear door and jumped to the platform. We breathed a sigh of relief and finally understood the show performed by our guide.

The German across from me pulled out a cigarette.

"*Strieckles?*" he asked, poking me.

I shook my head no, and returned to feigned sleep, my hand over my face so I could peek out through my fingers. The train rolled on through the night and the sun had begun its ascent when our stop was finally announced.

The German soldiers sharing our compartment began

to collect their gear, pulling duffel bags from the overhead compartment and smaller bags from under our feet. Joe and I stepped out into the corridor. The train rolled very slowly, and people opened their coach doors and jumped off at the various cross streets.

Our guide stood near the front of the car. He looked at us to make sure we saw him, and then stepped off at the next cross street. We followed, ducking our heads against the gently falling snow, and shuffling through the thin layer of white that coated the street.

We trailed along behind him, a little closer than planned because of the poor visibility. He never looked back. Turning off the main street, he led us up a side street into a bakery. We walked straight through the bakery and out the back door, eventually ending up in a small pension just off the kitchen area.

The man working there seemed to be expecting us. He took us into the empty kitchen and gave us hot coffee and some croissants with preserves. Our guide shook our hands, and then disappeared back into the street. We waited in a small alcove off the kitchen for our new host.
Simone, a young school teacher, spoke excellent English.

"You will stay with me until your companions catch up with you tomorrow or the next day," she said. "The hotel will provide you with a room until I get back from school."

We shared a small room on the first floor. Joe and I fell into the single bed, rolled over and slept until Simone came for us around four that afternoon. Leaving the hotel, her arms looped through ours, she led us through the streets to her small studio apartment.

The plan was for Simone to maintain her normal schedule, returning home after school to cook our dinner, then leaving around nine to spend the night with a girlfriend. Simone warned us that one of her neighbors was dating a member of the Gestapo.

"Be very careful," she told us before leaving. "Don't let her spot you here."

After lighting the fireplace for warmth that first night, we pulled the bed apart. One of us slept on the box springs, the other on the mattress on the floor. Simone returned before daylight. We ate breakfast then she left for school.

Ernie and Bob were due in that day, or the next day at the very latest. We waited patiently for their arrival. On Saturday night, when they still had not arrived, Simone began to get nervous.

News of their capture was slow in reaching the Perpignan Resistance workers helping us escape. On Sunday, Simone learned from her contact that Ernie and Bob left Marseilles the 24th, the night after we left. They were arrested by the Gestapo near the train station in Perpignan and turned over to the German army. Their guides, a young couple working with the Resistance, were executed. Bob and Ernie heard the orders given to the firing squad and the shots through the barred window of the interrogation room.

That was "Black Sunday." Hiding us in her apartment put Simone in mortal danger, but turning us out ensured our capture. The Perpignan ring had been broken, our escape jeopardized. She agonized over her dilemma but never once asked us to leave. The carefree girl that hid us three days ago was gone, in her place stood a woman fully aware of the implications of her actions.

On Monday, Simone heard from her contact that copies of our pictures had been found in the heel of the shoe of the executed guide and published in the local newspaper. The Gestapo was now looking for us and warned that anyone helping or harboring these "enemy agents" would be shot on sight.

Simone made arrangements to take time off from work and travel to her parents' home in a rural area east of

Bordeaux. She would leave when they moved us from her apartment. In the meantime, local Resistance workers plotted our escape. On Tuesday afternoon, Simone packed up two parcels of food, knit gloves and a scarf for our two-day trek over the Pyrenees mountains. She carefully tied the packages with string. She gave us each a water container and a medicine bottle filled with schnapps.

Around 5:30 that afternoon, a young man delivered the coded knock on the door and Simone let him in. We picked up our food bundles, tucked our scarves, gloves and schnapps into coat pockets and turned to say goodbye.

"*Au revoir*," Simone said, with a hug and a kiss on each one of our cheeks. "God go with you."

She was so warm and cheerful that I couldn't help but think, "Please God, don't let her down." Both Joe and I prayed that she would make good her own private escape to her parents' sanctuary and survive the war.

It was a moonless night and our guide wore dark clothing. We stayed close as he led us south, out of the city, across a field and into an area of high grass and spongy ground. After walking some distance, he told us to crouch down and wait.

A low whistle sounded in the distance. Soon we were joined by a group of American and British airmen. We followed their leader further into the grassy area. When we finally halted, this new guide gave us each a token, a French franc bank note torn in half.

"Keep it safe," he said. "Only give it to your guide when you are safely in Spain."

We continued walking and eventually met up with two mountain guides leading a group of French civilians and a Russian Jew. I had the feeling that our new guides, perhaps a Basque father and son, were professional smugglers. Luckily, one of the French civilians spoke numerous languages. He became our communication link with the guides. Orders were given directly to the Frenchman then whispered from one person to the next down our single-file line.

German sentries patrolled the area, so we walked very close to each other, silent in a single file. Our path turned into a road. The younger guide went ahead on reconnaissance, a soft whistle signaled safe passage and we hurried across the road. We continued in this fashion, across roads, around farms and through vineyards.

One of the Americans tripped and swore in a loud voice. A dog barked nearby and we all froze. It was a few minutes before we continued. When we cleared the vineyard, our guide stopped and turned to our interpreter.

"If anyone makes noise like that again, he will be left behind."

There was no question that our guide was serious. We considered ourselves properly warned.

We walked in silence for two hours then stopped for a 15-minute rest.

"*Allez vite*," our guide growled. Hurry up. Move.

We heard this so often, that we unofficially named our guides Allez #1, our leader, and Allez #2, the guide who brought up the rear and prodded the stragglers.

Our path took us through the foothills, perpendicular to the coast. Every time we heard a dog bark, our guide would stop. He seemed able to discern the local farm dogs from the German dogs accompanying soldiers on patrol.

At midnight, we stopped for a second rest. Joe and I opened our supplies and ate some bread and cheese. We barely had time to finish eating when our guide rousted us.

"*Allez vite*."

I tried to retie my bundle of food but couldn't get it to stay together. I took the scarf out of my pocket and wrapped it around the food, tying the corners securely.

As we started into the mountains, we heard dogs bay-ing in the distance. Our guide immediately changed directions. Allez #2 spread pepper on the trail.

We came to a rushing mountain stream filled with the runoff from melting snow. It wasn't deep but it was wide. Our guides took off their shoes and socks, then rolled up their pant legs as high as possible.

We followed suit, tying our shoestrings together and wrapping our shoes around our necks. The first few made it across without any real trouble, but some got the hems of their coats wet. I decided to remove my jacket and tie it around my neck as well.

I waded into the icy water, stepping from one submerged stone to another. The stones were rough and slippery. I slipped off one and went down into the cold water, losing the grip on my food packet. I was wet to the waist by the time I reached the other shore and my food had washed away down the stream.

One of the Frenchmen behind me slipped and apparently hit his head on a submerged rock. Swept away, he never struggled or attempted to swim to shore. He just disappeared into the dark night. The guide went downstream for a few minutes but came back alone.

"*Allez vite*," he said and we moved on.

My wet pants and sweater dripped down on my socks and shoes. Pretty soon my feet were soaked. Chilled to the bone, I started shivering. When we came to the next stream, I took off my socks but put my shoes back on. After crossing, I dumped the water out of my shoes and sloshed along with the group.

I couldn't stop shivering. Cold, exhausted, I kept moving, hoping that constant movement would keep me from freezing to death. I was worried about the lost food. I knew Joe would share his, but if we got pinned down by German patrols, or if the trip across the mountains took more than two days, we wouldn't have enough to eat.

Joe took the loss of food in stride, but his energy level lagged and we had trouble keeping up with the group. We were climbing now, in some steeper foothills, and the going was tough.

"You just leave me here, Lieutenant," he said, struggling to keep moving.

I wasn't about to leave him.

"*Allez, allez, vite, vite,*" the rear guide admonished us. We struggled along. Relief flooded my soul when I saw the eastern sky begin to lighten. Certain that we would travel only at night I looked forward to getting a little rest.

Dogs began to bark in the distance. Our guides stopped, and then started to backtrack, over the ground so recently gained. Allez #2 spread pepper. Eventually we stopped and waited, listening for the dogs and German footsteps.

With the dawn's light, we could see the mountains. They looked formidable in the daylight, with snow-covered peaks. We bedded down in an area of thick brush near some large boulders. After telling us to stay out of sight, remain quiet and not smoke, our guides disappeared. Exhausted, we stretched out in the morning sun and tried to sleep. As the day wore on, we ate a little and got to know our fellow travelers. My clothes were dry but my shoes were still wet.

I decided to cut a walking stick. I cut a little sapling that had a "Y" at the top. I trimmed the two branches, forming a crutch. Soon I would be very glad that I'd made this effort.

Joe and I ate conservatively and watched as our companions consumed their meals. One of the fellows pulled a crisp apple from his pack and began eating it. My mouth watered at the sound of his munching. When he threw the core away, I covered it with dirt and sand. After the man and his companions crawled away, I retrieved the apple, washed it off and ate it. My stomach growled its approval.

Around six that night, we formed a single-file line behind Allez #1 and started out on our second night of walking to Spain. Our trek took us up and down hills, the ground covered with shale and rocks, the upside often slick with ice and snow. We'd take two steps forward and slide back one, sometimes slipping, sliding and falling down the slope. My walking stick came in handy. I wished I had cut one for Joe.

The German patrols on the border were heavy and our guides admonished us to stay silent. We stopped to rest every two hours. Joe and I were lucky that we still had our own shoes. Some of the travelers had ill-fitting shoes and they suffered from blisters and frostbite.

We came into an area of heavy snow. The path was narrow, steep and rocky. One of the Frenchmen slipped and fell into the gully below. We could hear him falling, tumbling in the dark.

"Allez vite," our guides admonished. One of the Frenchman's friends turned back but our guide moved us forward. We never saw either of the Frenchmen again.

As we approached the border, a searchlight, perched on a peak above us, was turned on. We all dropped down, lying perfectly still, curled up like rocks. The light remained on for 10 or 15 minutes, then suddenly shut off. There were indeed Germans patrolling the border.

I was thirsty and out of water. Eating the snow didn't satisfy my thirst. My energy reached its lowest point and I begged Joe to continue on without me. He wouldn't consider it. He grabbed my arm, pushed and shoved from behind just to keep me moving.

"Spain is just over the next hill," our translator kept telling us.

Finally, around midnight, we stopped to rest. There was some water. We broke the thin ice and drank our fill. I must have been dehydrated, because the water helped me.

When we got up to move, Joe "hit the wall." He staggered and stumbled, often falling. It was my turn to pull and prod, staggering like two drunks.

At 1:30 in the morning, we actually saw the lights of Spain. It was March 2, 1944, and we were finally out of France. Our interpreter passed the word.

"Be extra quiet," he told us. "The Spanish patrols are to be feared." Officially neutral, the Spanish favored the Nazis and for a pittance would turn us over to the Gestapo.

"*Allez vite.*"

We continued single file down the hill, slipping and sliding on patches of ice. At three in the morning, we stopped near a deserted stone hut. The guides let us go inside for warmth. We soon started out again. A little before daybreak, we circled around a small village. The local dogs barked, but the guides paid no attention.

We stopped in an area of tall reeds. The marshy ground was soggy and our shoes were wet. We couldn't sit down, so we crouched on our haunches.

"Stay here," the translator told us. "The guide will get us some food."

Our guides appeared out of thin air, making us aware of how easily we could have been overtaken by enemy patrols. They brought a large bundle of fish and chips wrapped in newspapers and three or four bottles of wine.

I ate with abandon, scooping up food with my hands and gobbling it down. My stomach revolted. I turned away and vomited. Finally, when my system settled down, I took it a little easier, eating chips and drinking a little wine.

When we finished, Allez #1 and Allez #2 requested our "souvenirs." We gave them the torn French francs and they simply disappeared, leaving us in the hands of a local guide. What was left of our group split up after the guides left. The Frenchmen headed off for Figueres, Spain. Only we Americans and two British continued. They housed us at a farm for two nights and on the third day, a man came for us at dark.

We cut across fields and followed paths through farm villages, finally reaching a train station on the outskirts of a small town. The guide took us to coal cars attached to a freight train.

"You ride in here," he told us in passable English. "Watch for me to get off."

Five of our group climbed into one car, the guide, two others and I got in the coal car just ahead of them.

The ride was bumpy and the cars swayed as they rolled along the track. Coal dust settled on our skin, working its way into the pores, and infiltrating our lungs, making us cough. We traveled all night, stopping just as the sun made its appearance. We followed the guide across the rail yard, through a fence, to a small stream that ran through an adjacent pasture.

"Wash up," he said.

We did the best we could. It was nearly impossible to get all the coal dust off our face and hands. Luckily, Joe and I wore stocking caps, so our hair was pretty much dust-free.

He gave us each a ticket to Barcelona, and then showed us a picture of the British Consulate. Drawing a map of the area on the ground with a stick, he carefully traced out the route he wanted us to take.

"Memorize this route," he said. "The German Gestapo is very active in Barcelona. They will be on the lookout for evaders. If you are caught by the Spanish police, they will turn you over to the Germans for a price."

He looked at each of us. "Ride in separate compartments. Do not speak to each other. Avoid eye contact with anyone if you can."

We wandered into the nearby station, two at a time, and climbed aboard when they called our train. Joe and I entered a compartment with a family and immediately faked sleep. The conductor came by, punched our tickets and we went back to "sleep."

We arrived in Barcelona around 10:30 in the morning. We wandered out of the station and up the street, stopping to look in store windows like inconspicuous tourists. Walking slowly, following the memorized map, we turned onto the street where the British Consulate was located. We approached the Consulate on the opposite side of the street. My heart beat double time and I imagined the Gestapo was hiding just inside every doorway, waiting for us to pass.

When we were directly across from the Consulate, I whispered to Joe, "Let's go for it!"

We dashed across the street. The guard at the entrance opened the door and we ran inside. The guard indicated a stairway and we went to the second floor. At the top of the stairs, a British woman sat behind a desk.

"Are you from the frontier?" she asked.

"Yes."

She asked us to sign our name and rank in a large book, and then pushed a buzzer. A British man joined us.

"Are there any others?" he asked.

"Six more," I told him.

"Two have already come in," he said. "The other four should be along shortly."

He left the words "I hope" unsaid.

We arrived in England on Sunday, March 19, 1944— more than seven weeks after being shot down. It took a while to prove our identity and I was able to deliver the intelligence information given to me by the lovely Frenchwoman in Marseilles almost a month earlier.

We departed London on April 8th and, after stops in Iceland and Newfoundland, arrived in New York on April 10th. It was good to be home. I immediately sent a telegram to my parents stating that I was back in "God's Country" and would be home the next day.

I was blessed with a loving family that surrounded me with values that carried me through the best and worst of times. I lived my dream. I flew for enjoyment, flew to serve my country and flew for a living. And I have never forgotten what it means to be an American and free.

Wes flew for Continental Airlines for 37 years. After retirement, he enjoyed cruising with his second wife on his powerboat, *Sea Whiskers*. He and his late first wife, Dee, have two children and one granddaughter. Wes lives in Palos Verdes, California.

Decorations and Awards: Air Medal with three Oak Leaf Clusters, "winged boot," a British award.

ROBERT "BOB" JOHNSON

(BY CINDY JOHNSON WOODS)

—⟨⟨⟨⟩⟩⟩—

CLASSIFIED 4-F

In 1939, I barely graduated from high school. I was fairly intelligent, and could work hard on things I enjoyed, but schoolwork was not one of those things. In fact, while I could add up almost any column of numbers in my head, the principal of Bloomington High School in Illinois only agreed to pass me with a "D" in mathematics because I promised never to do anything that required the subject. I thanked the Man upstairs, as my father called him, for squeaking me through.

I had been working at the local Standard Oil service station part-time, and now I could be a full-time employee. I was a good mechanic, and I enjoyed helping people, so it was a perfect fit. Having gotten my pilot's license when I was a senior, I now had the money to go flying whenever I had the time.

Flying was like a puzzle for me, and I loved solving puzzles and riddles of every kind. Figuring out the wind direction, speed, and altitude was about the most fun I could think of.

When I was younger, my dad had been the city clerk for Bloomington. He had the opportunity to meet and work with attorneys, and found that law appealed to him. So he attended Wesleyan Law School to earn his law degree, taking classes taught by local attorneys after hours.

He graduated as president of his class. After he passed the bar exam, one of his professors, Adlai H. Rust, hired him as his law clerk. Before long, Dad was handling all Mr. Rust's "growth" work, so Mr. Rust would be free to concentrate on his biggest client: the State Farm Automobile Insurance Company.

State Farm grew rapidly in Bloomington, and in 1940, they hired Mr. Rust and Dad to handle their legal work exclusively.

And in 1941, I went to work for State Farm.

I made more at State Farm than I had at Standard Oil, but it wasn't as interesting. I did general office work, such as filing and distributing mail. I also helped keep the few office machines working properly.

Most forms were filled out by hand in those days, but there were a bank of typewriters that got quite a workout making multiple carbon copies. My job was to make sure the keys were straightened after they jammed together when the typists got going too fast for the machine. I was also in charge of untangling the keys on the company's one comptometer. It was sort of like a typewriter with numbers on the keys, and it was used to calculate sales totals and for actuarial work.

In December of 1941, the Japanese bombed Pearl Harbor and President Franklin Roosevelt declared a state of war. In early January, I decided to enlist in the service. When I told my dad about my intentions, he supported them wholeheartedly. And he gave me a piece of advice.

"Bob," he said solemnly, "I recommend that you enlist

in the Navy."

Since he had been an Army sergeant and had taught bayonet fighting in World War I, I asked him why the Navy instead of the Army.

He looked at me dead on with his one good eye and said, "A bunk and a hot meal beats K-rations in a foxhole any day."

Dad was an excellent social gambler. I thought back to the story he sometimes told of playing a game with a fairly good hand, but being short of money. He took out his glass eye and put it on the kitty, saying, "I see your bet." None of the other players wanted to touch his "ante," so he won the hand.

And I enlisted in the Navy.

They shipped us to Stevens Hotel in Chicago, where 976 of us were sworn in at the same time, a record for Navy enlistments at that point. I was assigned to the Great Lakes Naval Training Station in Chicago the next day, where I completed my basic training in a few weeks. It was hard work in cold weather, but I loved the feeling of serving my country.

After basic, I was reassigned to a school where I would be trained to repair airplane engines. I knew a little about them from my days of flying a Taylorcraft two-passenger plane, but I had never worked on anything bigger than about 40 horsepower. I was excited and ready to get going.

Before they shipped us out, we were held in what was called Out Going Unit (OGU) for a few days. During that short time, we were sent to Great Lakes Naval Hospital for a thorough physical exam, including chest X-rays. Even though I was 5'8" and only weighed 135 pounds, I was strong and healthy, so I wasn't worried. But my X-rays came back showing a considerable amount of scar tissue on my lungs.

Most of the rest of the enlistees were shipped out, while I was moved to Mainside Naval Hospital for additional tests. A doctor there finally determined that I had contracted tuberculosis some time in the past. It had healed, but there was too a great a chance that it might come back, so I was given an honorable medical discharge.

As soon as I got back home, I promptly registered as a volunteer draftee. Within a week, I was drafted into the Army. But they did their medical exam right up front. When they saw my X-rays, I was discharged with the same diagnosis. I was officially 4-F.[1]

Since military service was out of the question for me, I started looking for a job in defense work. There were several plants in the Chicago and Detroit areas, and I knocked on every door. But no one would hire me because of my medical discharge. Honorable or not, I could not get a job.

In the spring of 1942, I was in Detroit being turned down at every turn, when I went into the General Motors headquarters to use a pay phone. In the lobby, there was the usual bulletin board listing the employees for the building. I saw the name of the vice president of personnel relations listed. I was so frustrated that I decided to call him and tell him about my search.

I called the general switchboard and asked for his extension. Then I waited about five minutes before calling back. This time, I asked for his office directly.

His secretary answered. When I asked if Mr. Smith was in his office, she said that he was.

"Please tell him that Bob Johnson is downstairs and would like to see him," I said.

She put me on hold for what seemed like forever, then came back on the line.

---

1 Selective service classification declaring that the registrant is not acceptable for military service.

"Mr. Johnson," she said politely. "Mr. Smith said to ask that you please come on up."

I was surprised, but I figured that for once having a common name had worked to my advantage. I was right: he knew a man with the same name as mine and that's whom he was expecting.

But he shook my hand and invited me to sit down. I told him my story.

"I'm not a draft dodger!" I said. "I'm trying to get a defense job, but I can't get anyone to hire me. And several of the plants who have turned me down were GM factories."

He asked me about my life and interests. And he gave me the greatest advice in the world.

"Bob," he said, "when this war is over, this country is going to have a drastic shortage of engineers. I'd suggest that you go to college and become one now."

I had never even considered going to college. But as we talked, I started to understand that engineers solved puzzles. And, better yet, they also got to come up with puzzles that no one had ever solved before. Of course, Mr. Smith didn't mention that those puzzles all involved mathematics.

So I went back home, packed up my Model A, and moved to Ames, Iowa, to enroll as an aeronautical engineer at Iowa State College. It seems like the Man upstairs was still watching out for me.

My mother died when I was 16 and my sister, Rosemary, was 14. There was no medical insurance in those days, and even with a good salary, it took Dad 10 years to pay off all Mother's medical bills. When Rosemary wanted to go to Wesleyan, Dad and I pooled our money to pay her tuition.

But I knew it would be up to me to pay for my own education.

By June 1944, World War II was in full swing, and the government realized that it had been drafting the nation's future engineers. So the Navy put the V-12 program into effect. This program inducted student engineers into the Navy, but allowed them to stay on campus until they finished their degrees. After graduation, they were promoted to second lieutenant and were obligated to serve at least one year or until the end of the war, whichever came first.

It was hard to be in classes with some of these students because they were my age or younger and in the Navy. They often gave me a bad time, as though I had somehow avoided the draft. Even when I explained my circumstances, they like to tease me, and I tried not to mind.

About this time, I fell in love with a local girl, Charlotte Nutty, who was also an ISC student studying home economics. Like a proper gentleman, I asked her father for her hand, but he said she had to wait until she was 21. So we applied for our marriage license on her 21st birthday, April 5, 1945. Two days later, we were married at the Ames courthouse—without his permission or presence.

I was the proudest man on campus that day. Charlotte was great support and teased the V-12s right back. It didn't hurt that she was beautiful and smart. And she could laugh at anything.

We rented a two-room apartment for $30 a month. The two rooms were a bedroom and a just-about-everything-else room. The bathroom was down the hall and we shared it with three other tenants. Charlotte was rather modest, so we had some interesting times at first.

She quickly set to making our tiny space into a comfortable home, with curtains, couch pillows, and a tablecloth for the kitchen table where we ate and studied.

Since we didn't have any way to offset our rent, we both got jobs serving food at the Student Union for free meals and a little income. By working on campus, we also saved time by doing homework between our classes in the

Union's dining room.

The war ended in August 1945, and by September, I was deep into the heavy part of my engineering studies and doing quite well. I had come up with a project that I was researching, and one of my professors encouraged me to prepare a small thesis on it. He suggested that it would be good practice for the master's degree he hoped I would pursue.

I was flattered, and it sounded like an interesting thing to do, whether or not I continued my studies. So I began putting it together.

I had been elected president of the student chapter of the Institute of Aeronautical Sciences. Along with my other duties, I was responsible for organizing the annual joint meeting of all the engineering colleges. This included finding a nationally prominent speaker.

This joint meeting included all the mechanical, aero, electrical, chemical and civil engineering students, as well as their professors, the dean of engineering, and some Navy brass. I was lucky to get someone I was sure they would all enjoy. With that accomplished, I worked on finishing my thesis.

All went well until the day of the meeting. The weather was below zero and it was snowing heavily. I had planned for our speaker to come in early so I could take him on a tour of the campus. Now I wondered if he would get here in time for his presentation.

About noon, I got the call I was dreading. My speaker was in Chicago, and all flights were grounded because of weather. There was no way for him to make it to Ames.

Fortunately, I had a few hours before the evening meeting, but I was desperate for a speaker.

Charlotte and I went over the possibilities, including the faculty and deans. Most had either spoken recently, or had no new research to present that I knew of. I tried to solve the problem, but I was out of ideas.

Suddenly, Charlotte sat up and folded her hands in her lap. "Bob," she said slowly, "why don't you present your thesis?"

I looked at her as if she were crazy. But she just kept looking at me.

"I can't do that," I explained. "I'm not qualified."

She adjusted her shoulders. "Do you have another speaker?"

And I realized I didn't. So that evening, I gathered my notes and took them with me to the meeting.

Dinner was a success. The food was delicious, and the students were glad to have the time to hobnob with their faculty and each other. There was some one-upmanship going on, but everyone seemed to be having a great time.

When it came time for me to introduce our speaker, I went to the podium with a quick word to the Man upstairs. "Please let me pull this off," I pleaded.

"Thank you all for coming," I began. "It's always an honor to have our illustrious faculty and guests from the Navy with us."

A hearty round of applause swelled the room.

"I'm sorry to report that our speaker has been waylaid by the weather," I said. "He sends his apologies that the airlines are not able to accommodate his travel through a little snow."

Several jokes about aeronautics were made.

"So, rather than leave you without a speaker," I said, expecting the worst, "I'm going to share some research I've been doing on a new way to propel helicopters."

There was some conversation, but no one pulled me from the stage with a hook. After a minute or two, the room became quiet and I started my talk.

I had made an outline with numbers to reference the various sections of my research notes. I'd made many presentations before, and enjoyed doing it. But never to a room full of experts and all of my fellow engineering students. I did a good job, didn't lose my place, and felt like it was definitely better than no speaker at all.

When I was done, there was polite applause. Some thoughtful questions were asked about my engine that had no moving parts and worked at or above the speed of sound. I actually felt pretty good about pulling it off.

"Thank you all for coming," I said. "We'll look forward to seeing you again next year." And with that, I headed back to my table. Charlotte was beaming when I gave her a huge hug.

"You were wonderful," she said in my ear. "I knew you could do it."

I was ready to say that I had not had nearly as much faith as she did, when the dean of engineering, Thomas Agg, and Professor Wilbur Nelson, department head for aero engineering, came up to me.

"Bob, that was a very interesting talk you gave," Professor Nelson said. I looked at him and saw that he was not smiling. Before I could thank him, Dean Agg spoke up, "Please come to my office. And I'll need your notes."

I handed them to him, wondering what was going on.

I gave Charlotte another kiss. "Hopefully, this won't take long." And I followed the dean across campus to his office.

When I arrived, the room was crowded, and I had to slide in sideways. Luckily, I didn't take up much space.

Dean Agg didn't introduce me to the other men, which was unusual, and he seemed almost as nervous as I felt. I stood while Professor Nelson and a man in Navy brass looked over my notes. They pointed to various parts without speaking, turned pages, and pointed some more. I was sure they could all hear my heart pounding through my jacket.

After several awkward minutes, they handed my paperwork to Dean Agg, who set it on his desk.

"Bob," he said sharply, "I need to you to re-create these notes." I thought quickly about how to respond, but he went on. "You have until Monday at 9:00 AM to bring them to me."

The naval officer added, "And until that time, you are under house arrest."

Now I was too stunned to speak.

It would be hard enough to rebuild my notes. After all, the dean had some of my original work, and other parts had come from talks with visiting professors or faculty who were no longer here. In one case, the professor was not even alive anymore!

But house arrest? I couldn't begin to understand why.

"Do you understand me, Bob?" said the dean. "Monday morning, you must have your notes to me."

I said, "Yes, sir. May I go now? My wife is waiting for me to take her home."

They dismissed me. As I left the room, I thought I heard someone say something about original work. I would never have plagiarized anything. And I doubted that it would be a house arrest offense if I had.

The last thing I heard was "treason."

My next 48 hours were a blur.

Charlotte and I stayed up for hours that night, debating what it all meant, so I let her sleep in the next morning. I got up before dawn and gathered what notes I still had.

I put a stack of paper to one side of the table. It was 14 inches by 8½ inches, rough like a coloring book page, and marked in quarter inch grids with light blue ink.

I lined up my tools: A mechanical pencil, extra lead, erasers. My best slide rule, made of ivory and accurate to four places past the decimal. A clean ashtray, my pipe, tobacco, and tamping tools.

Then I began reworking my calculations. And I suddenly remembered that promise to my high school principal.

After half an hour, I was starting to think I should have kept that promise. I considered waking Charlotte, but it was only 6:00 AM. Instead, I called my dad.

When I had explained the situation to him, he was quiet for a minute or so. "Is it your own work?" he asked.

"Yes," I replied.

"All original?"

"Yes, sir."

"Can you look yourself in the mirror?" This was his true test of character. Dad always said you can lie to anyone, but could you look your own reflection in the eye?

"Yes, I can."

"Then do your best, Bob," he said, "and I believe it will be fine." I waited a moment, then he added, "And it never hurts to ask the Man upstairs for some help."

"Thanks, Dad," I said, and we hung up.

I kept working through the calculations, but they weren't coming out right. I erased parts and started working again, but they still weren't right. Then, feeling a little frustrated, I got a new sheet of paper and started again. I took a pull on my pipe, only to find it had gone out.

I was used to having all the answers. In fact, I prided myself on being able to figure out just about anything if I put my mind to it. And now, I couldn't even figure out my own formulas.

It was almost more than I could bear. I was tired and worried. What if I couldn't re-create my work? I thought about my carefully organized life crumbling because I couldn't hold it together. The word "treason" kept coming to my mind.

Charlotte got up quietly and I smelled coffee brewing as she made breakfast. Except for a kiss on my cheek, she didn't do anything to break my concentration.

I bit into a slice of toast and took a deep breath. "C'mon, Bob," I told myself. "It's just numbers. You can do this." And I started again. And again. The calculations just wouldn't come out right. I could see Charlotte knitting on the couch.

Usually going for a walk clears my head, but the snow was still too deep. And I was under house arrest. All of the sudden, our cozy apartment felt like a cage.

Just then, Charlotte said, "Oh, for heaven's sake!" She started laughing, something I've always found irresistible about her. She saw me looking at her and quickly apologized. "I'm sorry, honey," she said. "I didn't mean to interrupt you." Then she began pulling out the rows of yarn she had just been knitting.

Shocked, I asked, "What are you doing?"

She held up the circular skirt she was working on. "I dropped a stitch," she explained, laughing at herself again as she unraveled.

"Can't you just pick it up?" I asked.

"Sure," she said as she kept pulling. "But it won't be right." She looked at me, her eyes twinkling. "And if I did it once, I can do it again."

We both laughed. I moved over and sat beside her, helping rewind the wrinkled yarn onto her ball. I wrapped it over my fingers, like my mother had taught me as a boy, so it wouldn't be too tight. I hadn't thought of the technique in years.

In all, I think Charlotte pulled out about 12 long rows. And then she started knitting again without batting an eye.

I got up and refilled both our coffee cups, walking without looking down as we'd been taught at the Union, so I wouldn't spill into the saucers. I put down the cups, took her beautiful face in both my hands, and kissed her. "I love you," I said and kissed her again. "I love you, too," she said, and we kissed one more time.

I started back to work, my slide rule flying, and I finally managed to get the numbers to cooperate. Soon, those wide pages started filling with neatly printed calculations.

At dinner, we talked about restarting projects. "It seemed so easy for you to pull out those rows and start again," I said to Charlotte.

She picked up her knitting pattern. "That's because I have my pattern right here," she said. "*Yours* is locked in the dean's office."

I emptied out the bowl of my pipe into the ashtray, using the small metal reamer to remove the spent tobacco. I dipped into the can of tobacco—my one extravagance—to refill it. I turned to the next tool on the ring and concentrated on tamping the leaves just firm enough to light, but not so tight they would be hard to draw. Finally, I struck a wooden kitchen match and sucked until the tobacco was lit.

Then I got back to work. This time the calculations came easily.

It took both days to finish, but I felt like I'd captured enough of my work to prove it was my own.

On Monday morning, I gathered my notes and made sure I had everything in order. I doubted that Dean Agg would give me chance to come back for anything I forgot. I kissed Charlotte goodbye, wondering if the next time I saw her would be through bars.

"You're going to be wonderful," she assured me. "And I'm expecting you home for dinner," she called after me. "I'm making pot roast!"

Somehow that cheered me up.

I got to Dean Agg's office 15 minutes early, and the same men were already waiting inside.

I looked up quickly and thought, "Please don't let me down."

Dean Agg extended his hand; I gave him my notes.

"Thank you, Bob," he said. "Please wait outside while we go through your work." He closed the door firmly behind me.

I sat in the hard wooden chair, watching students and professors go by. On Friday, I'd felt like a hero. Today, I did not.

The hallway was cold and a little drafty—always a cause for jokes to engineering students. After all, shouldn't the engineering department have a perfectly engineered building?

Somehow the humor escaped me today.

I don't know how long I sat there, but finally it all got to be too much. I dozed off. And I snored.

When the Navy officer opened the door and found me sleeping, he shook my shoulder to wake me. I opened my eyes, and everything seemed all right for a minute. Then I realized where I was and jumped up.

"I'm so sorry," I said quickly, running a hand over my hair.

And the Navy brass finally cracked a smile.

"Please join us," Dean Agg said. I came in and sat in that crowded room. And waited.

"Mr. Johnson," said one of the other men. "We're from the FBI."

I stared, not knowing what to say.

He continued, "We've read through your work, and we're convinced that it is original."

"Of course it is!" I said, a little too loudly. "I would never plagiarize someone else's work."

Dean Agg nodded, "I didn't really think you had, Bob. But we had to be sure."

He went on to explain that the Navy had recently signed a contract with ISC to develop military aircraft engines. It was a top-secret project, requiring special security clearance. Imagine their surprise when I presented part of it to the all-engineering meeting. They had to be absolutely sure that no one had leaked the existing research to me.

And imagine my surprise when they told me that I had designed a ramjet engine concurrently with the Navy. Instead of arresting me, they offered me a job on the project named Bumble Bee. I immediately accepted.

I couldn't wait to tell Charlotte and Dad as much as I could.

When my security clearance arrived, I brought my badge home to show Charlotte. "Look," I said, "the Navy wouldn't have me when I enlisted, and now it's invited me to join."

I got to work closely with Professor Nelson, who was in charge of the project. I graduated in 1946, and started my master's degree.

Our research was completed in 1947, too late for WWII, and I was always sorry that I hadn't been able to help with the war effort.

Shortly after we finished, I was offered a job in California working with Shell Oil Company. So I left my master's unfinished, and Charlotte and I moved to Martinez, California. In 1949, while we lived there, I developed pneumonia. My regular doctor suggested I see a pulmonary specialist in Oakland.

As it turned out, the specialist was the same doctor who had diagnosed the scars on my lungs as TB, and who recommended my discharge from the Navy. He explained that, after the war, the Navy had done more research on the condition because so many young men were discharged for it. They found that the scarring was actually caused by coccidioidomycosis, or Valley Fever, not TB at all.

At first, I was angry that my life had been so affected by a mistaken diagnosis. But, as usual, Charlotte saw the funny side of it.

"Oh, Bob, aren't we lucky?" she said, laughing. "If you'd joined the Navy, we never would have met."

When we left his office, I actually thanked the doctor for explaining the situation. I was even grateful for his misdiagnosis.

Years later, I was learning to use the Internet and looked up Bumble Bee. Along with many listings about honey, I found one on Project Bumblebee. It seems that, while our ramjet engines never made it into WWII, they were the propulsion system behind the surface-to-air missiles used in Korea and Vietnam.

I realized that I actually had contributed to the war effort after all. By this time, both Dad and Charlotte were gone, but I knew that they were probably with the Man upstairs and just as proud as I was.

Bob became a successful sales engineer, specializing in materials science and aluminum production. During his career, he worked for Alcoa, Reynolds and Texas Aluminum Industries. After retiring, Bob started a second career in real estate. Charlotte passed away in 1960. Bob remarried and moved to St. George, Utah. He has two children, three grandchildren, and one great-grandchild.

BONNIE
(WILLIAMSON)
GWALTNEY

ROSIE THE RIVETER

n September 1, 1939, Hitler invaded Poland. Two days later, Great Britain and France declared war on Germany. I was 16 years old, living in Johnston County, North Carolina, and that war seemed very far away. You see, we Americans were disillusioned with war and determined to stay out of it. After all, we fought in the Great War—World War I—the war to end all wars.

Not only that, we were still in the final grips of the Great Depression. Millions of Americans struggled just to put food on their tables and a roof over their heads. My father was a builder by trade, and he worked every job he could find, when he could find one. My mother owned a tobacco farm but, with seven children, we could barely make ends meet.

But the war news from Europe was everywhere. Edward R. Murrow gave us constant updates on our battery-powered radios. When we could come up with a nickel to see a movie, the "News of the World" newsreels before the feature film were full of war reports. Even the pages of *Life* magazine bled with war photographs. We were surrounded by news of the war and none of it was good.

Thinking back, I realize that many of our politicians knew we would eventually get drawn in. In 1940, Congress passed a law that created a draft. This was the first peace-time draft in our history. Of course, nothing's ever all bad. The government started spending more money on defense. My father found work building barracks on military bases while the rest of the family worked on the farm. That really helped us.

I moved into a boardinghouse in Charlotte, North Carolina, in October 1941, to go to school. My parents encouraged us to get an education. Since I was good with numbers, I decided to study comptometry in business school. A comptometer was an adding machine with keys like a typewriter, except with numbers on them. I'd punch in someone's list of numbers, and the comptometer would total them up all nice and neat at the bottom of the paper. It was sort of fun, and it paid better than farming.

I remember that I was alone in the parlor of the boardinghouse, sitting in a rocking chair and listening to the radio, when the announcer broke into the program with startling news that the Japanese had bombed Pearl Harbor. I stopped rocking and sat still in a state of shock. For a while, I couldn't process the news.

"Yesterday, December 7, 1941, a date which will live in infamy . . ." President Franklin Delano Roosevelt announced on the radio that next day.

"I ask that the Congress declare that since the unprovoked and dastardly attack by Japan on Sunday, December 7, a state of war has existed between the United States and the Japanese Empire."

After that, things changed overnight. Everywhere I looked our boys were in military uniforms. Ships that once carried raw materials and manufactured goods now carried American troops. Everyday items grew scarce. And suddenly we had a whole bunch of new government agencies.

We began to ration sugar, rubber, gasoline, heating oil, coffee and other daily necessities. We all got ration coupons and had to use them to buy these things.

Factories stopped manufacturing peacetime goods like bicycles, toasters, waffle irons and zippers. Instead, they produced things needed for war: tanks, airplanes, ammunition and bombs.

To help get the raw materials for these wartime provisions, communities were encouraged to organize huge drives to collect salvaged scrap metal, newspapers, waste fat, aluminum, tin cans, rubber, nylons and silk stockings. We were all anxious to do our part. Our nation pulled together to win the war in Europe and the Pacific.

Slogans popped up everywhere: "Stockings for Victory." "Use it up, wear it out, make it do, or do without!"

An underlying sense of paranoia permeated the country. Warnings, such as "Loose lips sink ships!" reminded everyone that spies could be anywhere. We put blackout curtains over our windows. Civilian lookout patrols scanned the skies for enemy planes. Airplanes flew up and down our coastlines searching for Japanese and German submarines we knew might be hiding there.

There were a bunch of things we could do here at home to make us feel like we were contributing to the war effort. We held air-raid drills, got training in first aid and firefighting, as well as other important tasks.

Even though Pearl Harbor was really the only big attack on American soil, we were consumed with the war and its progress. Radio broadcasts, dominated by war news, reported actions in both theaters of war. Movies with war themes like *Thirty Seconds Over Tokyo* brought true stories of heroism into

local theaters, and popular songs like the "Boogie Woogie Bugle Boy" by the Andrews Sisters celebrated our soldiers.

The American workforce also started changing. Factories from all over the country advertised for workers. My brother Oliver read an ad for Douglas Aircraft Company in Santa Monica, California, and decided to thumb his way across the country to work on airplanes.

My sister Myrtle made 75 cents an hour as a teacher, while an office job in the factory paid $1.25. So as soon as school broke for the summer vacation, Myrtle followed Oliver out to Santa Monica.

Once Myrtle got settled in her job, she encouraged me to join her. I'd finished my classes in comptometry, so I decided to see what California offered. I boarded the train in North Carolina and headed across the country. It was a long, slow trip and the train was so full of servicemen that I was lucky to find a seat. Sometimes I sat on the steps in the doorway, my little weekender suitcase at my feet. Someone always carried a deck of cards, and we idled away the four-day trip playing games like Gin Rummy and Hearts. I got to see a lot of America going by outside the windows.

When I finally made it to California, I joined Oliver and Myrtle working at Douglas Aircraft. I had worked on the farm from the time I was eight years old until I graduated from high school. I was used to doing hard labor, plowing the cornfields with mules and sawing down trees, and I was a strong girl. So it was easy for me to secure a job as a riveter.

At first they had me working in the tail section of a plane, but I was average size and the space seemed too tight. I felt like I was being smothered. After just a couple of days training, I was assigned to the bomb bay doors of the A-20, called the Boston Bomber or Havoc depending on where in the war it got flown in combat.

My partner was named Betty and we soon became

close friends. As the riveter, my job was to insert the rivet into a pre-drilled hole and drive it through. Betty was the bucker. She held a metal bar, the bucking bar, against the bomb bay door. As I drove the rivet through, Betty held the bar firm. The pressure against the metal shaped the end of the rivet into a second head that held the sheets of metal skin coating the doors together.

We switched off pretty often. I'd pass her the rivet gun and she gave me the bucking bar. Betty and I worked really well together. They tried splitting us apart once, gave us each a new girl to train. But as a team, we produced more than almost anyone else, so they soon put us back together. Then we worked even harder so they wouldn't try it again!

America needed even more workers to keep up with the war efforts, and this changed our workforce. Handicapped workers found jobs on the assembly line and child labor laws were suspended. Midgets and dwarves were hired to work in tight spaces, like the tail section of planes where I was too tall. And millions of kids as young as 12 years old were hired.

My younger brother, Ray, had just finished his junior year of high school, and he decided to come work with us at Douglas. When he got there, the four of us rented an "overhead" apartment above a garage. Our little apartment was within walking distance of the Douglas plant, and our landlady, who lived in the big house, packed our lunch pails for work with fruit, a sandwich, a cookie and a thermos of juice.

We worked eight-hour days, six days a week. Every morning, we lined up at the gate of the plant. We had to have our badges and lunch pails checked before we could punch in for work. The factory ran 24 hours a day, seven days a week, and did we ever work. At the height of production, certain plants were producing a bomber an hour round the clock.

Some volunteers from Hollywood came and disguised

the Douglas plant to look like a neighborhood, in case enemy aircraft flew over it. They were pretty clever. The planes
and factories were hidden under this big framework made
out of wood and chicken wire. It was covered with cloth netting and had fake plywood buildings, trees and bushes poking up through it. From the air, it was supposed to look like
streets with houses on a hill. The netting was drab olive, so
everywhere we looked, we saw green: the planes, the netting.
I swear, even though the walls of the plant were bathed in
bright electric light, they seemed green.

The lighting inside kept the workspace bright, but the
noise was deafening. I had to yell for Betty to hear me. But
I loved it! I loved the hubbub, the work, feeling a part of the
war effort.

Most of us did. In fact, there was a kind of glamour
to being a "Rosie the Riveter." Songs, like the Four Vaga-
bonds' "Rosie the Riveter" played on the radio, making us
feel special.

> While other girls attend a favorite cocktail bar,
> Sipping dry martinis, munching caviar;
> There's a girl who's really putting them to shame—
> Rosie is her name.

> All day long, whether rain or shine,
> She's part of the assembly line,
> She's making history working for victory,
> Rosie, Rosie, Rosie, Rosie, Rosie, Rosie the riveter.

We ate lunch in shifts, and lots of times Douglas provided entertainment during our half-hour lunch break. Sometimes, bands would play on the outdoor stage. Kay Kayser,
the bandleader from North Carolina, came once. He was from
our part of the country and it felt like a little taste of home.

On other days the company held boxing exhibitions. We'd all sit in the bleachers and watch while we ate our sandwiches. Sometimes I'd find myself a spot of shade under a bomber wing and just enjoy the relative quiet of sitting outside.

Oliver, Ray, Myrtle and I had Sundays off, so Saturday nights were the best. We'd head down to Ocean Park in Santa Monica where they held dances at the Aragon Ballroom. We'd dance the night away to bands like Bob Crosby and Spike Jones. Some Saturday nights, we'd head down to the Palladium in Hollywood where Tommy Dorsey played. My brother took dancing lessons from the Arthur Murray Studio and he was a terrific dancer. I already knew how to do the jitterbug from high school, so we would dance together. Sometimes I got tired and would sit out a dance. Every now and then a fellow would sit down next to me and ask if Oliver was my husband. I'd tell him no, that Oliver was my brother, and I was just resting. I hardly ever danced with anyone but Oliver.

During this time period, the government began to recruit more women to work in factories. We were told that more women would be needed if America hoped to win the war.

Ads were put on the radio and in the newspapers, asking wives and mothers to come to work. Posters had slogans like "Women in the war: We can't win without them!" and "It's a man's and woman's world!"

Of course, this also meant that women who went to work still had to take care of their homes and children. Even if they had money and ration coupons, by the time they got off work and to the grocery stores, there was not much left to buy. So the government started asking store owners to stay open later and to "hold back" things for the working women.

I guess they were also worried that women workers might stop being soft and gentle, so they were encouraged to "Be feminine and ladylike even though you're filling a man's shoes!"

Lots of women were already working low-paying but important jobs. As they rushed to the factories to be patriotic, and make more money, they left their old jobs empty. This was good for the factories, but bad for the country. The government started telling women that they were really needed in the "essential" jobs, if America wanted to win the war.

In the fall of 1943, Oliver enlisted in the Navy. He asked me to care for his maroon Buick convertible. Of course, I couldn't really afford to drive it. Gasoline was a rationed item and you couldn't buy new tires. I rented a garage for five dollars a month, half the going rate for a nice room. I was relieved when a friend of Oliver's wrote him a letter, asking to buy the car.

"Yes, sell him the car," Oliver wrote. So I did. I was glad to get rid of the responsibility and the expense.

Douglas gave its employees pins to wear when family members enlisted in the service. The pins had stars for each family member in the armed forces. I wore a star for Oliver. Some of the workers had three and four stars on their pins.

Myrtle moved back to the East Coast in the summer of 1943 and stayed. That left Ray and me alone at Douglas Aircraft. In December 1943, Ray decided to go home and finish high school before joining the Army.

"I don't want to stay out here by myself," I told him. "I'm going with you."

I wanted to leave on Tuesday, December 13, 1943.

"Thirteen is an unlucky number!" Ray argued.

"Not for me!" I said. "Thirteen is my lucky number!"

And I was right.

The train that left on December 12th got in a terrible accident. We would have been caught in one of the worst train wrecks ever. As it was, it took us longer to get home because the accident was between New Orleans and North Carolina. We detoured to Florida and chugged up the East Coast to Raleigh, North Carolina. I'm sure glad we missed that accident!

It seemed to take forever, puffing away, thick black smoke trailing up through the smokestack and in through the cracks in the windows.

I took one of those essential jobs right after the new year. I started in January 1944. A bus company hired me to record the "end of the day" ticket numbers on the night shift.

Our busses were packed with soldiers and sailors crisscrossing the nation; some on passes to rejoin their families, others on their way to the front on foreign soil. My job wasn't as exciting as riveting bombers, but still helped them get where they needed to go.

The Germans surrendered on May 7, 1945, and after we dropped atomic bombs on Hiroshima and Nagasaki in August 1945, the Japanese signed official surrender papers on September 2, 1945. World War II was officially over, the United States transitioned back from wartime production to peacetime manufacturing.

Sewing machine factories stopped making bombs, vacuum cleaner factories stopped making machine guns and we were expected to return to our kitchens.

In 1945, as our boys came home, the defense jobs went away. And, of course, the government messages changed again. Now we were told it was a woman's duty to return home to take care of her husband and children. What the message didn't say was that it was so the men coming home could have the jobs.

The amazing opportunities women enjoyed in the workplace were pulled away as quickly as they'd been given. Some women left voluntarily, and didn't mind so much. But most were laid off. And lots of these newly jobless women were war widows with children to support. It was a long time before a lot of women started working again, and then they were usually in those essential jobs.

I was one of the lucky ones. During the night shift, I began to tabulate ticket numbers and figured the books for our auditor. He liked my work, so he recommended me for a promotion to become the auditor at the bus station in Suffolk, Virginia.

The war was a hard time for America, but we made the best of it. I got to travel across the country and do work that supported the war effort. I was happy to do my part.

I met a man in Suffolk, Virginia. We got married near the end of the war. The marriage didn't last, but we had a son and he's still the light of my life. And I ended up back in California. I like to visit Santa Monica. Of course, Douglas Aircraft is gone, but the memories are still there.

Bonnie moved back to California in 1962 and went to work for the Sears Catalog Store. She retired in 1979, and returned to the East Coast for 10 years before settling in Long Beach, California. Bonnie has one son, two grandchildren, and four great-grandchildren.

DAVID W. LESTER

—◊◊◊—

BATTLE OF THE BULGE

My great-great-grandfather, Col Davy Crockett, commanded Gen Andrew "Old Hickory" Jackson's Fifty-seventh Militia in the War of 1812. One hundred thirty-two years later, I fought next to "Old Hickory" veterans from WWI, descendents of the same men who fought alongside my ancestor.

Before the Japanese bombed Pearl Harbor, I worked as an airplane mechanic on the flight line of the US Army Air Corps B-24 bomber and the US Navy PBY-5A amphibians at Consolidated Aircraft in San Diego, California. I was given a critical defense deferment to discourage me from joining the military. However, by D-Day, June 6, 1944, Uncle Sam needed more cannon fodder than bombers for the invasion of Europe.

I entered the service, expecting to join the Army Air Corps. My hopes ended when a rosy-cheeked second lieutenant announced, "You're all in the infantry and there isn't a damned thing you can do about it."

I trained in the IRTC at Camp Blanding, Florida, with

descendants of immigrants from Russia, Mexico, China, Canada, Italy, France, Germany and a host of diversified backgrounds. A mixed lot, we were trained to kill the enemy with any weapon or our bare hands if necessary.

We crossed the Atlantic aboard the USS *Wakefield* in the late summer of 1944. Unescorted, we took the northern route through the Arctic Circle in hopes of avoiding German U-boats. In the early dawn before docking in Liverpool, we passed through a field of enemy parachute mines.

We were transported by train to Southampton, then on small inter-coastal vessels to France. Loaded on 40 and 8s—boxcars built to carry forty men or eight mules—we chugged through the French countryside toward Belgium.

One of the coldest winters in memory, we trudged through heavy snow over icy roads to a replacement depot in Belgium. By the time I joined my unit I suffered from frostbite and walking pneumonia and was immediately ordered to the Forty-seventh Field Hospital.

The Allied High Command considered the Ardennes forest a quiet sector and used it as a safe area for units that had already seen heavy fighting. As a result, the men stationed in this region were a mixture of inexperienced and battle-hardened troops.

The Thirtieth Infantry "Old Hickory" Division was the first to liberate Belgium, the first to liberate Holland, and the first to invade Germany. Old Hickory pushed the Germans back behind their own borders and spirits ran high among our troops. Rumors spread through the division that the war would be over by Christmas and we'd all be going home. They proved to be false rumors.

On December 16, 1944, the Germans launched the Ardennes Offensive. Focusing on lightly fortified segments of the US line in the Ardennes forest, the Germans hoped to split the Allied line in half, capture Antwerp, Belgium, cut off supplies to Allied armies by encircling them, and force the British and Americans to negotiate a separate peace treaty, leaving the Soviet Union out of the agreement.

Dietrich's Sixth SS Panzer Division hit at 0530 with a massive artillery barrage on the morning of January 25, 1944. By 0800, von Manteuffel's Fifth SS Panzer Division and Brandenberger's Seventh Army attacked the areas around Bastogne and Luxembourg, respectively. With the distinct advantage of surprise and a blanket of heavy fog that kept Allied aircraft grounded, the German troops wreaked havoc against our men.

When our casualties flooded the field hospital, they reclassified me as "walking wounded" and I was discharged with orders to rejoin my unit. In the States, I was trained as infantry, but after spending two weeks in the hospital, I was proselytized, along with two other men, by the 105th Engineer Combat Battalion and reassigned as a combat engineer. Capt James Rice welcomed me into Company A of the 105th Engineer Combat Battalion of the Thirtieth Infantry "Old Hickory" Division in General Hodges's US First Army. Lt Paul B. Jones, Third Platoon commander assigned Cpl. Emmett Carpenter as my mentor. Emmett taught me all I needed to know to become a competent combat engineer. I became a new member of the third squad of the Third Platoon.

My first combat experience came with the attack on Ligneuville. Our field artillery pounded the enemy troops. During the firefight, we entered the local hotel, crunching through broken glass as the enemy fled out the back door. A goose, roasting in the oven, filled the air, making my mouth water. The second wave of troops attacked, and a young GI entered the hotel. He sank to the floor, his rifle clattering against the wood.

Hess, our medic, hurried over and knelt next to the fallen GI.

"He's dead," Hess said.

He was just a boy and obviously a new recruit. His uniform showed almost no wear. There wasn't a mark on his body.

"Heart attack," Hess said. "A number of men die from heart attacks in combat."

We searched the hotel before leaving and discovered Peter Ruff, the proprietor, hiding in the cellar. Two American officers were in the cellar with him. The Germans planned to execute them, but our attack had saved their lives.

The Ardennes Offensive, later known as the Battle of the Bulge, was one of the bloodiest battles in the European theater during World War II. The multi-fronted battle lasted from December 16 until January 17, 1945. But to us, it seemed much longer.

We found ourselves sitting in foxholes under enemy fire in freezing weather. When a man had to relieve himself, he took care of his business in the foxhole and sat in his own waste or crawled out and lay on his side to pee. We were reluctant to start an open fire for fear the smoke would reveal our position, even when we pulled back to refit. We lived on pancake mix and K-rations. Clean, dry socks were a rare luxury. If you had an extra pair, you wrapped it around your stomach to keep it dry. We used empty K-ration boxes to warm our toes or heat water for coffee. We used precious water for drinking, not for washing or shaving. Our cheeks froze, making our speech incoherent. GI gloves were inadequate, making messages difficult to write. Breath condensed and froze inside microphones making them useless. Batteries froze. Our weapons froze. We froze. But when faced with uncontrollable situations, we simply adapted and kept moving.

Lieutenant Jones was an outstanding commander and I felt fortunate to be in his platoon. He was intelligent and took full advantage of his resources in men and material. He considered each man's ability before assigning a task. He led us with an unshakable courage.

On one reconnaissance mission, a snow bank directly in front of us stood up to surrender. It was a camouflaged enemy machine gun crew, left behind to cover a retreating Wermacht. Had they not already decided to surrender, they would have cut us down. It was the first time Jones felt in danger of being annihilated. He never showed fear. His confidence was contagious.

Stories circulated of enemy spies infiltrating Allied forces. In fact, Operation *Greif*, an enemy attempt to infiltrate American positions using English-speaking Germans impersonating Americans and British was moderately successful. The German imposters, soldiers dressed in Allied uniforms, complete with dog tags removed from corpses and POWs, made it behind Allied lines to change sign posts, misdirect traffic and generally cause disruption. Their attempt to seize bridges across the Meuse River was, fortunately, unsuccessful. But their presence caused concern throughout the Allied forces.

We heard direct reports of our men facing similar situations. Members of Old Hickory reported actual incidents involving German spies. After the Germans had retaken Stavelot, an enemy assault raged until the infantrymen in the 117th Regiment moved back in to stay. Positioned with a clear view of the Amblève River bridge, Sergeant Cassidy aimed his .50-caliber machine gun at three jeeps filled with soldiers dressed in GI olive drab uniforms. When the jeeps tried to cross, Cassidy opened fire, killing the driver of the first vehicle and wounding a number of men. As the rest of the troops gathered up the wounded and fled back into the trees, a confused GI yelled, "What in the hell are you guys doing?"

"They're Germans in GI uniforms," Cassidy retorted, "trying to infiltrate our lines."

Sensing that the enemy would return with panzers, Lieutenant Cofer gathered a few good men and waited for the cover of darkness to attach 1,000 pounds of TNT to a center span on the bridge. We scattered a few detonators throughout the explosives. Even with a chemical smoke screen, our men were targets for the enemy snipers.

When Cofer detonated the bridge, nearby buildings disintegrated into clouds of dust and the explosion echoed across the valley. An oncoming column of panzers and German troops performed an about-face and disappeared back into the trees. However, Schutzstaffel infantrymen continued headlong toward the river in a futile attempt to force a crossing. The 117th opened fire with their "50s" and the Amblève River ran red with German blood.

One of the combat engineer's jobs was to locate and disarm S-mines. The S-mine was one of the most diabolical enemy anti-personnel (AP) mines. When you stepped on its prongs, the first explosive propelled a second explosive chest high. That second explosion would kill or wound any and all within range.

We disdained the use of the SCR-625 mine detector to sweep for the S-mine while under enemy fire because its operator had to stand tall, a much too visible target. And so, to avoid snipers, we'd get down and dirty on our gut, scooping dirt with our belt buckles while crawling slowly with arms outstretched and sweeping the ground ahead, feeling for its prongs with our bare fingers, even under the snow when necessary. We used our bayonets to clear the device and inserted a small nail through its pinhole, then bent the nail to prevent it from falling out. This deactivated both of its explosives and then we could remove the mine from the area.

Combat engineers weren't always under fire. We spread gravel on black ice roadways to prevent vehicles from sliding into ditches. We filled bomb craters and repaired roads. We used our D-8 dozers to cut through hills and forests making roadways were none existed before.

When enemy troops occupied St. Eduaords Sanitarium, using it as an observation post to shell our main supply route, we requested artillery fire against the sanitarium's back wall to camouflage the chopping of trees. We used the lumber to build a road through the bog. We hauled truckloads of gravel and dumped it over the lumber, forming a solid surface. When we completed our project, we called for a Sherman tank. The driver poked the cannon through the sanitarium's back door and fired three quick rounds. The enemy fled, screaming down the road.

In the cellar, we found priests, civilians, Wermacht, and both GI and German medics. The medics were treating the Wermacht and American wounded. Belgians, GIs and Germans joined together to applaud our entry.

Shortly after our capture of St. Eduaords, I was ordered to lead a small patrol sent out to determine the feasibility of our use of our Sherman tanks through a fire break in the forest. To minimize the possibility of stepping on mines, I urged each man to step in the footprints of the man ahead. As we crossed through the forest, a sniper, hiding in a forestry tower, stood up and opened fire. He wounded two of our men. We returned fire and hit him. We hauled him down, but couldn't understand a word he said. He must have been a conscript from one of the countries conquered by the Nazis. His blood stained the snow beneath his body as life flowed away.

Stoumont was a bloody battle. Both American GIs and German troops suffered unthinkable deaths and wounds on its cobblestone streets. Panzers, maneuvering in battle, squashed the disabled and dying under grinding, pivoting tank treads. The streets actually ran red with blood and flesh seeped between the stones.

War brings men together. Hudgens came from a fami-

ly so far back in the hill country of South Carolina, he claimed
they had to "pipe daylight into them." He was an excellent
rifleman and one helluva soldier, but he could barely read or
write. I wrote letters for him and read the letters his family
wrote to him. We both seemed cut from the same mold, operating on the border of discipline.

When we heard about a panzer wedged between bridge
abutments, we both wanted to see it. It was helplessly stuck,
with the guttural sound of German voices emanating from its
radio. Hudgens tossed a grenade down its open hatch and the
tank exploded into a burning inferno.

While K-rations seemed to be our daily gruel, we
scrounged potatoes, eggs, or whatever we could find to supplement our meager fare. When Carpenter and I were returning
from a night patrol, we passed a camouflaged half-track with
a GI field kitchen bolted to its frame. The cooks were feeding
the Sherman tank crews who were hiding in the surrounding trees. Our armored friends appreciated combat engineers
who cleared enemy anti-tank mines from their routes. They
invited us to join them for a breakfast of coffee, powdered
eggs, sausage and a hot biscuit. I was searching for a dry spot
to sit when my biscuit slid off into the mud. I picked it up,
blew it dry and ate it.

"Your biscuit just fell in the mud of a former stable,"
one of the mess crew joked.

I didn't care. That biscuit tasted just fine.

After the Battle of the Bulge, we were trucked to
a huge coal mine where we stripped, showered and donned
clean uniforms, once again smelling like civilized human beings. The war wasn't over and we still had a job to do, but first,
we were given a few days leave in Kerkrade, Holland. We slept
between clean sheets, played ball, wrote letters home, loafed
around and strolled the streets unarmed.

Our brief respite passed all too quickly. The Roer River

needed crossing, and it was my job to help build the bridges required to cross it. Truck after truck brought infantry support bridge sections and stored them under camouflage nets near the crossing sites. Twelve combat infantry divisions, each with its own organic combat engineer battalion, prepared to build those bridges. We checked and rechecked every single item to minimize possible shortages.

The plan to cross the Roer called for a series of bridges to be built at predetermined sites. We sent patrols upstream to the Schwammenauel Dam to control the valves. Unfortunately, the Germans blew the gates and flooded the entire valley.

The flood forced a delay in our plans, but we closely monitored the river flow in an effort to determine when the flood would crest. In the meantime, we dug a trench about fifteen feet long and six feet deep and buried a dead man log[1] to secure one end of a steel anchor cable. The cable stretched across the turbulent river and was secured to a large tree on the opposite bank. Hundreds of engineers worked continuously, making almost no noise.

It was my job to verify the security of that steel cable. Vicious currents swirled unmercifully with the receding flood waters. T/4[2] Adam Burko and I set out in a two-man pneumatic boat. Burko paddled while I used my paddle as a rudder. About midstream, we hit an underwater obstruction. The boat capsized, flipping both of us into deep water. Our weapons plunged to the bottom of the river, and the boat skittered off downstream. Burko struggled toward the enemy shore and I tried to follow him. But my pants were caught on wire

---

1 A large tree trunk or log buried in a riverbank used to secure the cable for a temporary bridge.
2 Technician 4th Grade. The rank of technician was introduced into the Army to replace the ranks of private/specialist. Technicians were considered noncommissioned officers rather than enlisted personnel.

fencing. I could not break loose. Foaming, surging white water pulled me under, again and again. I'd spit water, take a
deep breath and try to break free. But the more I fought, the
more tightly the fence held. I soon became totally exhausted.
My strength gone, I knew I was going to drown.

I held my breath and ducked beneath the surface in a
final attempt to rip my pants free. I felt a hand grip the col-
lar of my field jacket and pull me toward shore. Praise God
almighty, Adam Burko saved my life. We sat on the shore on
the enemy side of the river and mulled over our fate. Do we
surrender and spend the rest of the war as POWs? Or do we
wait until our infantry crosses over and join them? As we pon-
dered our options, Sergeant Turnbaugh arrived in a large rescue boat. We soon found ourselves in dry uniforms, wrapped
in blankets, drinking hot soup, new weapons at our sides.

It took four engineers to carry the first bridge section
down to the river. We shackled a connecting line to the steel
anchor cable and slid that section into the river. Other sections quickly followed, until the first float touched the embankment on the enemy side of the river.

I could not carry both my rifle and the short ramp that
connected the bridge to the embankment, so I set the rifle
aside. I crossed the bridge to the enemy side of the river and
knelt in the mud, making sure the connection was secure.

I felt them before I saw them. Four Germans on patrol
materialized on the riverbank above me. They lobbed hand
grenades at the troops installing stanchions and safety rail-
ings on the bridge. Most of the hand grenades fell into the
river, resulting in harmless miniature geysers. However, several hit the bridge, wounding the GIs at work.

One of the grenades fell short, hitting near where I
was working and exploded. A small fragment hit my left leg,
ripping my pants; the blood soaked my sock and boot. Outnumbered and unarmed, I lay quietly in the mud until they

had exhausted their supply of grenades. They were so close that I could have kicked them into the river.

We completed the bridge 30 minutes before the assault began. At exactly 0330 on the 23rd of February 1945, thousands of artillery tubes simultaneously opened fire on predetermined targets beyond the river. Shells, sounding like a dozen freight trains, whistled overhead. Muzzle flashes from our cannons lit up the surroundings with such brilliance we could easily read our battle charts.

I was suddenly aware of thousands of infantrymen kneeling quietly behind us, their M-1 rifles and helmets gleaming ghostly in the night. It was an awesome sight; thousands of riflemen jammed shoulder to shoulder in total silence.

For 45 minutes, earsplitting artillery shells careened overhead, pounding targets already set aflame. When the firing ceased, a field of steel helmets rose as one and jogged quietly in columns toward their assigned crossing site. Lieutenant Jones stood firm.

"Keep a safe distance between yourself and the man ahead," he told each man. Lightweight infantry support bridging, if overloaded, could easily capsize.

The sudden silence was just as abruptly broken as enemy artillerymen scrambled from their bunkers and began the most hellacious artillery barrage I have ever experienced.

Completed bridges were filled with men jogging toward enemy-held positions. German observers kept us in their sights. My job was to repair broken sections. Enemy shells severed lines, destroying one bridge after another. We rebuilt them by physically pushing or pulling bridge sections back into place.

Medics moved in to treat the wounded and Graves Registration troops removed the dead. Direct hits disintegrated men and bridges alike. Many were reported missing in action. Riflemen caught halfway across a crumbling bridge, unable to shed heavy combat gear, splashed to their death. We threw lines and saved a few, but could not save them all.

Infantrymen attempted to assess the situation by avoiding damaged bridges and scrambling toward the nearest available crossing. Few needed urging to move rapidly. Most knew to clear impact areas. A number of bridge sections broke off and floated downstream.

Plywood utility boats, manned by 10 mostly unskilled men lacking floatation devices, became victims of enemy fire. Many capsized and the men disappeared. Eventually, someone in command requested and received alligators, tracked amphibious vehicles designed to carry 10 men. They successfully hauled men safely across the river.

Two hundred and fifty engineers were killed in action and hundreds were wounded. Riflemen losses were staggering with thousands killed and wounded. Operation Grenade, the Roer River crossing, was one of the bloodiest river crossings by the Thirtieth Infantry "Old Hickory" Division.

When the floodwaters finally receded, pools formed in swamp areas and cadavers mixed with debris piled up. The smell of death mingled with cordite.

Combat engineers follow their organic infantry units, and when we caught up with the 117th, we discovered that Captain Rice had been severely wounded and that Lt Leland Cofer was in command. Under Cofer's leadership, the situation changed. We never had another man listed killed in action. They may have died at home or in some hospital somewhere, but none died on the battlefield.

After crossing the Roer River, the Third Squad was given the dubious honor of liberating an 88 mm anti-aircraft gun in Krauthausen. We were following a path up the river on the enemy side when a mortar round fell nearby. Haspel and I dove for the same ditch. I fell on top of him.

He started cussing then stopped. "I'm sorry, Lester,"

he said. "It's not you, it's this damn ditch! It's full of manure!"

We saw firsthand the devastation of our artillery fire. The field was pockmarked with shell holes, trees were shredded, farm animals lay dead and the village was completely demolished. We decided to look on the bright side. Their trees were pruned, their animals butchered, their field freshly plowed and their homes air conditioned for the coming summer.

We entered the village under the horizontal camouflaged muzzle of an 88 mm anti-aircraft cannon. We found the crew, three Hitler Youths,[3] in their bunker. They offered no resistance. However, Wermacht defenders of the village had fled toward the Hambach Forest.

While following them into the forest, we passed an infantry platoon that seemed a little reluctant to continue.

"Men, I'm taking my radio operator and runner through that forest and I want every man of you to follow!"

Their leader took off and they quickly followed.

A roadblock of felled trees blocked the way. As combat engineers, it was our job to remove it and to dig up the mines so our tanks could pass. Two Sherman tanks idled nearby. "Pappy" Morgan, our truck driver, arrived with our tools and we began sawing and chopping. But before we could clear all the mines, a British tank, equipped with mine flailing chains, pounded its way through the minefield. Unfortunately, the tank hit a mine, lost some chains and a track and was stopped. An arrogant Brit climbed out and, in total defiance and utter contempt of the Germans, stood atop the turret and lit a cigarette in full view of enemy artillery observers.

As we worked to clear the mines, we could hear isolat-

---

3 Hitler Youth, or *Hitler-Jugend*, was a paramilitary organization of the Nazi Party made up of boys primarily between the ages of 14 and 18.

ed enemy troops in the forest pleading, "*Kamerad? Kamerad?*"

We didn't have time to take prisoners, so we ignored them, even though they kept firing.

When the road was finally cleared, our two Sherman tanks clanked up with their NCOs standing tall in the turret, in spite of the hostile surroundings. I saw a Panzerfaust make a direct hit on the first tank, splattering the bloody guts of its commander all over the turret. The second Sherman spun around, but it too was hit, incinerating its crew.

We were totally exhausted. We hadn't slept in four days and needed shelter large enough to spend the night. We commandeered a farmer's barn, roasting some chickens to add to our K-Rations. I was standing at the gate around midnight, when it swung open. A young boy walked through, coming face to face with the muzzle of my rifle.

"Please don't shoot him!" The farmer begged for the life of his only son, an AWOL *Hitler-Jugend*.

Enemy troops were fleeing toward the Rhine when Captain Cofer and Lieutenant Jones left on a three-day pass to Paris. A young lieutenant took temporary command. He sent Sergeant Scott and Private First Class Hornbeck to remove demolitions from a railroad beyond the village of Oberempt. When they bumped into a German patrol, Hornbeck ran and Scotty dove into a deep rut.

Hornbeck returned to camp, leaving Scotty to fend for himself. That really ticked me off. Scotty and I had been through a lot together.

"I'll go find Scotty," I told the lieutenant, who seemed to be numb to the situation.

Hornbeck pointed in the general direction and I set out alone. I passed enemy tanks hidden in a ravine, but easily avoided them. I found Scotty lying in a deep rut. He'd been wounded in the Battle of the Bulge and hadn't fully recovered. When he saw me, he broke down. He refused to get up. He lay face down, clawing the dirt with both hands.

I could hear enemy patrols rustling through the brush. When the enemy activity quieted, Scotty finally calmed down enough to let me help him toward our line. Once clear of the enemy, he became more coherent.

"Please don't tell anyone," he begged. No one wanted to be labeled with "combat fatigue."

I promised.

Later, between the Roer and Rhine crossings, Scotty led a five-man reconnaissance team. Our radio operator had been hospitalized and, because I knew the codes, I carried the radio. We started up a mild slope, when a jeep driver towing a trailer loaded with white phosphorous mortar shells started following us. We stopped at a stone schoolhouse and the driver parked his vehicle. Claiming to be lost, he asked to join us.

Almost immediately, an enemy shell hit the jeep, igniting the mortar shells with a blinding flash. Every man of us dove into an open cellar door. I tried to make radio contact with our unit, but a piece of shrapnel had embedded in the radio circuitry and the radio was dead.

We attempted to organize a defense, but were held down by continuous enemy artillery fire. When the Germans vanished with the breaking dawn, we crawled out of the cellar to scout around and discovered a fixed base 88 mm anti-aircraft cannon surrounded by empty shell casings. The schoolhouse had been demolished, the jeep and trailer reduced to a smoldering hulk.

Lieutenant Jones and Sergeant Turnbaugh joined us. After a short critique, we followed them toward a nearby mountain lodge. We made our way up a path that narrowed and came to a fork. As we neared the fork, a young boy leapt out of the tall brush and ran toward the lodge. A quick investigation revealed a machine gun on a tripod aimed down the road that we had just walked.

We moved on toward the Rhine and found quarters in the village of Wallach near Wessel. Cofer kept us busy setting beehive charges along the edge of the river to break the sharp embankment down into a slope to give our alligators and other amphibious vehicles a better ramp from which to cross.

In March 1945, we heard the sound of a thousand bees and looked up to see an aluminum overcast with over 20,000 C-46s and C-47s towing hundreds of glider infantry. As they flew above the Rhine, 88 mm flak filled the sky. I saw air crews and paratroopers shot down. I believe that many of them knew in their own hearts that they would not live to see another day. Parachutes from disabled and burning aircraft blossomed. Gliders were cut loose to fend for themselves over hostile territory. Many would crash-land, their crews at the mercy of angry civilians.

Aerial photographs of the opposite shoreline revealed row after row of enemy foxholes. Nevertheless, our job was to cross the river. I climbed into an alligator and waited for the nervous driver to get it started. When it wouldn't start, two other engineers and I boarded a compass-equipped storm boat driven by a wild-eyed Texan. He navigated through a chemical smoke screen, putting us ashore at our designated landing site. Fortunately, the enemy chose not to defend that particular area. The foxholes were empty. We cleared the beach, and waited to welcome our infantry. General Harrison was among the first to arrive. He climbed the embankment, turned his back to the enemy and welcomed his troops.

Thousands died at the Roer River crossing, but we only lost 31 crossing the Rhine. It wasn't without some humor. One boat hit the beach and a soldier quickly stepped ashore. He was marooned when the helmsman suddenly backed off to land elsewhere. Troops from a following boat found him wandering on the beach and, thinking he was a German in a GI uniform, captured him. They took his rifle and held him under strict guard until someone from his unit identified him.

Civilians were told to hang white sheets from their windows to indicate a peaceful reception. If we came upon a house without the white of surrender, we would search it for "dangerous" weapons like binoculars, cameras and food. One village welcomed us by applauding our entry.

Armored units led the way to deal with any hostilities. Thousands of trucks followed, bumper to bumper. They held enough supplies to support Allied armies splitting Germany apart. Fuel to "keep the drive alive" was of critical concern.

We paused in Hanover for a quick relief and were surprised to find a fully uniformed Wermacht officer hanging around town. His English was perfect. When we questioned him about his presence in Hanover, he mumbled something about remaining behind to care for his mistress.

We pressed on toward the Elbe River, passing thousands of Wermacht troops in open fields surrounded by wire fencing and guarded by a single GI with a carbine. Huge columns of grey coats filled the autobahn center dividers. They were hiking toward distant destinations.

Roadblocks were rare and we seldom needed to deactivate explosive devices. We entered one small Hansel and Gretel village. Faces appeared at windows, then quickly disappeared. When we withdrew, the village baker offered each of us a freshly baked biscuit. The farms in this area were neat and the equipment seemed to be of high quality. Almost all of the farms and villages were intact, not suffering from the devastating damage witnessed earlier.

In Brunswick, General Hobbs negotiated with General Veith; however, the German refused to surrender his troops. We attacked but the German soldiers didn't have much heart left in the battle. I rounded a corner and saw two unarmed men in a small disabled armored vehicle. A civilian ran from a large bunker, spotted me, and ran right back in. I followed him,

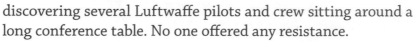

discovering several Luftwaffe pilots and crew sitting around a long conference table. No one offered any resistance.

Our 743rd tanks were on a roll. We followed them into two Allied POW enclosures. We rolled down a two-lane country road and spotted an obvious internment camp beyond the trees. German guards must have known we were coming. They threw the gates open and ran toward a nearby village. Four prisoners struggled painfully toward us. Suddenly, the guards stopped, turned and deliberately shot all four in the back, then took off at a run. They were far beyond the range of our M-1 rifles, so we couldn't return fire.

We entered the compound and saw 20 emaciated skeletons lying on a dirt floor in their own fecal matter and urine. The stench was sickening. Unable to comprehend our arrival, they stared at us with vacant eyes. Mortarano, one of our men fluent in German, questioned them. They were good Germans who somehow provoked the Nazis and were suffering the same fate as their Jewish sisters and brothers. We notified the proper authorities and moved on.

Our 743rd Tank Battalion discovered two abandoned steam locomotives on parallel tracks in the forest near Magdeburg. The 18 coaches were filled with over 1,400 refugees bound for the gas chamber at Buchenwald. Some of our soldiers fired up the train's boilers and transferred the refugees to a medical recovery center in a nearby Luftwaffe airbase hospital.

We arrived at Rogätz, near Magdeburg, just before dark and immediately set out digging four .30-caliber machine gun positions with radios equally spaced around a house. I was assigned to man one of the guns later that evening, so I decided to do a little personal scanning with my newly liberated 8×45 binoculars. While scrutinizing the canal area, I spotted four men approaching our position with weapons. Two adults and two *Hitler-Jugend* picked their way toward our camp. I requested crossfire and waited for them to come into range. We fired a quick burst into the dirt beside them. The two adults ran, leaving the kids squirming on the ground. We heard two shots. The next morning, we discovered that the boys had committed suicide, one with a blue steel Belgium automatic, the other with a quick disconnect barrel Spanish automatic. I kept the blue steel.

After a K-ration breakfast, we were preparing to leave for Magdeburg when one of our maintenance engineers arrived with a carbine pressed to the back of an elderly German he had rousted from a small garden shed. Hooting and shouting, we congratulated the engineer on his quick actions. We pulled out, and when the engineer raised his left hand to wave, he accidentally pulled the trigger with his right hand. A .30-caliber round hit the German's lower back. We never found out the outcome of that incident.

The Germans decided to defend Magdeburg, but when General Hobbs threatened to send a squadron of B-24s over the already bombed-out city, they capitulated. In April 1945, Magdeburg was declared an open city. We moved in to stay. My squad took up living quarters in a rather palatial house, over the Fräulein's vocal objections. We remained fully armed, carrying live ammo.

When I purloined the Fräulein's portable typewriter, she complained to the Counter Intelligence Corp. Captain Cofer suggested I return the typewriter, apologize and dig six holes in the ground, six-by-six-by-six. My shovel had hardly warmed to the task when I observed scores of released Wermacht troops heading home down a nearby road. I didn't smoke, therefore my swapping bag was filled with K-ration cigarettes. When I offered the first few *soldaten* a genuine American smoke, they were eager to dig and happily agreed to complete the task.

Combat engineers were called upon to round up enemy explosives and dispose of them. We filled craters left by

British bombers with explosives, added a few detonators to guarantee a clean blow, and then warned the citizenry to protect their windows.

While I was still in the crater scattering detonators, someone yelled, "Fire in the hole!"

I scrambled to climb out, my fingers clawing the loose sand in an attempt to clear the area. Once out, I dove into a ditch. The explosion bounced us off the ground and sent a huge smoke ring skyward.

We cleared Magdeburg's streets of plundering *Jugend*. A patrol scouting in the countryside discovered a Heinkel HE-162 jet airplane factory in a salt mine under the village of Geln. My camera recorded 15 jets on the line near ready to fly.

We had no food or medicine for retreating Germans, but with the Russians hot on their tails, they crossed our lines in increasing numbers. A few days before, they were eager to kill us, but now they sought amnesty among us. We blew the large Elbe bridge, yet they still came. When the Russians arrived, we swapped uniform insignia and sampled their vodka. Even a nip of the stuff was enough to blow the top of my head off and I swore off booze forever. I took pictures of smiling Russian troops in various uniforms.

We celebrated V-E Day on May 8, 1945. Corks popped and Lieutenant Jones offered me a shot of scotch. Cigars made the rounds and chow halls were wide open. Some of the guys were shaking hands, slapping shoulders and getting a little drunk. Mostly, Emmett and I just sat and watched the Elbe River flow and talked about nothing particular. We promised to meet up after the war, but we never did.

Our battalion assumed temporary occupation duties at Ranis, Germany, a picturesque village in the Harz Mountains near the Czechoslovakian border. We found comfortable quarters in a former *Hitler-Jugend* training facility. We repaired local bridges, roads and other infrastructures. We toured an ancient castle overlooking the valley and discovered women still having babies for old Adolph Hitler's defunct Thousand Year Reich. A German Red Cross nurse told me about the "Nazi Mother Medal." Women were decorated for giving birth: bronze for a few, silver for a few more and gold for a whole bunch.[4] We shared the castle ghost stories and enjoyed the beautiful sunset.

Captain Cofer remembered my typewriter caper in Magdeburg and sent me to assist our company clerk, who was in the process of upgrading service records of every man in Company A. My tasks were relatively easy, although the clerk kept my nose to the grindstone every day except Sunday. On Sundays, I would hike local trails, avoiding the deep forest. I left that area to the ghosts and legends.

As garrison troops, we abided by regular Army rituals. Our bugler was the best in the battalion. Ramseur set his mess area up on the main street, directly beneath the window of the Company A clerk's office. Local *hausfrauen* and their *kinder* stood ready to claim old coffee grounds for their own use. Hard-hearted Sergeant Ramseur was known to order that all edible leftover food be reserved for the particularly disabled, aging Germans in the village.

The beer garden was reserved and well stocked for engineers only. Two men, inseparable in combat, began fighting over some insignificant detail, pulled knives and began carving each other. A bloody sight, they were arrested and sent to the stockade to cool off. When they returned, they acted as though nothing had happened.

Our stay in Ranis was pleasant. When it came time to pack up and head for Camp Oklahoma City near Paris, Pappy

---

4 Bronze: one to five children; silver: six to seven children; and gold: eight or more children.

Morgan fell in line behind Captain Cofer's jeep. We climbed the serpentine roads toward the high country. The views were magnificent. After one tight turn, Captain Cofer jumped to attention. We looked ahead and saw Old Blood and Guts himself, Gen George S. Patton, decked out in full uniform with his famous ivory-handled pistols on his hips. Surrounded by a dozen GIs in Class A uniforms toting tommy guns, Patton raised his arms in a prizefighter pose.

"Thanks, men! I couldn't have done it without you!"

Rolling down from the mountains toward Frankfurt, we passed several Messerschmitt Me-262 fighters/bombers concealed under camouflage alongside the autobahn. They were part of the "Eagle's Nest."[5]

We entered Camp Oklahoma City, and Pappy parked our squad truck and walked away without looking back. On a pass to Paris, I ran into Phillips. He'd been a shy lad from Arkansas when I first met him. He'd changed. On that day, I saw a self-assured man decorated with a Combat Infantry Badge, Silver Star, Bronze Star and Purple Heart. You never can tell what a man will do when faced with combat.

I sailed home on the *Queen Mary*. The Statue of Liberty was one of the most beautiful sights I've ever seen. I really appreciated it when Consolidated Aircraft (now Convair) welcomed me back to the flight line in San Diego. I worked on the XL-13 STOL (short take-off and landing) liaison aircraft project for US Army Aviation. It was good to be home.

---

5 Hitler's mountain-top hideaway near Berchtesgaden.

David returned to Convair in 1946. He was assigned to the development of the Stinson XL-13, short take-off and landing (STOL). When that contract expired, David moved to Pasadena, California, and helped overhaul a Lockheed P-38 for the 1948 National Air Races in Cleveland, Ohio. After the air races, he accepted a position with Aerojet General and spent 18 years developing space propulsion systems. He spent the next 18 years with Collins Radio, Rockwell, Conexant and Boeing, surviving each merger. He married Mary Ruth Hayes in 1951. She passed away in 2008. David and Mary have four children, five grandchildren, and two great-grandchildren.

Decorations and Awards: Bronze Star with V device, Bronze Star, Meritorious Service Medal, WWII Victory Medal, European Campaign Bar with three Bronze Stars, Belgium Fourragere (Designated Thirtieth Infantry "Old Hickory" Division), Army of Occupation Medal

EDITH (SAIRS) McCLURE

ARMY NURSE IN ENGLAND

I wasn't sure how I ended up an Army nurse stationed in Devizes, England. I joined the Army Air Corps in California. After spending three to five months bouncing from one Air Corps base to another in the southern United States, the heartbreaking order came.

"The Air Force doesn't need any more nurses. We've assigned you to the Army's 141st Hospital Group."

A short time later, our small group of Army nurses left New York City for Europe. We didn't know our destination, only that our new assignment would take us to the European theater. Even though I wasn't with the Air Force, I was excited to be a direct part of the American war effort. We traveled in a convoy of ships, crossing the Atlantic on fairly calm seas. When we landed in London, drivers immediately took us to the small town of Devizes.

Our hospital handled a number of psychiatric cases, men suffering from shell shock. It also held a separate wing for German prisoners of war. I sometimes wondered how the close proximity of German soldiers affected our boys.

I stood outside the door to the POW ward and waited for Peter, the Army corpsman who generally accompanied me on rounds with the German patients.

"Lousy weather," Peter said, removing his slicker. "Don't know if I'll ever get used to this rain."

I smiled. Boston, where I'd grown up, had its share of rain, so the British weather didn't faze me.

We entered the prisoners' ward together. I could feel the muscles in my neck and shoulders tighten as I looked around the room at the rows of beds. Six enlisted soldiers and eight officers shared the windowless room, which held fourteen to sixteen beds. The only light came from electric overhead fixtures.

An enlisted soldier, tangled in the top sheet, whimpered. I approached his bed, instinctively aware of the men at my back. Touching my hand gently to the young man's forehead, I felt the heat of fever.

"*Wasser,*" he pleaded, "*Ich benotige wasser.*"

I leaned closer. "What is it you want?"

The young German looked at me, his eyes glassy, "*Wasser, bitte.*"

"What does he want?" I asked the patient lying in the next bed.

The officer's unflinching blue eyes bore into mine, but he maintained his silence.

"Please help me," I implored. "What is it he needs?"

The officer turned away. I wanted to stamp my foot in frustration, or better yet, slap the haughty look off his face. I knew many of the German officers spoke English. Staring at the arrogant profile, the high cheekbones and firm chin, I resisted the urge to slap him. It would be so easy for him to help the soldier in the next bed. Was it pride that stopped him? Unwillingness to help an American woman? Or was it beneath the SS officer to aid an enlisted man?

I used a damp cloth to wipe the soldier's face and straightened the sheets. Feeling helpless, I cautiously moved around the room, doing what I could to assist those in need of attention.

"He wanted water," Peter said when we closed the door to the POW ward.

I knew Peter spoke fluent German. The fact that the prisoners lacked that knowledge gave the staff a small advantage. I shook my head in frustration.

"Why wouldn't the officer just tell me that? Couldn't he see the man was suffering?"

"They live by different rules," Peter said, trying to manage his own irritation. "We'll send water around the ward with the next shift."

I reached out and touched Peter's arm. "Thank you," I said, then turned to enter the next ward.

Compassion drew many people into the medical field, but it was imperative for a nurse to remain objective. I held no love for the German prisoners and conversely, I couldn't help feeling a special bond with some of the American boys.

Paul was one of those cases. A young infantryman, he'd been in the psych ward for weeks, and no one had broken through the cocoon of silence that imprisoned him. I stopped by his bed. Paul's eyes remained closed and his face devoid of expression. I wondered what horrors were locked inside his head. It seemed impossible that, with all the medical advances available, we were still unable to reach one lost boy.

The hospital in Devizes was marginal, but certainly not nearly as primitive as the facility in El Centro, California, where I worked before enlisting in the service. Just barely north of the Mexican border, the small town was flooded with itinerant farm laborers. The operating rooms were far from sterile, with nurses frequently wielding fly swatters to

keep insects off the incisions. And, although we tried to keep
the wards clean, the relentless wind tucked sand between the
sheets and blanketed every flat surface. Yet patients in that
rustic setting thrived. Was it the quiet humor of the population? Or their unshaken belief that everything would always
be okay?

I brushed the hair from Paul's forehead. "You're going
to be alright," I promised, then whispered a secret prayer for
his recovery.

The days followed each other in endless repetition. The
patients rotated in and out of the hospital, most of their own
accord, some in coffins. A few of the German soldiers died;
mostly those who refused food or water. I did my best to help
those I could, but I never felt secure on the ward.

"Stay away from the blond officer in the corner," Peter warned me. "He frequently talks of raping you. And don't
get too close to the German in the third bed; he has anger
issues . . . you aren't safe."

I regularly checked the bulletin board in the hallway,
where news from the front was posted. On the good days for
the Allies, German hostility in the ward was flagrant. Unsub-
stantiated rumors of the "Final Solution" circulated through
the hospital, and every effort was made to keep Jewish staff
far away from the prisoners.

But nothing changed with Paul. Frequently, my system on caffeine overload and weary from lack of sleep, I
would spend hours sitting beside his bed, holding his hand
and whispering encouragement.

The medical team in the psychiatric ward decided to
try and bring Paul back by injecting Sodium Pentothal, the
truth drug. I was there when they gave him the injection,
searching for answers that might provide a key to unlock his
mental prison.

Paul spoke out in anger as he recalled in horrific detail

the German attack on his foxhole. The hand grenade that exploded, injuring him, and blowing apart his closest buddy.

After treatment, Paul retreated to his own private hell, again withdrawn and mute.

I couldn't help but wonder what he'd been like before the war. Had he been fun-loving and full of high jinks like the boys from the Eighty-second Airborne? I remembered the relative innocence of those boys in training, not yet exposed to the realities of war. I smiled at the memory of two boys returning to the orthopedic ward after a night's furlough. Labeling them intoxicated would have been an understatement. They were dead drunk when they passed the nurses station and headed to their ward.

"What the heck," I thought as I bid them goodnight. They'll be off to war in such a short time, let them enjoy themselves.

My thoughts weren't so charitable when they held a lit cigarette to the fire alarm a little while later, and the sprinkler system rained down on the patients in the orthopedic ward. Plaster casts melted as water showered the boys in traction.

"You should have known better," my commanding officer reprimanded after calling me into his office.

I hadn't signed the orders releasing them from the ward earlier that evening, but he wasn't looking for excuses, he was looking for someone to blame.

Now, in retrospect, I could view the incident with humor. The casts were repaired, the bones mended. How easy it was to heal some injuries.

I looked down at Paul. And yet how hard to mend others.

Some days later, I stood in shock when Peter informed me that Paul had committed suicide during the night. I could honestly say that I'd done everything I could to help the boy, but it hadn't been enough. It was strange the way war made some people stronger and broke others.

I turned away and escaped to the yard outside the makeshift hospital buildings. The smell of the damp earth filled my nostrils. I brushed away a persistent fly and thought about the simple joy shared by the laborers in El Centro, the unshakable belief that life was good. What, I wondered, would war have done to those people? Would they have survived and become stronger, or given up like Paul? What happened to the boys of the Eighty-second Airborne? Were they still filled with high jinks and joy? Or did the war rob them of their youth? And what, I wondered, was it doing to me?

I wiped my cheeks and straightened my cap. "When was the time for tears?" I wondered. It was not now; there were other patients waiting. I squared my shoulders and stepped back into the hospital where Peter waited to escort me to the prisoners' ward.

Edith married George Sairs shortly after WWII ended. She continued to work part-time as a nurse, returning to full-time when George started his own company. She eventually went to work with George at Intercity Personnel Associates (IPA). When George passed away in 1982, Edith became president of IPA. She was one of the first women to run a personnel company in a male-dominated industry. Edith married Charles "Mac" McClure, one of the Doolittle Raiders, in 1987. Mac died in 1999. Edith lives in Tucson, Arizona. She has five stepchildren, 10 grandchildren, and 23 great-grandchildren.

ROBERT "BOB" A. HOOVER

ESCAPE FROM STALAG LUFT I

During the last six months of World War II in Europe, the pilots and crew members who were going on missions were instructed by the intelligence people to pass the word if they were shot down. General Eisenhower had put out an order that there would be no more attempts at escape because he felt the war was getting into a wind-down position and that the risk was too great on the POWs if they got on the open countryside versus staying in the prison camps and having our forces come in and recover them.

Well, there were some of us who had been attempting to escape for so long that our sole motivation for living was to get out. And by the time I escaped, 15 months after being captured, I was one of 200 out of the 10,000 prisoners at Stalag Luft I who had never given up, in spite of the general's orders.

I'd like to hastily add that our prison was like a country club compared to the POW camps from conflicts with Japan or Korea or Vietnam. But some of us, because of our enthusiasm for trying to get out, were constantly mistreated. The Germans had a lot of different ways of looking at life. After one of my escape attempts, they took my guards and put them in the "cooler," or solitary confinement. And boy, it didn't make it easy for me because the guards who were being punished were the same guards who were keeping me in confinement. I got beat up a lot of times in situations like that.

We all have our heroes, men who inspire us, and for me that hero was Col Russ Spicer. He was the senior officer at my prison camp at the time and just the finest gentleman you could ever hope to meet. He had been shot down in a P-51 over the North Sea.

Well, shortly after he became commandant of our camp, we heard about a battle that had taken place where our forces had been caught in a German pincer and the Germans, instead of capturing and taking our men prisoners, went in and shot everybody. Thousands of American troops were murdered. But there were two servicemen who faked being dead and were recovered by our forces when they moved into that area.

When word got back to us through new prisoners coming in, Russ stood up at roll call and, in front of the German guards, described Nazi war atrocities, including the mass murder of our men.

The Germans "are a bunch of murderous, no-good liars, and if we have to stay here for 10 years to see all the Germans killed, then it'll be worth it."

That speech earned him a death sentence. He spent nine months in the cooler, waking up every morning and wondering if that was the day he would be executed. His bravery earned my undying respect. He was finally released when the Americans liberated the POW camp.

I worked with a lot of different fellows on the escape committee and we would assist each other. About two weeks before the war ended, you could hear the Russian big guns, cannons going off as they invaded Stettin (Szczecin), which was a hundred miles away. The guards started deserting and where there had been six guards on a fence in a given section of the prison camp, there were now three or four. It kept getting worse toward the end there.

Well, I created a diversion with some of the people I worked with by having them stage a fight. All of the attention of the guards in the towers was focused on the big fight, where three or four people pretended to beat each other up, throwing things and creating quite a distraction.

That was my signal to go for the fence. Two people joined me, a Canadian and Jerry Ennis, another pilot from my outfit.

We chose the far corner of the compound, where we were least likely to have anybody pay attention to us. We took boards from under one of the buildings and put them across the top of the coiled wire between the two fences. We got over the fence and down the other side, and then ran.

The prison camp at Stalag Luft I was near the little town of Barth on the Baltic Sea, on a peninsula. The only way off was to get across the water to the mainland. So we went through the woods and found some vines, like grapevines, and some logs. We tied them together and built a makeshift raft.

The Baltic Sea at that time was pretty cold; it was April and the water was close to freezing. We decided one person would sit on the raft and hold the clothes. Two of us got down in the water and propelled this thing across to the mainland. It wasn't very far, maybe a thousand feet. We got across and pulled on dry clothes. That helped.

We headed through the open countryside away from Barth, and then found a place to sleep near a building that looked deserted. We couldn't get inside.

The next day we were getting pretty hungry. We came upon a farmhouse and I knocked on the door. A lady opened the door.

"Do you understand English?" I asked.

"A little bit."

So I told her that we had just gotten away and that we thought the war was over. "Can you give us something to eat?" I asked.

She spoke English pretty well, so we could understand her. She gave us some potatoes and eggs.

After eating, I asked her if she had any paper and a pen or pencil. She understood and gave me a sheet of paper and a pen. I wrote a note:

> To Whom It May Concern:
> This lady has been very generous and helped us
> in our escape. I would like to make sure that
> you treat her with great kindness because she
> assisted us.

I signed it and handed it back to her. She didn't read it. We thanked her and I shook her hand. We started down this little old dirt road from the farmhouse to the main road, which was another dirt road. She came running out of her house, waving her arms and yelling to us.

I turned back, wondering what was wrong with her. When I got up to her, she showed me the note.

"I read your note," she said. "I want you to have this because you may need it more than I do."

She gave me a little pistol with three cartridges. I thanked her profusely, shook her hand again and off we went. Well, that gun was the greatest thing that could have ever happened to us.

We found three bicycles. The Canadian decided he had a better chance on his own, so he took off. Jerry and I continued alone, in and out of the Russian lines. That in itself was a nightmare.

To set the stage of understanding this whole situation, I want to tell you a little about the Russians. The Russian troops were called storm troopers, just like the Germans, and, believe it or not, they were on horse-drawn wagons. They would go in and ravage towns, rape the women and kill the people.

One town we stopped in, a woman recognized our uniforms, even though they were tattered. Her hand was wrapped in a bloody cloth. While standing there, she unwrapped the bandage to reveal the severed stump of her ring finger. The Russians wanted her wedding ring and couldn't get it off, so they cut off her finger.

"I speak English," she told us. "I want to show you some things."

We spoke for a few minutes about the Russian storm troops who had been in the area just the day before.

"I want you to take this home with you as a memory forever," she said.

The first place she took us was a department store. All the bodies in there had their throats methodically slit. Men, women and children died right where they lay. Some of them slumped over a counter, over chairs, lying on the floor.

"They did nothing," she said.

We stared at those bodies, unable to comprehend the Russian brutality.

"I want to show you one more thing."

She took us to a large round reservoir, like we have for drainage in our country. It was solid with bodies that had been machine-gunned. Civilians.

We left and soon caught up with the storm troopers. Thankfully, they ignored us. We went into one house where some Russian soldiers were gathered around a flush toilet. The tank was mounted on the wall and the Russians kept pulling the chain, watching the water flush through the bowl. They'd never seen a flush toilet before. They were so primitive. It was unbelievable. It might have been funny, except I kept seeing the bodies in the department store and reservoir.

As we made our way west toward the American line, things went from bad to worse. Jerry and I found a farmhouse and decided to stop for the night. The Germans had built walls around the main house and barns. The walls were 10 or 12 feet high with gates, much like a compound. We went in and found this big barn with horse-drawn wagons. There were about 50 free Frenchmen inside—conscripted labor. The Germans went into France, collected all these people and sent them to Germany to clean up the rubble from our bombings.

They were trying to get back to France, found this enclosure and thought it was a safe place to camp. One of the women spoke pretty good English and Jerry spoke French. We visited with them and learned a lot about what was going on in Germany. The one woman told us stories about her experiences, and boy, they had been through some terrible times.

Well, it got dark and everybody went up into the hayloft. There must have been 50 people in there, tucked into the hay. We no more than got to sleep when we heard this rumbling. Russian tanks came right through the wall. Storm troops piled out, swarmed into the barn and grabbed pitchforks. They started punching the pitchforks into the hay. They hit someone, heard him scream, and then fired machine guns into the hay.

The Russians had a lantern. Everybody started surrendering. They took this woman who appeared to be about ready to give birth, slit her throat and then lined up. I don't know, about 10 or 15 Russian soldiers raped this dead woman.

They came over to the wall where Jerry and I were still hidden in the hay. We stood and held up our hands. We tried to communicate, tell them that we were Americans. I kept pointing to their shoes and their clothing—it was GI issue.

I tried to explain that we were the same because we had the same uniforms and stuff. I don't know how we got by with it, but they didn't disturb us any further. For reasons beyond our comprehension, they left most of those Frenchmen dead, took everything they wanted from the little compound, climbed into their tanks and drove away.

Jerry and I got back on our bicycles and rode off, accompanied by new memories of Russian atrocities.

A day or so later, we were riding our bicycles and I saw some revetments. Revetments are created by building up mounds of dirt on three sides and putting camouflage over the top. That's were you hide your airplanes from the enemy. There was one right after another and they were filled with German Focke-Wulf FW-190s.

The airfield was practically deserted. I'd see somebody walking over there, see somebody walking over here, but there were no guards or anything protecting the field.

"Jerry," I said, "this is what I've dreamed of!"

While in prison camp, I met a fellow named Gus Lundquist. Gus had been a test pilot at Wright Field. He was given an assignment to go to London and conduct test flights on all the captured German airplanes. He wrote evaluations of each one. He'd flown 10 hours in the FW-190 before talking his commander into letting him go on a combat mission. As a test pilot, Gus was not supposed to fly combat, but he was a gung-ho person and really wanted to go on a mission. Luckily the Germans never figured out his background!

My dying ambition from the very beginning of my flying career was to become a test pilot at Wright Field. I wanted that so much that I told my commanding officer, Col Marvin McNichols.

"Bob," Marvin said, "if you can survive the war, I'll make that happen somehow, someway."

When I discovered that Gus was a test pilot and incarcerated at Stalag Luft I, I looked him up. He confessed that he had flown the FW-190 before being shot down. There was an airfield near our prison camp where they operated FW-190s. I fanaticized about escaping and somehow stealing an airplane from that field—which would have been impossible—and flying out of Germany.

"Jerry, I'm going to see if I can find one of these airplanes and see if I can remember everything Gus tried to show me with his sketches in the dirt."

Well, in every revetment I went to, the airplanes were too badly damaged. Finally, I found one that didn't appear to have anything damaged that was vital to flight. It was full of fuel.

"Boy," I thought, "this is it!

I climbed into the cockpit and looked around. I was puzzled. Even though Gus had briefed me, everything was in German and I couldn't figure it out.

"Jerry, I don't remember enough to even know how to start this thing!"

"Well, what are you going to do?"

Jerry already told me he didn't want to go with me. He was done with flying. He'd taught French in high school before coming into the service and wanted to go back to teaching.

"The first German who walks by here, if he has on coveralls like a mechanic," I said, "I'm going to bring him in here with the use of this gun."

"Okay," Jerry said.

And we waited and waited and finally somebody walked by.

"Halt!" I yelled.

The German turned around. I had the gun pointed at him and motioned for him to come in. Well, we couldn't communicate with him. We both tried.

"I'm going to use my French on him," Jerry said.

The man spoke French. So Jerry told him what we wanted to do. He told him to help me start the airplane. I didn't have a parachute and I didn't have a cushion—so when I was seated in the cockpit, I could just barely see out. Normally, you have your head up above the canopy rails so you can look out the windshield. Jerry told this fellow that I needed a cushion. I already searched the other planes and hadn't found one anywhere up and down the line. This fellow told us he didn't know where to find them.

"You're going to help him start that engine," Jerry said in French to the mechanic. "If he doesn't get airborne, it's going to cost you your life."

And so the fellow helped me start the engine. And once I got the engine going, I just took off. Other stories have been told that I taxied out. I did not taxi out. I stayed right there in the revetment, got the engine going full power and just roared straight out.

The stupidity of what I was doing registered just about the time I got off the ground. I got the wheels up and it suddenly dawned on me that I was the biggest target that anybody ever had. I was sitting helpless in a German airplane and some second lieutenant right out of flight training was going to come along and knock me down.

Well, the sky was overcast up to what I guessed to be 4,000 feet, so I climbed up underneath the cloud level and just stayed there so that nobody could see me coming if they were looking down out of the clouds. I headed north until I hit the North Sea, and then I turned west. The airplane was full of fuel but I had no navigation, no maps, no charts or anything. I thought I'd pass over some airfields, but even if they were deserted, I couldn't land because I knew the Germans mined their airfields after they deserted them.

I thought, "I've got to go until I see windmills so I know that I am in Holland." I knew Holland was opposed to the Germans because they've been occupied by them. When I finally saw windmills, I couldn't find any runways. I was getting low on fuel and the gages were all bouncing off zero. I circled an area that looked pretty smooth, like a good place to land. I put the wheels down and the flaps down. I came in and got it on the ground alright. Then I looked up and saw a ditch that I hadn't noticed from the air. I knew if I went into the ditch that the airplane would flip upside down and I'd be trapped in it with no way to get out. So I ground-looped it, which means I booted[1] full rudder while applying the brake and the aircraft swerved away from the ditch and wiped out the landing gear. The plane was sitting on her belly. I breathed a sigh of relief. Even though I was disappointed about the loss of the airplane—I really wanted to come back to one of our airfields in that plane—I had finally escaped.

I had noticed a road on the other side of a thick stand of trees while still in the air. I got out of the airplane and started walking in that direction. I wanted to get on the road and see if I could hail down some vehicle.

About that time, I looked around and there were a number of farmers with pitchforks running at me from every direction. They thought I was a German. I had my hands up and kept trying to communicate. No way to do so. I kept pointing over to the road and kept walking. They just followed me. When we got to the road, we stood there, the farmers jabbering amongst themselves about what the next step should be. Luckily, no one had a gun or anything. They were just standing there with their pitchforks pointed at me when a British truck drove up. Of course, I saw the truck coming from some distance, and when it got up close, I started waving my arms. They slowed down.

---

1 Pushed the rudder pedal down as far as it would go.

"I'm an American!" I yelled. "They think I'm a German."

They stopped and I told them what happened, indicating the airplane on the other side of the trees.

"It's okay, old chap," one of them said. "Just get in. We'll take care of you."

And so they did. They took me to their camp and fed me. I thanked them profusely.

"I'm going to hitchhike to Camp Lucky Strike," I said.

The Americans took most of the liberated POWs to camps, where they attempted to rehabilitate them. Camp Lucky Strike was the biggest. Most of us were skin and bones. That was the only bad thing about being a POW. We were hungry and cold most of the time. But the average person in a German POW camp, if he just wanted to be docile and wait for the war to end, only went through being hungry and cold. They weren't mistreated—thank goodness. That wasn't true of the Japanese prisons or the POW camps from other conflicts.

Well, I was on my way to Camp Lucky Strike, hitchhiking on military trucks, riding as far as I could until they needed to turn off somewhere. They'd stop and I'd get out and stick my thumb out again. I was on the main road and this one truck stopped. There was an American on board. His name was Nelson Gidding. He recognized me because I was getting pretty well known for all my escape attempts. He was a writer and put on a play, *Hit the Bottle*, an all-male thing in the prison camp, just as an amusement. Everybody was looking for some amusement. I didn't know him, but I did remember that play. We started talking.

"Tell you what we'll do," Nelson said. "Let's go to Le Havre."

I didn't really want to go to Camp Lucky Strike and Nelson didn't either. It was like going to a prison camp where you were still confined, only you were getting fed.

We got on a train, sat in one of the little compartments and started visiting with the other travelers.

"You look familiar to me," one of the men said.

"Well, I don't know where it would be from," I said. "What do you do?"

"I'm with the Merchant Marines and I'm the navigator on a ship. I went through flight training and got washed out."

"Where did you go to flight training?"

"That's where I know you from!" He went on to tell us that he joined the Merchant Marines after washing out and was the third mate on his ship. "My ship is in Le Havre," he said. "I'm going to Paris for two days, and then I'm coming back to the ship.

"We're sailing to the United States in a few days. I can smuggle you on board. I'll make all the arrangements. You'll be Stevedores. We'll load you up with things to take on board and I'll be waiting for you. I'll put you in a room and get food brought in to you."

And so we thought, "Oh boy! This is just heaven!"

Well, Nelson couldn't stand the confinement of the room on board.

"I'm going to go out and walk around the ship," he said one afternoon.

"Nelson, you're taking a big gamble."

And sure enough, he went by this little stand where you hand in a ticket and you can get candy bars, cigarettes, and stuff like that. He was standing in line, waiting for his turn, not knowing that you needed a coupon to get what you wanted from the stand. There was a captain with Army intelligence standing in the same line and when Nelson went up to the counter, the captain overheard the conversation.

"I don't know what you're talking about," Nelson responded when the clerk asked for his coupon.

"We can't serve you anything if you don't have a coupon," the clerk said.

"Okay," Nelson said. He turned and walked away.

The intelligence officer followed him back to the room and put us under house arrest. They took us down to the brig. It had bars on the windows. The third mate found out, so we still got good food and everything. But he did bring us bad news.

"We're not going to the United States. We've got to go back to England."

Nelson and I were shaking our heads, looking at each other. "What are we going to do?"

"I sure didn't know this," the third mate said. "The orders got changed after we spoke. But I'll get you off just like I got you on. The Army will be getting off first."

So we ended up in England. Nelson had gone to school there. Oxford, I think. And his family had some contacts in very high places. We went to Sir Carry Evans's home. Sir Evans gave us some money and we went out and got new uniforms. We went all over London and were living it up like kings!

"Nelson," I said one afternoon, "I'm going to Bournemouth." I wanted to find my brother, Leroy. When I checked with headquarters in France, I learned that he had never left England. I took a train to Bournemouth and found him. Leroy told me that our mother was very ill.

I had not planned on going home. I was having fun in England and wanted to have fun for a while longer, especially after not seeing any women for 15 months! I was a bachelor and living it up.

But after talking with Leroy, I told Nelson, "I'm going to have to go home."

Believe it or not, we got back on that same ship. It had already made a trip to the States and back. I turned myself in and they kept me in the hospital for three days doing some psychiatric tests.

"These questions I'm going to ask you are somewhat

personal," the doctor told me.

"Fire away!" I said.

"These are psychiatric questions about how the prison camp has affected you. Did you dream about women while you were in prison camp?"

"All the time."

"Well, who were you dreaming of?"

Trying to be a smart aleck, I responded, "Well, kissing Eleanor Roosevelt through a picket fence."

"I think you're sick," the doctor said.

"I was trying to be funny!"

The trip home was heaven without dying. You know, being free. Getting to eat all that good food. It was wonderful.

Anyway, that's the story of the escape. People make it out as if I'd done something heroic and everything I did was just not very smart at all. But I was only 23.

★ ★ ★ ★

There's actually another story that I prefer to talk about. It's about a man named Tom Watts, and he kept a diary every day of all the things that happened to us.

I was assigned to a British unit in England for a couple of months before being transferred to Africa. Once in Africa, I was selected to test out the airplanes and asked if they could release Tom Watts to assist me. We hoped to go into combat together as a team. We'd flown together before. I knew his skills and he knew mine and we trusted one another. Tom wanted to join me and he did.

They called us test pilots, but we were more like production test pilots. Sort of like where a car is built and somebody drives it around the block to see that everything is okay.

The airplanes were being assembled by indigenous labor and we didn't have enough inspectors to make sure ev-

erything was put together properly. We first started out with
P-40s and P-39s.

We flew those airplanes and we had one incident, accident or belly landing after another. We just didn't have enough
people to get the assembly of the planes right. So we really had
to be diligent before we got in an airplane and took off.

Anyway, we went from there to ferrying airplanes to
the front line. We'd take a new airplane out to them as a replacement for an airplane that had battle damage. One morning, we had to take two planes to a field down near Constan-
tine in North Africa. The area was south of Algiers, where the
Atlas mountain range dips into the Mediterranean Sea.

Anyway, we got there with the new airplanes and
turned them over.

"Instead of going back in a Gooney Bird," the commander said, "we've got two battle-damaged P-40s that we'd
like you to take back to the depot for rehab."

We said okay and took off. We didn't have enough fuel
to go around the enemy lines, so we decided to fly directly
over them. The only way to get back was through those big
Atlas Mountains.

We were going along fine when, all of a sudden, Tom
called me.

"Bob, I've got a real rough engine."

"Tom, I haven't seen anyplace we could land since we
took off. We could turn around, but if you've got a sick engine
there's no way of going back."

"What do you think of that plateau on top of that little
mountain over there?"

"You hang on to your glide speed with what little power you have and I'll take a look at it."

I veered off and took a look.

"It's gonna be risky," I said. "But I think you might get
away without killing yourself."

"Well, I don't have any choice. I've got to get down."

Bailing out wasn't an option. If you bail out in these mountains nobody will ever find you.

"Go for it," I said.

Tom headed in the direction of the plateau. And by golly, he got on the ground and got it stopped. The airplane was intact.

"I'm safe!"

"Is there enough room for me to land?" I asked.

"I'm sure there is but I don't know if we can get off."

"Well, I'm going to give it a go. I'll land and pick you up. But forget your parachute because there isn't any room for one."

I landed and made it, keeping the engine running. Tom ran over and climbed in. I took the straps off my parachute and used it as a seat cushion. Tom climbed up and sat down on my back with his knees hooked underneath my shoulders, his feet tucked into the seat next to my body. With the two of us in the cockpit—of course, there wasn't room for two of us in that plane—we couldn't close the canopy. Tom's head stuck out above the windshield and mine was jammed against the gunsight. We got off. It was cold going across the top of those mountains. We got to Algiers and I called a Mayday.

"I've got an emergency. I'm going to have to put her down. I'm getting low on fuel."

I got it down okay and taxied in with the fire truck following me. Tom's face was wind burned and the corners of his mouth were torn by the force of the wind. My face, well, I never thought it would be the same again. I had a crick in my neck. They gave me the bronze star with a V for valor. But the real reward was knowing that Tom was safe.

They fixed that plane and the fellow who took it off the plateau didn't make it. He ended up in the neighboring mountain side.

On January 24, 1944, Tom Watts was shot down near the coast of Calvi, Corsica. He successfully bailed out of his plane, but the high winds dragged him into a reef of rocks offshore. When I flew over the reef, I could see his body in the crystal-clear water. Tom died doing what he loved most, flying fighters. Tom will always be remembered as a great patriot.

Bob realized his dream of becoming a test pilot for the Army Air Force. He flew captured German and Japanese planes and flew the chase plane in the Bell X-1 program when the sound barrier was broken for the first time. He continued as a test pilot for North American Aviation. Jimmy Doolittle called Bob "the best stick-and-rudder man who ever lived." In subsequent years, he entertained airshow audiences around the world. Bob was listed as the third greatest pilot of all time by the *Air and Space* magazine Centennial of Flight issue, behind Jimmy Doolittle and Noel Wien and before Charles Lindbergh and Chuck Yeager. He and his wife, Colleen, have two children and four grandchildren. They live in Palos Verdes, California.

Decorations and Awards: MILITARY—Distinguished Flying Cross, Soldier's Medal for Valor, Air Medal with Oak Leaf Clusters, Purple Heart, French Croix de Guerre.

CIVILIAN—National Aviation Hall of Fame, Lindbergh Medal, International Council of Air Shows Hall of Fame, Society of Experimental Test Pilots, Kitty Hawk Award, Arthur Godfrey Aviation Pilot of the Year, Flying Tiger Pilot Award, Lloyd P. Nolan Lifetime Achievement in Aviation Award, Cliff Henderson National Aircraft Exposition Award, Godfrey L. Cabot Outstanding Contributions to the Science of Aerospace Award, Bill Barber Award for Showmanship, ICAS Art Scholl Award for Showmanship, Honorary Member of the Original Eagle Squadron, Award of Merit from the American Fighter Aces Association, Honorary Member of the Thunderbirds and Blue Angels

CARMELITA POPE

———❧———

USO ACTRESS IN THE MEDITERRANEAN THEATER

I was Corliss Archer. I could feel her essence pulsing through my body as I sat in the audience watching George Abbott's production of *Kiss and Tell*. Corliss Archer—the all-American girl that our soldiers and sailors were risking their lives to protect.

I headed backstage as soon as the play ended and demanded to see someone in charge.

"Do you have a script?" I asked the bemused stage manager. "I would like to read the part of Corliss Archer for you because I think I should play it!"

"Yeah, I'll give you a script." Obviously a little surprised by my brazenness, he managed to hide his smile. "Come back in a week and read it for me."

So I did. A week later, I stood in the middle of that stage in Chicago and read the part of Corliss Archer and I loved it. I *loved* it!

"Gee, you *are* Corliss Archer," he said to me when I finished that reading. "But there's nothing open."

He actually seemed as disappointed as I felt. As I turned to go, he brightened and called out to me.

"When George Abbott comes into town, which he does often, I'll have him listen to you. You get up on this stage and read that part for him."

Which I did about two weeks later.

"The next opening I have is yours," Mr. Abbott told me after that reading. My feet didn't touch the ground until I got home.

You see my father played vaudeville while earning his law degree. He gave up show business to practice law, but he loved the theater and vowed that his children would have the opportunity to perform. George Abbott gave me that opportunity when he hired me as an understudy for the Chicago production of *Kiss and Tell*.

About six months after joining the company, I learned that George Abbott was putting together a cast of *Kiss and Tell* for the USO. You see, this was 1944 and there was a war going on and I wanted to do what I could for our troops. I called Mr. Abbott in New York and asked for that part.

"Oh Carmelita, I wish I'd known," he told me on the phone. "We're all cast. The whole company. And we're in rehearsal."

"I see," I said, heartbroken.

"But, I'll tell you what. If we send another company out, I'll let you know."

I didn't hear from him for two weeks and then he called.

"Take your physical!" George said, the long-distance phone line crackling. "You're going overseas!"

"What happened to the cast?" I asked.

"I fired them!" He said. "They weren't up to par. I want good people going over there! If this show is going to have my name on it, I only want good people going."

I was a little nervous about telling my parents. I hadn't said anything about going overseas or wanting to do something for our troops.

"Well," I thought to myself, "they're either going to say no or be happy about it."

My mother was a little taken aback, but my dad thought it was wonderful. He was a true patriot and instilled in his children that you don't take anything away from this country—you give. I think maybe President Kennedy got his idea from my dad!

My mother came with me to New York. We took the train from Chicago. We booked a little roomette on a train filled with Americans in uniform. My nerves tingled with excitement. This was my first time in New York. It was enchanting!

Some of our relatives met us at the station. I had rehearsal in an hour and we had trouble finding the rehearsal hall. We eventually found it and I couldn't wait for the elevator. I ran up the stairs and I ran so fast that I ended up on the roof of the building! I went right by the floor where I needed to get off! When I calmed down and found the right room, we started rehearsal.

As an understudy, I knew all the girls' parts, but I was ecstatic when I learned that I would play the lead, Corliss Archer! Finally!

My mother stayed with me in New York for a few weeks and we had a wonderful time. When George Abbott decided we were ready to take the show to the troops, he arranged for our company to do about six performances in the New York area before shipping out.

We performed at Mitchel Field, two shows at Camp Kilmer, one night at Camp George Meade, and one final performance at Hunter College.

On the morning of our final show, I woke up feeling very sick. I got worse as the day proceeded, so that afternoon,

I called the hotel doctor. My temperature hit 104° on ther-mometer and every inch of my body ached—even the roots of my hair. The doctor gave me a dose of sulfa, the medical cure-all in those days.

"Stay in bed for three or four days, and you'll be al-right," he told me before leaving the room.

Well, the minute that door shut, I climbed out of bed and threw on my clothes. I felt horrible, but once we started and I looked out at all those wonderful sailors, I forgot I was sick and the show went on.

Someone told one of the officers about my illness and he arranged for a car to take me back to the hotel so I wouldn't have to ride the train.

"Here were two of the most adorable sailors driving me home," I wrote to my mother later that night, "and I was so sick, I didn't even notice." Now that's sick!

Before we were scheduled for an overseas assignment, we were fitted for USO uniforms. We wore the same uniform as the Women's Army Corps, only ours sported insignia des-ignating us as USO. On our identification cards, we held the rank of captain but we weren't really part of the service. Des-ignating a rank was mainly a precaution in case we were cap-tured by the enemy. You see, officers generally receive better treatment than enlisted personnel.

No one knew where they would send us. We stayed around New York waiting for orders. I spent that New Year's Eve in Times Square, crushed to death by the crowd. It was the most thrilling moment of my life because, when they played "The Star-Spangled Banner," I was in uniform and I stood there proudly saluting my flag.

Our alert finally came around the 8th of January. They loaded us up on a train with three other USO companies. None of us knew our destination. I wanted a compass so I could tell our direction. It wasn't until they gave us our passports that I

discovered our assignment would be the Mediterranean Theater of Operations.

Thrilled qualifies as an understatement. I am a first
generation American. My father was born in Italy and my
mother's mother came to America to teach Italian, as a professor at DePaul University. She taught there for 25 years. My parents were very excited when I told them about my assignment.

The train dropped us off in Newport News, Virginia,
and we reported to Fort Eustis for training. Now, up until this
point, I had been billeted in hotels, pampered with room service and daily maids. When we arrived at Fort Eustis, the girls
in our company were turned over to a tough little sergeant.
She took us into the barracks.

"Pick a cot," she told us.

"A cot?" I thought to myself. "I'm going to sleep on a
cot?"

I set my backpack on a thin mattress covered by a drab
olive, itchy blanket.

"Now we're going to line up for the latrine," she continued.

"Line up for the latrine?" I asked. She just looked at
me. I found it easy to read the message in her expression.

She made us march to the latrine. Think about it. We
were actors, we didn't know what we were doing, and here she
had us marching to the latrine.

"Oh, my heavens!" I thought to myself when we arrived. "I'm never going to be able to do this!"

None of the toilets were tucked into private stalls; they
were all just in an open room. And the showers were communal. It took me a few days to get my thoughts in order, but after
that, well, you know, it just didn't matter anymore. We all ended up in those showers together, singing and talking and scrub-
bing each other's backs. It was quite a learning experience!

January is bitterly cold in Virginia. My roommate Vi

and I, on a particularly cold afternoon, decided to light the stove in the barracks.

"Let's get some heat in this place," I told her.

So we filled the stove with all kinds of wood that we found outside and struck a match. We were really happy. The room began to warm up and we started to thaw out.

"I think we better look at that stove," Vi said to me. "It looks funny."

Well, not only was the stove red, but the pipe going all the way up to the ceiling glowed bright red.

"Look at this notice," one of the other girls said.

"THIS BARRACKS WILL BURN IN FOUR MINUTES."

We immediately ran to the latrine for water and dumped it on the fire. After that we decided to put up with the cold. We were very afraid to light that stove again!

Part of our training included instructions in the use of gas masks. Captain Pleasant was our instructor. He came into the barracks, lined us up and marched us over to the gas chamber.

"You are going to learn how to put on gas masks," he told us.

"Oh, we don't have to do this," we girls told him and poured on the charm. Nothing worked with Captain Pleasant.

"Oh, yes you do!" he said.

He issued each of us a gas mask and showed us how to put it on.

"Now we're going into the gas chamber," he said.

"Oh no! Not the gas chamber!"

"You have to," he explained. "You need to know what it smells like."

So we went in, each of us decked out in green rubber and metal masks, like aliens from outer space.

"Make sure your mask doesn't leak," he told us. "Is everybody comfortable?"

We nodded our heads yes.

"Now take them off."

"No! We're not taking them off!"

Captain Pleasant put his arms across the door and said, "Unless you take your gas masks off, you are staying here!"

So, one by one, we took our gas masks off and ran out of the gas chamber. Captain Pleasant sure didn't live up to his name!

After about four days of orientation, they lined us up to get on the ship. We wore our heavy woolen uniforms and trench coats. They issued us belts with a canteen, mess kit, first-aid kit, mosquito netting, and gas mask hanging like Christmas ornaments from little clips. They passed out helmets, which, of course, we automatically tilted to one side.

"No! Straight!" they yelled. So we straightened them. And boy they were heavy!

I wore my long underwear, hoping to keep my pack as light as possible. Our ship, the USS *General Richardson*, carried 5,000 soldiers and sailors. Of course, we wanted to look wonderful. But we stood there in the pouring rain and waited until all the troops boarded.

By the time we walked up the gangplank, our hair was dripping water, our clothes were soaked and the helmet made us crouch down like frightened turtles. We were the saddest-looking group in the world!

They kept us segregated from the enlisted personnel. I didn't think that was right so I paid a visit to the captain one day and confronted him.

"I'm here to entertain the enlisted men," I told him firmly, "and I want to be able to talk to them."

"You follow orders," he said to me. "I'm the captain of this ship—not you!"

Well, I was very unhappy, but I'd been told. It wasn't until much later that I learned that many of the enlisted men were from US prisons. They'd been offered leniency and a pass out of prison if they agreed to enlist in the armed services. So, of course, the captain wanted to keep us safe, he just neglected to tell us that little piece of information.

American planes escorted us for the first two days, and then we found ourselves alone, zigzagging across the Atlantic in hopes of avoiding German submarines.

We girls loved sitting on the deck and frequently played cribbage. One afternoon I looked out over the water.

"You know, that looks like a periscope out there," I said pointing to a spot not far from our ship.

Moments later every gun on our ship went off and the alarm chased us below deck.

About 20 minutes later, the "all clear" sounded and we returned to our game. It felt like an awfully close call and we were mighty glad when we got close to Europe and American planes based on the continent flew out to escort us into port, guiding us and protecting us in case anything else happened.

We berthed in the Bay of Naples. It was a thrill for me because I had heard so much about Italy from my family. My grandmother always spoke Italian to me and, of course, like all stupid young people, I always answered in English.

"Someday you're going to be sorry," she told me.

But I fell into it. I could understand everything, and with a little practice, could speak fairly well. And I had fun with it!

I wore an American uniform, and one day, while in an Italian shop, a woman turned to her friend and said in Italian, "What kind of uniform is that?"

"It's an Army uniform," I told her in Italian. "I'm with the USO."

Boy was she shocked! I laughed all the way back to the base!

We got off the ship in Naples and I drank my first cup

of coffee—ever! It was cold, very cold out. We were wrapped up in our woolen uniforms and trench coats, wearing our helmets, dangling gas masks, mess kits and mosquito netting from our belts and freezing. Boy did that cup of coffee taste good!

We were billeted in tents in Caserta and it rained like mad, nothing but mud everywhere you looked. But we didn't care. After all, we'd survived the barracks at Fort Eustis, giving us immunity to almost anything!

We were anxious to do the show, but they sent our scenery and costumes to the front line by mistake. We sat around for a couple of days, and then decided, what the heck; we could do the show without the scenery! The entire play, all three acts, takes place on the Archers' front porch. All we needed was a couch and a couple of chairs and we could do the play almost anywhere.

So we got some furniture and put it together. The only snag came when Corliss wears shorts and the dialogue focuses on those shorts. Well, with my wardrobe on the front line, I didn't have any shorts to wear in the play.

"Don't worry, I'll fix it," our special services officer told me. "I'll get you something to wear."

And he did. He brought me a pair of men's khaki satin shorts and, of course, they were awfully big on me. Well, we did the show and when I came out in those Army shorts—remember the audience is composed of a thousand guys—they laughed so hard that they almost broke up the show. We couldn't go on for a long time. It was great! What a night!

That was the beginning of our entertaining there. And you know, there isn't an audience in the world like those kids. One night, we played to the Navy and at the end of the show, during our curtain call, every one of those sailors threw his hat in the air. From the stage it looked like cloud of white. What a thrill!

They were so appreciative. But it made me a little sad,

too. When we arrived at the theater, there would be a line of soldiers that reached around the block. Some of them came the night before and slept in the street so they could get into the show and get a good seat. They were so devoted. Never before and never again did a curtain call give me that kind of thrill!

Most of the time we had makeshift dressing rooms, just bare bones. Sometimes they were in tents. But once in a while, we would be lucky and play in a theater with fancy dressing rooms. You know, Italy is famous for its wonderful operas and we did have some beautiful theaters with great acoustics. We played in the Santa Maria Opera House in Naples, where Enrico Caruso sang. They assigned his dressing room to me, the one where he autographed the wall. They must have papered around it a hundred times, just cut a hole in the wallpaper. I'll bet that signature is still there.

The Santa Maria Opera House has a box in the center for the king and queen with the Savoy insignia prominently displayed. Well one night, General Marshall, General McNarney, and General White attended our performance and sat in that royal box. I received lovely letters from them thanking us for such a great performance. The best thing about *Kiss and Tell* is that it tells the story of an all-American family. Funny and wholesome, I'm sure it made some of the boys pretty homesick while reminding them what they were fighting for.

Corliss Archer had a little dog and in one scene, he accompanied her onstage. Americans love animals and most of the troops kept company mascots. Some of them were really strange-looking, half-starved street dogs that the troops fed and pampered. Well, we'd ask the groups we entertained if they had a mascot and, whenever we could, we used their dog onstage. The troops got the biggest kick out of seeing their company pet up on stage with me.

On our voyage across the Atlantic, Vi and I met a dashing young pilot. Myers J. Reynolds III had flown over a hundred missions. After a brief visit home, he received orders to return to his squadron. He was a magnificent-looking, charming young man. Outgoing and friendly, he easily befriended the company. He went by the nickname "Chum."

Myers knew he would not survive another tour. He stayed on in Naples, AWOL, for five days with our company before his crew chief came down to collect him.

"Myers, you need to get back to base before they court martial you!"

Reluctantly, Chum returned to base.

Vi and I made plans to meet him in Sorrento about two weeks later. He never showed up. After waiting all day, we called his base.

"Myers is missing in action."

I knew he didn't make it.

A few weeks later, his crew chief knocked on my door, very early in the morning. He'd come all the way down to Rome to tell me in person that Myers's body had been recovered and he was buried in Milan.

Vi and I visited his grave after the war. We brought plants and flowers and planted them. Before we left, we took white pebbles, and in the center of his grave we made wings, the same insignia he wore on his uniform.

"Oh, what a handsome man he was," the caretaker at the cemetery told us.

And he was a dashing, beautiful young man in the prime of his life who knew, before he returned to that base and climbed into his plane, that he would make the ultimate sacrifice for his country.

We took the show to Palermo, Sicily, and I ran into a friend from college who had enlisted in the Navy shortly after we entered the war.

"Oh!" I told him, happy to see a familiar face. "I'm going to have a party for you!"

And I did, in my room. I invited a lot of people, put out food and poured wine. We had a wonderful time!

When he left that evening and entered the lobby, the shore patrol arrested him and hauled him off to the brig. I was frantic to learn that his only crime was being an enlisted man in an officers' hotel.

Well, I was so upset about this incident that I went to Father Murphy, a fellow Chicagoan, and asked him to intercede. I even went to my friend's captain and begged for leniency. I did everything I could to get him out of jail. Eventually, he sent me a message.

"I'm only in here for a couple of weeks and it was well worth it!" he wrote. "I'd do it again!"

It didn't have a bad ending but I was certainly upset about it. I hated to leave Palermo with my good friend languishing in jail.

We frequently did two shows a day, so when we had the opportunity to take a little time off, Vi and I jumped at it. Some friends we made in the Eighteenth Troop Carrier Squadron were billeted in a beautiful villa on the Mediterranean in the picturesque town of Rosignano. It was an absolutely gorgeous, gorgeous place. They gave us this little cupola on the top of the villa with a sweeping view of the Mediterranean Sea. We spent a week there teaching their chef how to cook spam in creative ways, like breading it, or using it in salads.

We were close enough to the airfield that we could see those planes take off on missions. It was sad to stand on the airstrip and count the planes going and then count them coming back.

I really wanted to go up with them and see the flak firsthand. So one night, I talked my friends into letting me stow away on a C-47. Our mission required us to drop ammunition and equipment to the Italian partisans helping the Allied troops on the far side of the front line.

Of course, we didn't have the commander's permission. He flew the lead plane, so I pretty much tried to stay out of sight. The planes took off in V formation. We went over the front line, and started dropping the supplies. All of a sudden I heard, "Bang! Bang! Bang!"

"OK, Carmelita," the pilot said, "you can see flak now."

I stuck my head up and looked around. "Oh! That's flak!" It was exciting but really scary, too.

And right at that moment, the commander looked over at us.

"Oh my heavens!" I thought. "I'm going to be court-martialed and so will everybody on this plane!"

When we landed, I whipped over to this lovely villa where they had a beautiful bar fixed up for the troops. I ran in and sat down.

"Give me a drink," I said, looking around a semi-dark room filled with airmen. "Remember, I've been here for two hours!"

An angry captain strolled in a few minutes later.

"What were you doing on this mission?"

"Mission?" I asked, innocence personified. "What mission? I've been here for two hours. Haven't I, boys?"

"Oh yeah," everybody in the bar responded. "She's been here. That's her third drink!"

Well, he was pretty red-faced, but he didn't do anything about it. I didn't care if I got in trouble, but I didn't want anybody else to!

In between all of our shows, we visited the hospitals. In fact, sometimes we did our shows in hospitals. As long as we had space to walk around, we could perform right there in the ward. And they were so grateful.

It was wonderful talking with those wounded soldiers. Sometimes we'd pop up and sit on the side of their beds. We'd talk about American girls. They'd tell us about their girlfriends and wives and children. It was very, very touching.

While in Naples, I ran into Frank Chesrow, a family friend. He was a pharmacist stationed at the hospital. He thought it would be helpful for me to see the electroshock treatments used on some of the shell-shocked young men. I was eager at first, but by the third one, my knees gave out and I just couldn't watch it again.

I held a special place in my heart for the boys suffering from shell shock. I spent a lot of time in the mental wards, just visiting with those boys. At first, the administration worried.

"Oh, we'll send a military policeman in with you."

"No, no. Have him outside," I begged. "If something happens, I'll call for him. I just want to talk to this young man."

I found that the most rewarding. And it was very endearing. One man reached out and asked, "Can I just touch your hair?"

And his hand was so gentle. I must have reminded him of his sweetheart.

Our visits gave these boys a little remembrance of home. A little look at America. Most of them hadn't seen American women for a long time—for some of them it had been years.

I only had one incident where one of the men got belligerent.

"You shouldn't be here," he said, his voice trembling with anger as he pushed me against the wall. "We're here to keep you home and safe. You shouldn't be here!"

"We all want to volunteer and do our part," I told him. "I'm an entertainer. This is all I can do."

He wasn't happy about us being there. But that was the only time anyone complained.

Frank Chesrow kept an eye on me for my family. One day he called me.

"Now, tomorrow I'm going to pick you up and I'm going to introduce you to somebody. I cannot tell you who it is but it is a very important person." He said. "You are going to have to speak Italian all day long!"

I couldn't begin to guess! I knew only two things about this mystery person—an Italian who was very important.

The next morning, Frank picked me up in a jeep. We went out into the hills outside of Naples. We wound around and around and I kept asking, "Where are we going? Where are we going?"

"It's a secret! I can't tell you."

Finally, we arrived at a gated entrance flanked by two Italian guards decked out in colorful uniforms. They put their guns out, then, spotting Frank, pulled them back.

"Oh! *Dottore* Chesrow! Come in! Come in!"

As we drove through the gate, Frank looked over and said, "You are going to meet the queen of Italy."

I stared at him with my mouth hanging open—not quite believing. The queen was in exile. Her husband and sons had fled the country. I guess some of the Italians knew she was there, but they protected her.

"But," he said, "you must speak Italian because she doesn't speak a word of English."

Oh my heavens! She was a lovely, lovely woman. Absolutely beautiful! In her seventies and a surgeon, she still practiced medicine. She would tie a babushka over her hair and go out to take care of the sick. Frank supplied her with medications and they became great friends.

"I have a secret to tell you when you leave," she said. "I can't tell you now."

"A secret?" I kept wondering. "What is this secret? What is this surprise?"

We sat down over tea. I kept dragging up all the Italian words my grandmother tried so hard to teach me. It was very difficult!

"You know," she said to me, "you speak very well. Your

grandmother taught you the Tuscan Italian, which is the pure Italian."

But of course she did! She taught the Italian language in a university!

Just before leaving, I turned to the queen and asked, "What is the secret?"

And in beautiful English she told me, "I speak English, but Frank wanted you to speak Italian all day!"

A laugh bubbled up from deep inside me. "And now," I said, "I have a favor to ask of you. My grandmother grew up in this country and never met anyone from the royal family. Would you give me a picture to take home to her?"

And she did. She signed it "Elena."

I gave it to my grandmother. As she grew older and older and her mind grew a little dull and she hardly knew me anymore, she would tell me the story of her granddaughter who went to Italy to entertain the American Army. "And that granddaughter," she would brag, "spent a day with the queen of Italy." Then she would hold up the picture, almost worn out from showing it.

On April 25, 1945, our company performed in Cesenatico, Italy. Everywhere I went on base, people would ask, "Have you met Major Cass?" Or they would tell me, "You have to meet Major Cass."

And I thought, "This isn't going to work. If everybody wants me to meet him, well, I probably won't like him."

Maj Benjamin Cassiday's commanding officer called him aside one day and explained that the girls from the USO show wanted a ride in a B-25. There weren't many B-25 pilots stationed at Cesenatico, so Major Cass was ordered to take them up.

"I'm Major Cassiday," he said to me the first time we met. "I'm going to fly your company, so if you want to go, get in."

He was cocky, self-assured, with that "I couldn't care less" attitude and I liked him. I liked him very much. In fact, my heart sank to my socks!

I rode in the right seat on that flight. Vi sat up front with us and suffered from motion sickness. But I felt fine— more than fine. I would have been flying without the plane.

Cass and I had dinner together that night, and breakfast the next morning. In fact, we spent as much time together as possible. Everybody around could tell that we were in love.

In fact, a three-piece ensemble in the dining room played "Here Comes the Bride" when we walked in one evening before the show.

I was in Italy when the war ended. Oh, the jubilation! I don't think we had the euphoria there that they enjoyed in the States, because these soldiers and sailors knew that this wasn't the end for them. The war still raged in the Pacific and they could be transferred there at a moment's notice. But we all celebrated that night.

We knew that nobody would watch our show that night so they gave us the day off.

Cass flew Vi and me down to Rome and we celebrated with thousands of troops in the streets. We weren't supposed to go and when we returned our special service officer called us into his office.

"You were not authorized to go to Rome," he said as we entered the room.

"How did you know where we went?" I asked.

"Well, because they saw you at the train station."

"Train station? We weren't at the train station! We flew down in a B-25!"

Two other girls from our company were seen at the train station. I don't know if they ever got caught, but they should have!

The day after the war ended, our company moved to

Milan. They flew us up to do our show. We landed in a muddy field and trudged through about two feet of mud with our equipment.

We went to the hotel where our group was billeted and it was a very strange thing. I opened the closet door and it was filled with German uniforms. An officer's Luger and ammunition and insignia, everything, was just sitting there, waiting for his return. That night, I wrote a letter to my parents.

"You know, this German, this soldier, left in a big hurry! Do you suppose he's coming back tonight to collect his gear?"

As I wrote, I scared myself half to death. My roommate was out with friends. I went looking for a maid.

"May I have a key to my room?" I asked in my best Italian.

"Oh no!" she said. "The German never returned it!"

"Oh my heavens!" I thought to myself. "He's got the key. His uniforms are here. His ammunition is here. What will I do?"

I pushed every movable piece of furniture in front of the door and waited up for my roommate. I was very happy when she came back!

That next morning, after a restless night, I woke up with a very sore throat.

"You know," I said to Vi, "before the show, I'd like to see a doctor and have him check my throat."

I had seen a Red Cross flag a block away. "Let's go there," I said to Vi, "and see if they have a doctor available."

There was a line of guys in front of the Red Cross building. Vi and I got in line. Most of the guys kept looking at us. It made us feel a little funny. We couldn't figure out why they kept staring. Finally, I wormed my way up to the desk and the sergeant sitting there gave me an incredulous look.

"What are you doing here?"

"Well, I woke up this morning and I have a really bad

sore throat and I'm doing a show tonight for the guys, and I'd really like to see a doctor."

"Lady, we don't even have a tongue depressor here!"

All of a sudden I realized I was at a pro station and they were passing out prophylactics to the troops. Well, we had to walk out of that Red Cross station, past all those guys still in line. My face turned bright red!

We were in Foggia when I first met Frank Sinatra. Foggia is in the south of Italy, very sandy and very, very hot. This was July 1945.

We cancelled our performance that night and attended his show. He stood out there in the middle of a sandstorm and sang for two hours. At the end of each song, someone would pass him a glass of water. His mouth was so full of sand from singing he would rinse it out and spit black.

I really have a lot of respect for that man. He could have ruined his vocal cords. But he kept singing for our troops.

Our hotel lacked air conditioning so we all slept with our doors open. It was the only way you could survive. Sinatra's room was two doors down from ours. Vi and I spent a lot of time walking up and down the hall just to sneak a peek at him sleeping. He was very skinny with large kneecaps. But he was charismatic and extremely handsome in person.

They blocked a special section off for him in the dining room. That first night, he picked up his silverware and napkin and carried it over to our table.

"I don't want to sit here all by myself. You guys are having fun! I'm coming over to eat with you."

Cass and I continued to see each other every chance we got. Sometimes he'd fly down to see me, sometimes he'd pick me up and we'd spend our time at his base in Cesenatico. The war ended and our time together grew short.

I believe that we have soul mates, but sometimes the cards we are dealt just don't quite work out. Within two weeks of meeting, Cass asked me to marry him. His family dated back generations in Hawaii. He was born and raised there. I studied to be an actress from the time I turned five years old. My goal was to see my name in lights on Broadway. As a West Point graduate, his destiny was to be an Air Force fighter pilot.

"You have to marry me, Carmelita."

"I don't know. I'm an actress. My life right now is in New York." I told him. "We're going to have to wait."

He swallowed and said no more.

Our company flew home via Africa. We landed in Casablanca after being reported lost in a horrible rainstorm. I suffered from a terrible cold and fell asleep on the descent. The pressure of landing punctured my eardrum.

I performed that night without being able to hear a single word that anyone said onstage. Luckily we'd done the show so many times I could read lips and deliver my lines.

Vi and I made it back to Chicago. I stayed busy at first by making phone calls for the boys.

"Call my wife," they asked when they heard I was going home. "Call my girlfriend, call my mother."

My mother even made calls. I sent her letters with phone numbers. "Tell so-and-so's mother that he's alright. I saw him in Rome or Milan or Sicily and he was healthy."

Many of the soldiers coming home passed through Chicago. They would stop and visit.

I never missed a show the entire time I was with the USO in Italy. I've done a lot of shows since then but I've never played to an audience like that. Not even when my name was in lights on Broadway. Sometimes, in those bare-bones theaters up close to the front line, we had to retime the entire show because the laughs were so tremendous, and they wouldn't stop, so you couldn't go on. We would have 10, 15 curtain calls. It was thrilling to hear the laughter, shouting and applause. And when I close my eyes, I can still see those troops, hear their voices, feel the applause. And a piece of my heart still belongs to each and every one of them.

> Carmelita went on to play Stella opposite her long time friend, Marlon Brando, in *A Streetcar Named Desire* on Broadway. She returned to Chicago after her stint on Broadway and worked in television. She appeared in the first soap opera, *Hawkins Falls, Population 6200*; played on the first panel show, *Down You Go*; and acted in hundreds of commercials. Carmelita retired from show business in 1988. She moved to Florida and then to Boise to be near her son. She is the director of the Veterans' History Project at the Warhawk Air Museum in Nampa, Idaho. She has two sons and four grandchildren. Now that they are both single, Carmelita and Ben Cassiday are back together.

VIOLET "VI" COWDEN

WOMEN AIR SERVICE PILOTS
(WASP)

I am sure God must grin when he watches a hawk fly. On wings spread wide, it soars above the earth with grace and majesty. And with deadly accuracy, it swoops down upon its prey. Perhaps there is no creature so magnificent.

I can't remember a time that I didn't envy the hawk, didn't yearn to soar, and swoop, and climb through the clouds with such pure elation. As I sat on the stoop of our little sod farmhouse in South Dakota, I dreamed of escaping the bonds of earth. I would watch with fascination as my hawk would swoop down, zero in on a little chicken, snatch him up and fly away.

"Oh," I would say to myself, "if only I could do that!"

So you can imagine my delight when a barnstormer landed his little Cessna on our picnic grounds during my senior year of high school.

Our nation was in the grips of the Great Depression and we had little disposable cash. But my boyfriend paid the five dollars that opened the door to my future. Perhaps there are no words to describe that first flight.

I went on to college. Worked my way through and earned my teaching credential. I taught first grade in a little school in Akaska, South Dakota. I earned $110 a month. My rent came to $10, so I had enough left over to buy clothes and other luxuries. Within a short time, I decided that my clothing needs were more than satisfied and, if I budgeted wisely, I could afford flying lessons. I put away $10 a month, and in a fairly short time, I earned my private pilot's license.

The airfield was six miles out of town. I didn't own a car so I rode my bicycle to the field early in the mornings; just slipped out of bed and started the day.

The children knew.

"You've been flying," they would greet me at the beginning of class.

"How did you know that?"

"Why, you're so happy!"

On December 7, 1941, I sat listening to Artie Shaw's music on the radio before church. An urgent announcement interrupted the program: the Japanese had bombed Pearl Harbor. I could not believe it. I thought after suffering through the Great War that the world had become a more civilized place.

"This isn't going to happen again," I told myself. "It's just not right."

On December 8, 1941, President Roosevelt and Congress declared war on Germany and Japan. I sent a wire to Washington, D.C.

"I have my pilot's license and I am ready to serve." Surely we needed planes to fly up and down our Pacific and Atlantic coasts, on the lookout for enemy submarines.

I didn't hear back from Washington, so I made my way out to California to stay with my sister, who was expecting her first child.

That's where I was when I received a call from Jacqueline Cochran. With the blessings of General Hap Arnold, Jackie formed a women's flying organization for the purpose of training women, thus releasing male pilots for combat missions. The Women Airforce Service Pilots (WASP) would ferry planes from the factories to points of debarkation for shipment overseas. Would I be interested?

Would I be interested in spending my waking hours flying without having to pay for the fuel? I had never heard of WASP before, but I didn't need time to consider the answer.

"Where do I sign up?" I asked.

The first step required an interview with Mrs. Hayward, one of Jackie's Hollywood friends. I walked up to the front door of a home that could only be described as an elegant California mansion.

"Oh my!" I thought as I rang the doorbell and listened to chimes reverberate through the spacious interior.

Mrs. Hayward asked me a lot of questions about my upbringing and experience as a pilot. She sized me up, seemingly satisfied with my answers so far, then looked me directly in the eye and asked, "What would you do to get into this program?"

I looked around her enormous living room with its beautiful furniture and soaring windows.

"If you asked me to scrub your house with a toothbrush," I said, re-establishing eye contact, "I would do it."

I reported to Long Beach for my physical.

"You're in excellent health. Twenty-twenty vision with perfect depth perception," the doctor reported. "But I can't pass you."

"Why not?" I asked, my heart pounding against my ribs in an attempt to escape.

"The minimum weight for a WASP is 100 pounds." He consulted his notes. "You weigh 92."

"Give me a week!" I pleaded. With my German-Russian heritage, I was certain I could put on eight extra pounds in a week's time. My sister, an excellent cook, joined my crusade with shared determination. I ate everything in sight, but, on the morning of my weigh-in, I came up just a tad short.

"Give me that bunch of bananas," I told my sister. I ate every one and followed them with as much water as I could force down my throat.

"Well, you made it!" the doctor said when I climbed on the scale in my scant little hospital gown.

"I should have!" I said, pulling the gown tight over my bulging stomach. "Look at this belly!"

He started to laugh. "That's the funniest thing I've ever seen!" he said shaking his head. "Do you mind if I call in another doctor?"

"Not before you sign that paper!" I told him cradling my distended stomach with both hands.

I'd like to tell you that I knew exactly what I was getting into when I signed up for the WASP program. But I didn't. You see, the fledgling organization grew out of a merger between Nancy Love's Women's Auxiliary Ferrying Squadron (WAFS) and Jacqueline Cochran's Women's Flying Training Detachment (WFTD) at Avenger Field in Sweetwater, Texas. Both Love and Cochran believed that there was a "sound, beneficial place for women in the air—not to compete with or displace the men pilots, but to supplement them." Over 25,000 women applied for this program. Standards were set much higher for women pilots than for their male counterparts. The training was rigorous and only 1,830 applicants made the cut. By the time they finished, almost 50% of them had washed out, leaving 1,074 graduates.

But I didn't know any of this when I borrowed money from my sister to pay for the train ticket to Sweetwater, Texas. The Army furnished transportation from the train station to Avenger Field. Two GIs picked me up in an open truck. I expected the passenger to give up his seat and allow me to ride in the cab. However, I found myself in one of two seats in the back, with my little suitcase tucked between my feet.

A thought came to me as we bumped along the dry, rutted road. I am not competing with women anymore: I am out there competing in the men's world. I am asking for a man's job, so I have to start thinking that I'm not the girl, I'm the person that has a job to do and I have to do it as well, or possibly better, than most men. In fact, starting at that exact moment, bouncing around in the back of an Army truck, I needed to prove to the world that I could do it.

My heart sank with that first look at my new home. Sweetwater, Texas, is the rattlesnake capital of the world. Dusty, dry, and hot, the landscape stretched for miles in every direction in an unvarying shade of sand punctuated with tumbleweeds. I took one look and wanted to turn around and go home. If I'd had any money left, I just might have done that.

Especially after I saw the planes! "They're so big!" I said to myself. "I don't think I can do this!"

I shared a room in the barracks with five other girls. I was lucky; my rickety metal single bed was next to the window, so I wasn't cramped in the middle. A communal shower with four heads separated us from six other girls in an identical room on the opposite side. It was so hot, there were days when we showered with our clothes on and let the evaporation cool our overheated bodies.

I'd arrived a week late, and by the time I got there, size 40 jumpsuits were about the only thing left. I wrapped a belt around my middle and rolled up the sleeves of my khaki wardrobe. I knew I looked ridiculous, but I didn't care; Uncle Sam was about to provide me with a steady supply of airplanes and lots of gas.

The male instructors made training very difficult and washed out students for unnecessary things. Some of the girls entered the program with thousands of hours of flying time and still washed out. Each day of training I knew would be my last. None of us believed we would make it through.

The program required check rides with male pilots. There were four of us in a flight and my friend Betty was a basket case.

"I don't think I can take this anymore," she said, gripping my hand. "I just can't do it."

"Sure you can, Betty," I told her. "Look—I'll go first."

I went first and passed.

"Betty, it really isn't hard," I told her after landing. "All we did was what they taught us, nothing particularly difficult. The hardest part is the landing."

"You didn't think it was hard?" Parker, one of the check pilots asked. He towered over me with an expression that radiated displeasure.

"Well," I said, "we just did the same things we do every day in our training."

The next morning I showed up at the flight line and had a check ride.

I went out and did fairly well. I didn't mess up the landing and I followed the check pilot's instructions without any problems. He didn't say one word.

I found myself scheduled for another check ride the following day and I thought, "Oh brother!"

The next day I had a check ride and the day after that. For a week solid, every morning began with a check ride. Not once did the check pilot comment on my flying. By the end of the week, I couldn't keep anything in my stomach, not even water. And I was really upset.

"I am going to get through this," I told myself. I dug deep inside that well of determination so carefully nurtured by my parents. "I have to do this! I am going to do this!"

I climbed up in that P-19 and flew the socks off that little plane. My check pilot remained silent. But he didn't wash me out.

When Jacqueline Cochran pinned on my wings, I covered them with my hand and said, "No one is ever going to take them away from me."

We represented all women. It always bothered me when women expected certain privileges just because they were women. The WASPs competed in a man's world and carved out a place in it for women. We proved that an airplane couldn't tell the difference between a male or female pilot, only between a good one and a bad one.

But flying was still a man's world. When I arrived at Avenger Field, male cadets still trained there. We weren't allowed to talk to them or even recognize them. It seemed like a silly rule, but one I could keep.

On my way to the Post Exchange one dry, dusty afternoon, one of the cadets whistled at me. I turned and gave him a dirty look. About that time, Jackie Cochran spotted me and called me into her office.

"You aren't supposed to talk to the cadets," she said.

"I wasn't talking to him. I just looked at him."

"Well," she said with a touch of mischief in her eyes, "you're not supposed to look at them either!"

Forty-five-mile-an-hour crosswinds swept Love Field. Grounded, we sat around the flight room waiting for the winds to change or the weather to improve. Groups of girls visited, laughter bubbling up from shared exploits.

"Let's go flying." A self-assured check pilot, with an overlarge chip on his shoulder, loomed over me.

"Nobody's flying today!" I answered.

"Well, if you can't fly in 45-mile-an-hour crosswinds, you can't fly."

Can you imagine? I think he looked around that room and picked me out because I'm tiny. But my spirit wasn't tiny.

"I will show you!" I thought, my eyes never leaving his.

It was an old airplane, a twin engine with a big tail wheel. The wind blew so hard that the tail kept whipping around and it took all my strength—arms and legs and everything—to hold her steady just to taxi onto the runway. As we rolled into take-off position, he shut down one engine, forcing a single engine procedure on take-off. I feathered the one engine and upped the power on the other side. It took some doing, but I got her airborne on the first try.

"Let me shoot a landing," he said.

I relinquished the controls. He made a good landing.

"Now you do it," he told me.

Well, I really greased the plane on my landing.[1] I nursed my anger and tapped a strength that came from that well deep inside me.

"OK, shoot another one."

So I did. I could have flown a bathtub that day, and I think he knew it.

"Let's go back to the field," he said.

We went back to the field and check pilot Williams pulled him aside. I could tell Williams was angry and hoped he wouldn't cause a scene.

"Well, how'd she do?" Williams asked, a little pulse beating in his cheek betraying his anger.

"You know, she can fly!"

---

1 Made a perfect landing.

My first assignment was ferrying a plane from Love Field to Newark, New Jersey. Our basic training included only a few cross-country flights and they were relatively short.

"I'm not sure I can do this," I told my commanding officer.

"Sure you can, Vi. Look," she spread a map out on the table, "do you think you can fly from here to Columbus?"

I looked at the map. "Sure, I can do that."

"OK, how about from Columbus to Pittsburgh?"

I studied the map. It wasn't that far. "I can do that."

"Well, how about from Pittsburgh to Newark?"

"I can do that, too."

"OK, now let's put it all together."

And I did. In fact, in a relatively short time, I became so accustomed to cross-country flights that I could fly from Dallas or Long Beach to Newark without maps. I knew all the calls, how far between checkpoints and just how long it would take. It became so routine that sometimes, when we flew in groups, we'd have picnics in the air. A bunch of us would pick up box lunches from the Red Cross and take them with us.

"I'm eating my sandwich," someone would call out over the radio, and we would all eat our sandwiches.

"I'm eating my apple."

I swear you could hear the crunch of crisp apples in that silent bowl of the sky. Each of us sat in our own plane enjoying a picnic over the airwaves. We had such fun!

After paying my dues, I earned the right to lead some of the flights. I worked out the flight plans and kept the group together. When I was in charge, I would take off first, using the radio to communicate with my fellow pilots. Each mission required code names and I'd call out, sometimes over a restricted frequency, "Leader Coconut took off."

"Coconut One took off," the next pilot called out.

"Coconut Two took off."

"Coconut Three took off."

And so on, until finally we would hear from the tower.

"Will the Coconuts please get off this frequency!"

But by that time, we were together and on our way.

Oh, I love flying! And I love the clouds. Sometimes I would be flying in a group and see a pretty cloud. I'd scoot over and take a closer look at it. And I'd hear one of the other pilots on the radio say, "That's Vi out there sitting on the clouds again!"

I was one of only 114 women selected for pursuit training. Men and women trained together and were broken into units of four per instructor. There were three men in my group of four, and with these guys, I felt equal. I mean, they accepted me as a fellow pilot. But our instructor had never flown with a woman before and was a basket case.

"Well, how's she doing?" one of the guys would ask.

"I don't know," our instructor would answer. "I just don't know if she can cut it."

You are washed out in three days if you can't make the grade. And on that third day, I was really worried.

"Well," I thought to myself, "this is probably going to be it."

I went up with our instructor that morning and he was on the controls the whole time. I mean, I never got the feel of that airplane—ever.

When we landed, he looked over at me and said, "You know, that was a lousy landing."

"I know," I said. "That was yours. You know, you haven't let me fly one time! I never got a chance to fly at all!"

He looked at me, "I've never flown with a woman before. I just knew I couldn't let you go. I would feel responsible if something happened to you."

"Well look," I said, realizing that I had nothing to lose. "I'm here. I'm volunteering. And if I am stupid enough to make a mistake, it's not your fault. It's mine."

"Well," he said after a moment of silent contemplation, "you can fly again tomorrow."

He was really surprised that I could fly. It never occurred to him that a woman would be able to fly a pursuit plane.

And that's exactly what I did! My orders would have me taking a P-51 from Dallas, Texas, to Long Beach, California. In Long Beach, I would pick up a different plane and fly to Newark, New Jersey. Or we'd fly to Wichita, Kansas, to pick up a Bamboo Bomber. We'd kick the tires and if the wings didn't fall off, we'd climb in. Once you got your orders, you checked out an airplane. I mean, what you really did was buy that airplane. It was yours. If you had to stop halfway to your delivery point, you sent a message back to the base so they would know where that airplane was and where you were.

One night I sent a message that said, "Delivered a P-51. Mother and plane doing fine." The guy reading the messages at about four o'clock that morning got a kick out of it.

I was an eager beaver and would happily pass on my seven-dollar per diem and sleep overnight on an airliner so I could start another round of deliveries the next morning. The WASPs had very high priority with the airlines. Only the presidential party could bump us. One time, I kept track of my meals: I didn't eat two meals in the same state for three days.

I only experienced one close call. I flew from Dallas to Long Beach. I called in for my landing instructions and the tower called back.

"You're on fire. You need to circle the field and we'll clear the area for your landing."

I couldn't see the fire, but I circled as instructed and set the plane down on the runway. My training taught me to evacuate as soon as possible, so I grabbed the plane's papers, my sock full of make-up and scrambled out. I stood there about 10 feet away from my plane—its locked wheel on fire, spewing smoke from the friction—with my ship's papers in one hand and my sock of make-up in the other. "Oh, my gosh!" I thought to myself. "I'm such a girl!"

I never lost that quality . . . I mean being a girl. My room in the barracks at Love Field reflected my feminine side. It came with a single metal bed and a board along one wall for hanging clothes. I fixed that room up. I made a bedspread and curtains for the window and a curtain to hang over the make-shift closet. It looked so cute! Even my base commander appreciated my efforts.

One night he asked me to hang around the barracks to greet some special guests. I wasn't happy about the assignment.

"But there's a dance tonight!" I argued. "I want to go to the dance!"

"I think they'll come in early and you can still go to the dance."

I could hear the music from the club as I sat fuming in my room. But it all worked out in the long run. President Truman had called Gen "Vinegar Joe" Stilwell back to Washington. The general, his pilot, copilot and their wives were our guests for the night. I felt really bad for the women. Here they'd flown in from San Francisco with their black negligees and plans for a romantic rendezvous, and they were stuck in our barracks!

"What are you flying?" Vinegar Joe asked me.

"The P-51."

"I can't believe you're flying the Mustang!" he said. "I think that's wonderful!"

He asked me to join them for breakfast and I did. What an amazing man!

General Stilwell wasn't the only one who didn't realize

women were flying pursuit planes. I landed the P-51 at one field, pulled over to the hangar area, and a guy jumped on the wing.

"Where's the pilot?" he asked.

"What do you think?" I responded. "That the pilot jumped out and I was just playing around and decided to jump in?"

I was flying on December 20, 1944—the day they disbanded the WASPs. I could not believe we were being deactivated. I stood at the airfield and looked across a sea of P-51s just waiting to be delivered. Most of the guys coming back were bomber pilots, not yet cleared in pursuit planes. We volunteered to deliver them. For a dollar a year, we would have flown those things for them . . . heck, forget the dollar!

It was the saddest day of my life. You see, I had this job to do, and it was just about finished, and they told us to go home. Just like that.

I think I felt the prejudice at that time more than any other. I felt that I was doing a great job, helping my country, sacrificing my ordinary life. Then a decision was made: they no longer needed me. I almost felt like what we did didn't matter that much. It was so easy for them to disband us. Like we were used, but not appreciated. I think most of the WASPs felt that way for a time.

But we did matter. Our job was important. It just took 33 years for us to get our veterans benefits.

And now, when I look up at a hawk soaring, I share his exultation. In fact, at 89, I jumped out of a plane with the Golden Knights. My partner was a black aviator and as we were drifting down, floating through that capsule of air, it dawned on me just how much things had changed.

"Mike, do you remember all the prejudice against black pilots and all the prejudice against women pilots? And here we are just floating down together and having such a wonderful time."

And he said, "You know, Vi, things have changed."

Vi returned to the field of education after the WASPs disbanded. She married Scott Cowden in 1958 and settled in Huntington Beach, California. Vi is on the board of directors for the Bolsa Chica Land Trust and the board of directors for the Yanks Air Museum in Chino, California. She celebrated her 89th birthday by jumping out of an airplane with the Golden Knights, and her 90th birthday hang gliding with her granddaughter. Scott passed away in 2008. She and Scott have one daughter and three grandchildren.

CLAUDE C. DAVIS

—⟨∘/∘/∘⟩—

TUSKEGEE AIRMAN

My boyhood was joyful. I grew up in a small mining village in western Pennsylvania, where my father worked in the coal mines. My parents were strict and they made us walk a chalk line—straight up and down—they didn't tolerate any foolishness. Your character meant a whole lot.

It was a wonderful place to grow up. Winters filled with sled riding and ice skating on the creek and summers spent swimming in a swimming hole. We'd hunt in the fall. Sometimes we had to hunt just to get something to eat when Dad was on strike.

"Son, we're not poor," he'd tell me, "just broke."

Ours was mostly a community made up of European immigrants. My family was one of about 10 African-American families in the whole village. My best friend, Leo Barnaby, was a sandy-haired Italian. There wasn't much focus on color. We were just kids doing what kids did everywhere.

I was eight years old when I decided what I didn't want

to do with my life.

"What do you want to do when you grow up?" my father asked one day. "What do you want to be?"

"Dad, I don't know." I told him. "All I know is what I'm not going to be."

"What are you not going to be?"

"I'm not going to be a coal miner."

"I don't blame you, son," he said, ruffling my hair. "Find some other way to make a living."

"I will, Dad. I'll find something."

And I did. I went to high school in Oakmont, Pennsylvania. The school was exactly five miles away from my house. My sister and I used to drive together in the mornings in our old Plymouth automobile. I played football after school and practice lasted a good hour and a half. She didn't want to wait for me, so I ran home. We lived near the Allegheny River, so I had to cross over the river on a bridge and run into the woods way up in the hills. It was dark and I ran by myself, but there was no crime then, you didn't have to worry about anybody bothering you or anything like that. Every now and then one of the guys would drive me home from practice. Now that was a real luxury.

I had chores to do when I got home—cutting wood and banking the fire so my mother could just light it in the morning and feed Dad so he could go off to work. I kept up with my books, maintained a solid B average. At night we'd go to sleep and start it all over again the next day.

I was a running back on the football team and played safety on defense. I think the five-mile run every evening increased my endurance. That, combined with my good grades, got me three scholarship offers. I chose Wilberforce. It was the oldest predominately African-American university in the United States. It turned out to be a wonderful choice for me.

The school didn't have much money, so my football

scholarship consisted of meals at the training table and a free room in the dorm. In the off-season, I needed to find a way to supplement my income. I turned to the National Youth Administration (NYA) and my job waiting tables paid 25 cents an hour. But even in those days I was a bit of a hustler. I started a car washing business on campus. For 50 cents, I'd wash your car and for $2.50, I'd simonize it.

Then I read an article in a magazine. If you sold two suits, they gave you a third free. Well, I signed my name and they said, "OK, Davis, you're it."

After I got dressed up, I sold the extra suits. Then I started selling women's skirts.

I still kept the car wash business going, mostly washing the professors' cars. All during the week in my downtime I'd wash somebody's car, and on Saturdays and Sundays I'd really get into it. Then I had the suit business going on the side. I was doing pretty well, well enough to send 10 or 15 dollars a month home to my family.

After my sophomore year, I quit football and joined ROTC. I decided to become a military officer and that seemed like the best way to get there. Every year they selected seven of the top students in military science and tactics to go into an advanced upper curriculum that led to a commission. I was selected at the end of my sophomore year, in 1940.

I graduated college in June 1942. I received a bachelor's degree in English literature, a commission as a second lieutenant in the United States Army and orders to report to active duty all on the same day. I didn't know it yet, but I was on my way to becoming a Tuskegee Airman.

I'd been dating my college sweetheart for a couple of years. One day I looked at her and said, "Let's get married." And we did, a week after we graduated from college. We did the whole thing—a full blown church wedding in military dress uniform with sabers and all the trimmings. I was 22 years old, a married man and a lieutenant in the United States Army. I had it all.

They sent me to Fort Knox, Kentucky. They didn't know what to do with African-American officers at the time. There were only a handful of us in the United States. The service was segregated and opportunities for African-Americans were limited.

My childhood didn't expose me to much prejudice. I got my first real taste of it in the service. I remember standing in front of the all-white mess at Fort Knox, looking through the glass door. I could see a group of captured Nazi prisoners of war, in their blue jumpsuits and white caps, eating inside. They were supposed to be the enemy, but here I was the one being kept out. It was sobering to say the least. That's when my father's words came to me: "Don't get mad. Get smart."

After some deliberation, they decided to make a tank officer out of me, sent me to a week-long tank communication school. When I finished that course, they sent me to Camp Joseph T. Robertson in Little Rock, Arkansas, and then on to Fort Huachuca in Arizona. I was a signal officer in the Ninety-second Infantry Division, a mortar platoon leader specializing in communication. The war was going pretty quickly.

My assignment as platoon leader only lasted a few weeks. My commanding officer realized that I had a college degree. He decided to send me to Fort Benning, Georgia, for some advanced military work.

Let me tell you, that training at Fort Benning was really something. They teach you to keep your head down while the machine guns are firing. You had to crawl with your rifle under overhead fire. You stayed down on your belly and didn't rise up because they were using live ammunition. You rise up and you're dead. You just try to be a good worm.

Well, while I was at Fort Benning, a memo came down from the War Department looking for pilots. They didn't say what kind of pilots—not white pilots or blue pilots or Eskimo pilots—they just said pilots.

I thought, "This infantry isn't the most comfortable way of making a living." So I signed "Claude C. Davis" on the line.

I returned to Fort Huachuca. Then, out of the blue, about three weeks later, orders came from the War Department ordering Lt Claude C. Davis to pilot training as an officer at Tuskegee Army Airfield, Alabama.

Up to this point, I'd never been higher than two stories off the ground in my life. I hadn't even been in a high-rise building. But I was going to fly airplanes!

I had my orders. My wife and I packed up our belongings from our little rented apartment in Tombstone, climbed into our Chevrolet coupe and headed across the country.

We stopped in Dallas for a hamburger and across the street from the hamburger joint was a used car lot. Well, I just looked over there and saw the most beautiful Buick convertible, dark blue with red leather seats and all the bells and whistles.

"Wow! Look at that!" I said to my wife.

"Oh, it sure is pretty!" she said.

So we drove over there just to take a look. The salesman came right over and shook my hand.

"Howdy," I said.

"Howdy, Lieutenant," he replied.

"How much is that?" I asked, indicating the Buick. I don't quite remember what we paid for it.

I turned to my wife and asked, "Honey, do you want it?"

"Yeah," she answered.

"Do you have any money?" the salesman asked.

"No, but I'll trade you my car."

The Chevrolet was a nice coupe and all paid for. So I

traded it right there. We put our baggage in the convertible and continued our trip to Alabama.

My wife had relatives who lived on campus in the little town of Tuskegee. We got a room with them and life was going well. I had a pretty car, a pretty wife, was a lieutenant in the Army Air Corps training to be a pilot. Yes, life was good.

By the time I finished pre-flight, my wife was getting bored. She decided to go home to Chicago. She left me there and we got divorced not too long after that. I moved into the barracks and started primary training. We flew PT-19s, low-wing trainers that had flaps. I think ours was the first class that flew the PT-19, the classes before us trained in the PT-17, a biplane with narrow landing gear that liked to ground-loop on you.

My instructor was Jimmy Taylor. He happened to be one of the only African American instructors at Tuskegee. We got to be mighty good friends.

There were fourteen student officers in my class, officers that came from artillery, infantry and other basic divisions. Most of the instructors didn't want us to fly. Thirteen of the fourteen washed out of primary. I was the only one that finished.

I made mistakes. At one point I broke a rule. It was a beautiful morning, about nine o'clock. My instructor had four students. I was one of the four.

The sky was deep blue and there were fluffy white clouds up there. We had an assignment to practice stalls.

"Don't go above the clouds," Jimmy Taylor said.

Well, I practiced stalls and after a while I got bored. I looked up there at those puffy white clouds and thought, "I'd sure like to know what it looks like on top of those pretty little clouds."

"Don't do it," the voice in my head said. But curiosity got the better of me. I couldn't think of a reason not to check them out.

That was about five or six thousand feet. I climbed up on top of those clouds and it was so pretty—just beautiful—those white puffs. The sky was deep blue and I was enjoying myself.

Now, while this was happening, the clouds closed in. Whoosh! All I could see was a sea of white cotton. I'm lost. I don't have a horizon. I've only got about 15 hours of solo time. I didn't know a thing about instrumentation or landing on instruments or anything like that. In fact, the field wasn't even equipped for instrument landings. No radar or anything.

I suddenly realized why he told us not to go above the clouds! I wasn't afraid, but I figured I had to do something. I had a limited supply of fuel. I started bucking through the clouds, not so steep, mind you. Lightning flashed every so often. I went down slowly and then I finally broke through. Now this is where the Lord comes in. Boy, he helped me so much.

When I broke out of those clouds, I was right over a cotton field that had been harvested. There were farmhouses nearby. I could have come down anywhere. I didn't know where I was. But I ended up over an open field.

I landed and all the farmers rushed toward me.

"Now, where are you from, boy?"

"How far am I from Tuskegee?"

"Oh, it's 85 miles."

I was in Georgia—85 miles away from the base!

"There's a road over there," one of the farmers said pointing across the field. "About three miles away. It'll take you right back to Tuskegee. You hear me, boy?"

"Yes siree! I hear you!"

Now the field was bordered with a wooden crisscross fence. I had about 300 yards of open field, but it was soft, sandy loam. I had the sense to go as far back as possible, drop 15 degrees of flap, run up the rpms, hold my brakes and let it jump out. That was the best I could do. So here I was doing this and doing that, but my wheels were sinking in a couple of inches in that soft loam. There was a line of tall pine trees at the end of the field. I couldn't get my speed up fast enough. About two-thirds of the way, my wheels broke ground and I almost stalled. I pulled that stick back pretty far because I needed to clear those trees. They were coming up fast. I hung on. Then a little space opened up between two pines and I eased over the fence, through the hole in those trees. Like I said, the Lord was with me.

I climbed up to about a thousand feet, flew back over the field, waved to those people and they waved back. Then I got over road he told me about and flew that road like a car— all the way back to the post.

When I got back, my instructor, Jimmy Taylor, was waiting. By this time a pilot's fuel, if he had stayed in the air, would be exhausted. They knew how much fuel I had and assumed I had crashed. He was glad to see me. When I landed one of those cotton stalks was still in my ailerons.

"Where have you been?" he asked, and then held up his hand. "Don't tell me! They don't grow those crops up there in those clouds."

We weren't supposed to land. If we did, we'd be washed out.

"Get those stalks out quick. Don't let anybody see them and don't tell anybody where you've been."

"OK, Jimmy!" I said.

So I got the stalks out.

Basic training followed primary. We flew BT-13s. Our training now included some instrumentation and combat flying techniques. The Germans were using the Immelmann turn, a maneuver that allowed them to dive in an aircraft, pull up into a half loop, complete a slow roll from an inverted to an upright position, then come around and get on a fighter's tail. The Germans were doing it very well and our instructors wanted us to master it too.

I did two or three and it seemed pretty easy. So I decided to try one at a slower speed. I didn't realize that it was the speed in the dive that made it easy, just like they taught us to do it. I was dropping at about 20 miles per hour, going into a much softer maneuver when the plane stalled. She was falling and I couldn't get my nose down. She was coming down, really screaming. I started out at about 6,000 feet. It took some time to get lift on those wings. Now I didn't want to black out—if I pulled back on that stick too much the blood would leave my head and I'd lose control. I'm down way too low to risk that. I'm coming straight down and the ground is coming up rather quickly—I mean the ground was really coming up, moving my way! By the time I got everything squared away— she got lift and I got control—I must have been three or four hundred feet off the ground.

Well, I definitely had a little help from Him.

I made some good moves too. And by the time I finished basic, I'd settled down a little—wasn't quite so wild. When I entered advanced, it was time to transition into combat aircraft and we needed to make a choice.

"OK, Davis. Do you want to be a fighter pilot or a bomber pilot?"

The choice was difficult. The 332nd Fighter Group was setting records in Europe for enemy kills. But by this time they'd formed the 477th Bombardment Group and African-American pilots were offered a chance to fly bombers. I took the opportunity to think it over.

"Well," I said, "I think I'd like to be a bomber pilot." So I signed up for training in bombers and eventual assignment to the 477th.

I didn't get washed out. I finished the course in pretty good shape. Now, if I had gotten washed out, I would have had to go back to the infantry. By this time the Ninety-second Infantry Division was in Italy fighting the Germans. As a platoon leader, I would have been on the front line with binoculars directing fire on the enemy over the heads of friendly troops. And of course, I would have been a prime target for enemy snipers who wanted to kill me in order to stop the fire from our artillery boys.

But I finished in pretty good shape and received orders to Douglas Army Airfield in Arizona for the transition into war planes. The old Army system dictated that officers were not supposed to date enlisted personnel, but our commanding officer gave us special permission to do so. We didn't ask for it, he just put himself in our place. There weren't many black women civilians in the nearby town and no black female officers. However, a company of black WACs (Women's Army Corps) were stationed at the base. One of them was a pretty young corporal.

One Sunday I took her to lunch at Agua Prieta, a little Mexican town down on the border. We were watching a softball game when in came a bit of a storm. There were a few showers, nothing big. We didn't want to get our uniforms wet so we ducked under a tree. That was the last thing we remembered. Lightning struck the tree, ricocheted into our bodies and knocked us flat. We were lying on the ground when the Mexicans found us. We shook it off and got back to the base where we stopped in at the clinic. Both of us were okay, but there were little burn marks everywhere we had the metal insignias of rank and her metal zipper left light burns on her skin.

At the completion of transition, I found myself assigned to the 477th Bombardment Group, the all-black group made possible by Executive Order 8802. For the first time, blacks received training as multi-engine pilots, navigators, bombardiers, gunners and radiomen. I paired up with the flight leader as copilot, and then took over the crew when he was promoted to commanding officer of the 616th. We flew out of Godman Field, Kentucky. The short runways and lack of hangar space at Godman proved to be inadequate for the B-25s assigned to the group.

The war in the Pacific was going strong and the 477th received orders to complete training at Freeman Field, Indiana, followed by assignment in the Pacific theater. It wasn't the bullets that bothered me, but I was mighty worried about the possible shortage of fuel required to fly from Los Angeles to Hawaii. With 300 gallons under each wing and about 900 gallons in the belly, we would just barely make the hop over the ocean with nothing to spare. It kept coming down to the water. "How were we going to get there?"

Freeman was a much better field. Beautiful long runways, no obstructions, no buildings to bother you, just bring her on in. The problem was the officers' club. Colonel Selway ordered that two clubs be designated as "officers' clubs." The original officer's club, Officers' Club #2, would service white officers and instruction supervisors only. The former non commissioned officer (NCO) club, Officers' Club #1, was for the black officers and trainees. This club was quickly dubbed "Uncle Tom's Cabin." We had never been welcome in the all-white officers' clubs, but at Fort Knox and Godman Field, we had places to go for meals.

A nonviolent protest was organized. The black officers arrived in small groups, entered the luxurious officer's club designated for whites, and ordered drinks. Refused service, the black officers were placed under arrest in quarters. When placed under arrest, the black officers quietly left the club and returned to the barracks. Every one of them conducted themselves as officers and gentlemen. Don't get mad. Get smart.

Sixty-one black officers were arrested that night. Out of those 61 officers, three were court-martialed on relatively minor offenses, and one was convicted. Orders, directly from President Truman, came down through the ranks releasing the officers from house arrest.

The ensuing investigation and prosecution took three months. By the time the issues were settled, the United States Air Force dropped two atom bombs on Japan. Our orders were cancelled and I didn't have to worry about that flight to Hawaii.

As a direct result of the Freeman Field Mutiny, the white command structure of the 447th was removed. On July 1, 1945, Col Benjamin O. Davis Jr. officially took command. In 1948, President Truman signed Executive Order 9918, racially integrating the United States Armed Forces.

They sent me to Fort Lewis in Washington when the war ended. I was assigned to the 386th Engineering Battalion as the public relations officer, the only black officer in the battalion. I separated from active service about four months later and signed up for the reserves. I had remarried by then and some of my wife's relatives lived in Berkeley. We decided to drive down to California on our way to Pennsylvania. We never left.

I found an apartment in the San Francisco Bay Area and eventually went to work for Acme Beer. I was the first African-American sales representative for beer in California. I kept hustling and ended up building my little sideline real-estate business into a full-time career. I still live in California, only now I'm down in the southern part of the state.

The Lord has been good to me and to my family and I'm enjoying the good life. I look back on the war years with mostly good memories and I'm mighty proud to be one of the Tuskegee Airmen.

Always enterprising, Claude enjoyed a number of careers. Hired by the Acme Brewing Company in 1950, Claude was the first African American to work for the brewing industry in California. He retired from the brewing business in 1962, and established his first real estate office in Los Angeles, California. Claude still works part-time as a realtor. He recently published his first book, *Wing Tips*. Written for young adults, it is the story of his experiences as a Tuskegee Airman. Claude has four children, six grandchildren, and two great-grandchildren.

THOMAS "TOM" C. GRIFFIN

SHOT DOWN OVER SICILY

When Americans rekindled an interest in World War II and asked me to share my stories, they focused on the Doolittle Raid in April 1942. But for me, that raid was only the beginning.

My return trip from bombing Japan and bailing out over China took me completely around the world. The War Department, hoping to capitalize on the high a grateful nation experienced after our first tangible victory in the Pacific, sent me on a publicity tour for war bonds. Treated like a celebrity, I visited factories, hobnobbed at formal banquets and generally did my part to raise money for the war.

There was no question that I would return to combat, but first the Army Air Corps granted me a two-week leave. I joined Bob and Aileen Bush, friends from high school, at their lake cabin in Dowagiac, Michigan. Aileen invited her cousin Esther. In retrospect, I can't remember exactly what happened during those two weeks, but I know Esther made my immediate future more bearable.

On the heels of my little vacation, I received orders to report to Baton Rouge, Louisiana, where an outfit of B-26 Marauders prepared for their assignment to General Doolittle's newly formed Twelfth Air Force in North Africa. The 319th Bomb Group trained over the summer and then departed for Fort Wayne, Indiana, in late September 1942, where our planes were equipped for the hazardous transatlantic flight over Labrador, Greenland and Iceland to an airfield in England.

They sent us out in groups of six or seven crews over a period of six weeks. We encountered terrible weather on the trip. Plagued by ice storms and poor visibility, we limped over the perilous northern route. By the time the group arrived in England, we had lost a number of planes and crews. Based on our heavy losses, the Army Air Corps never again sent twin-engine bombers over the northern route that late in the year.

After the publicity tours and stateside training, I was happy to get back into the battle. After all, I joined the Air Force to defend our country, but I soon found myself up to my neck in misadventure.

The Allied invasion of North Africa, Operation Torch, began on November 8th. The 319th flew out of Oran from an airstrip right on the sparkling Mediterranean. I wasn't the only Doolittle Raider in the Twelfth Air Force. Bill Bower, Paul Leonard, Dick Miller, Davy Jones and a few others found themselves again under Doolittle's command. A special bond existed between the Doolittle Raiders and the Boss that carried over to our service in the Twelfth.

The Achilles heel of the entire Axis's North African campaign was the shipping of supplies on merchant vessels, so we developed methods to attack those supply lines. One of the best techniques turned out to be skip bombing.

In January 1943, we spent two weeks dropping bombs from Marauders 50 feet off the ground at 170 miles per hour over the Sahara Desert. The sand acted much the same as water. The bombs bounced off the surface into a designated target.

This training took us to Algeria near the town of Youkes-les-Bains, where senior Allied officers often gathered for high-level meetings. We were there when General Doolittle arrived with his personal crew.

The airfield attracted regular attention from the Luftwaffe, which dropped bombs on a nightly basis. Holes dug into the ground near the planes offered our only shelter and when the Germans flew over, we'd just jump in. I was maybe 100 feet away from Paul Leonard when a bomb dropped directly into his hole. Leonard had been Doolittle's crew chief on the Raid and had continued to serve as his personal crew chief in North Africa. Doolittle found what little was left of Paul when he returned to the field that next morning. It was a sad day for all of us.

Skip bombing proved an effective technique against enemy ships. Our unit, assigned to interdict supplies coming out of Italy down into the Algerian and Saharan districts supplying Erwin Rommel and his forces, used skip bombing runs successfully. The bombs, fitted with six-second delayed fuses, allowed us to hit our objective then clear the superstructure of the target ship before exploding.

However, unlike the inert targets used for practice in the desert, enemy ships shot back and rarely did our planes complete a bombing run unscathed.

My job as navigator required me to set the course, then make my way into the nose and man a .50-caliber machine gun. On one run, we encountered our target, a German supply ship, about 30 miles out of Bizerte. Charley Meyers, our pilot, skimmed the water at 170 miles per hour while our bombardier released the bombs.

From the nose, I swept the freighter's deck with a shower of bullets. When Charley pulled up over the superstructure, we encountered heavy flak. The Marauder vibrated as metal projectiles pierced the thin aluminum skin of the plane. Enemy fire knocked out one engine. Hydraulic fluid leaked from the lines and the bomb bay doors yawned open.

An explosion shook the ship and I turned my attention away from my gun toward the cockpit. A 20 mm shell penetrated the windshield, exploding between the pilot and copilot. Blood ran down their faces. Charley brushed the blood out of his eyes and then pulled back on the controls, lifting the nose skyward. The one remaining engine labored with the effort but held steady.

We flew along the Atlas Mountains, where the foothills skirted the Atlantic, dipping their toes into the surf, in search of an airfield about 130 miles west of Bizerte, or any hospitable stretch of sand long enough to set down a B-26. Before reaching a suitable landing site, our one good engine prematurely quit and we went into the water.

Now, a B-26 does not float. We hit the water and those big, heavy engines pulled her under. We'd opened the overhead hatch before going in, so we didn't have to worry about our escape route. I was the last one out of the plane. I guess I hit my head on the bulkhead and it knocked me out. The rush of water must have forced me out through the open hatch, because when I came to, I was floating. The cold water wrapped my flight suit around my legs and sucked at my boots. Scanning the surface, I counted four other heads, so I knew we had all made it out of the plane before she went under.

The copilot's injuries were much more extensive than our pilot's. Charley swam ashore unassisted, but the top turret gunner and I rigged up a float for the copilot. We balanced him on a cushion from the cockpit. Holding tight to the pillow, we backstroked him in to shore. It took a good hour and a half to make it to safety. Luckily, the shark-infested waters off the coast of Africa remained free of finned predators.

Not everybody was that lucky. On January 25, 1943, two days before we found ourselves swimming for shore, my closest buddy, Dick Miller, was killed when a shell came through the nose of his B-26 and exploded next to him. The rest of the crew survived.

By May 1943, we joined the Allied effort to secure Sicily, where the Luftwaffe dominated the skies and ground troops kept a stranglehold on the island. Massive bombing raids were executed to soften German holdings and prepare for Operation Husky, the Allied invasion of Sicily. Our target on July 4, 1943, was an airfield near Catania in eastern Sicily. Based in Sardinia, our squadron consisted of 40 B-26s accompanied by a number of P-38s. We picked up a bunch of English Spitfires out of Malta on the way. The Germans met us with Messerschmitt ME-109s and Focke-Wulf FW-190s. A massive air battle ensued.

We were in the lead plane, flying at 10,000 feet. Our formation had planes as high as 12,000 and as low as 8,000. We flew in a cone shape, scattered in layers so enemy flak had a hard time finding us and shooting us down.

Our group commander, Colonel Aring, flew with us. Perched in the tail, he focused on the tight formation of his planes. As soon as I completed my duties as navigator, I climbed gingerly to the rear of the plane and leaned out the waist gunner's window with my box camera, snapping pictures of our bomb patterns so we'd know what we had done that day.

Flak struck the sides of the plane, sounding like handfuls of marbles ricocheting off the metal surface. Bullets pinged against the fuselage and wings. I was recording the damage below when our plane sustained a direct hit.

Rocked by the explosion, tongues of fire quickly spread throughout the plane, consuming any flammable surface. Thick, acrid smoke gobbled up the breathable air. Waves of fear ran up my spine when I thought of my parachute tucked in the navigator's compartment in the front of the plane. It took a full 30 seconds to register that I had a second chute stashed in the tail. I crawled over and clipped it to my harness.

This wasn't one of those times when you wondered, "Are we going to stay in the air or what?" If we stayed we'd be 100% dead. I climbed to the open hatch and prepared to follow my crewmembers out of the plane.

I wore a German helmet because you needed to wear headphones in the plane. The best the American supply could produce was regular GI helmets, which did not flare out for headphones. You had to jam those helmets down over your earphones and it was very uncomfortable. We would wait to jam them down until we got into an area where we were under attack or in anti-aircraft explosions. But my German helmet, a tanker helmet, flared out so that my headphones could sit there and I was perfectly comfortable.

But it had swastikas on either side. As I lowered myself out of that burning plane, the thought struck me.

"If they capture me down there with this helmet on, they'll shoot me as a spy."

With that thought rattling around, I pulled myself back into the plane, removed my helmet with both hands, and gently placed it beside the open hatch.

"Griffin," Colonel Aring yelled, "get the hell out of this plane! You're blocking the hatch!"

So I jumped. We all made it out.

We were at 10,000 feet when our engines exploded, about 8,000 when we bailed. I pulled the ripcord and floated down over a wheat field. German soldiers manning anti-aircraft guns left their posts and scurried toward the descending parachutes. Occasionally one would stop and take a potshot. I know, because the bullets would whiz by my head.

But I faced a more immediate problem than random

shots from the field. An ME-109 headed directly toward me. I watched the wings for flashes of red fire and waited for the bullets to tear into me. On his first pass, guns jammed, he pulled up, just barely missing my chute. Pass after pass, the pursuit plane flew directly toward me, pulling up at the last minute.

He came closer and closer with each pass and I realized that since his guns were jammed, he was trying to dump the air from my parachute.

"What's the matter with this character?" I asked myself as I hung there helpless, shaking my clenched fist at this aggressive enemy in what I believed would be my last gesture.

After the sixth or seventh pass, he flew off. When my feet touched the ground, he made a final pass, wagging his wings about 50 feet over my head.

Staggering to gain a foothold, a gust of wind caught my chute and pulled me across the wheat field. German soldiers ran toward me from every corner. Struggling to stay standing, I caught the shroud lines and collapsed the parachute. By the time I gained control, soldiers surrounded me, guns ready. Any possible attempt at escape would spell suicide.

On July 4, 1943, I became a guest of Hitler and the Third Reich. Within a half an hour of being shot down, I stood in a gazebo in the middle of a fruit orchard drinking cold lemonade and smoking a German captain's cigar.

He couldn't speak English, I couldn't yet speak German, but we got along quite well.

Later that day, the captain delivered me by open command car to a general's office in Catania. I gave him my name, rank and serial number, the only information required under the Geneva Convention. Then, feeling I didn't have much to lose, asked the general, "*Herr* General, do you give your pursuit pilots orders to shoot us down when we bail out of our planes? Because one of your pilots tried awfully hard to shoot me out of the sky and if his guns hadn't been jammed, he would have killed me!"

"*Herr Hauptmann* Griffin," the general replied in perfect English, "he wasn't trying to shoot you down. He was taking your picture!"

They held us in Catania overnight and then flew us to Frankfurt to an interrogation center the next morning. I think they decided ahead of time how they would interrogate you—if they planned to be mean and tough or sweet-talk you and try to get whatever they could by being nice.

Now with me they decided to be real nice, but not without some serious discomfort first. When we arrived in Frankfurt, they took us to a *lager*. A long hall bisected the building with doors leading to small rooms on either side. They placed me in a cell with the radiator going full blast.

The temperature in Frankfurt during July lingered around 100° Fahrenheit. The radiator in my cell kicked that up to at least a 125°. Slowly roasting from the oven-like temperatures, I couldn't get comfortable. Sweat poured down my sides, and fingers run through my hair left trenches bordered with wet locks on a sticky scalp. There was no possible way to sleep. I banged on my cell door, calling to the guard.

Finally, after a seemingly endless delay, a German guard came over. I couldn't speak a word of German and he obviously didn't speak English. I pointed to the radiator.

"Hot!" I complained, fanning my face. In pantomime, I turned an air knob to the off position. "Please turn it off."

Of course, he paid no attention. Without a word, he turned and walked away.

When they brought me into the interrogation room the next morning, I was furious. A German officer sat behind a desk. He indicated an empty chair.

"Please sit down," he ordered in English.

I sat, unable to contain my temper.

"What kind of chickenshit is this? Making us sit in a hot cell?"

"Ah, *Herr Hauptmann* Griffin, you mean the radiator?" the officer in charge responded. "I can't imagine why they'd do that! I'll look into that and see it doesn't happen again."

That's how it started off.

I was amazed by how much they already knew about me. They knew I was one of the Doolittle Raiders. I'm sure if there had been a submarine available, they would have shipped me to Japan just for the brownie points. Had they captured Jimmy Doolittle, they would have commandeered a sub.

A bench ran along the side of the room where four high-ranking German officers sat, ramrod straight, side by side. During the next 22 months, I never met another prisoner who had a bench full of officers observe their interrogation.

The interrogation stuck to generalities and the interrogating officer remained cordial. There wasn't much they were going to get from me.

"*Herr Hauptmann* Griffin," the officer asked, "when will this war end?"

"I think it will take about 18 or 20 months."

"Well, what will end it?" he asked.

"It will take that long for us to defeat you people."

And that was the end of it. We let it go at that. It didn't amount to much. But I was lucky. They'd get somebody else in there and just grill them unmercifully. I always remembered that I was lucky.

Captured Allied crews were sent to various prison camps from the interrogation center. After several days of questioning, the four officers from my crew went to Stalag Luft III, the German Air Force prisoner of war camp built to house Allied airmen. One hundred miles southeast of Berlin, the prison first housed RAF officers. By the time we arrived, the Germans built a second *lager* south of the original complex for the Americans, separating us from our British counterparts.

We felt it was our duty to escape. Barring that possibility, it was our policy to make the Germans use the maximum number of guards possible to keep us contained. With these goals in mind, we divided into groups focused on escape activity. We had escape groups of one kind or another working at all times—digging tunnels, securing escape supplies, building radios.

Digging the tunnels was dangerous, dirty work. To avoid detection, we needed to dig a shaft 30 feet down through sandy soil, then go 300 or 400 feet out. We'd shore up the tunnels with boards from our beds. A string of electric lights allowed for limited visibility. It was quite an operation because two men had to go to the face of the tunnel for the digging. They would fill sandbags and place them on little makeshift railroad cars. Workers at the top pulled the cars to the surface and placed the sand in long tubes secured with string ties at each end.

Those assigned to distribution would sling the tubes over their necks, tuck them down their pant legs and releasing small amounts of sand in a steady flow, spreading it throughout the prison yard.

The Americans never broke a tunnel, but the British chaps in the neighboring camp successfully broke "Harry" in March 1944. One night, 76 RAF officers crawled through the tunnel to initial freedom in what would later be known as the Great Escape.

Outraged, Hitler ordered the men shot as an example. Seventy-three were captured and sent back to Stalag Luft III. Fifty were executed by the Germans and their ashes returned to the prison. Only three made their way out of Germany to freedom.

I did some digging and my share of distributing the sand, but my primary job was to secure items delivered by mail from the mythical Aunt Tillie. Playing the odds, the American government assigned certain airmen as recipients of escape materials should they be captured. We had four of these men in our *lager.*

When mail arrived for one of them with a return address from Aunt Tillie in Peoria, or wherever, the boys on mail duty would snag the package before the Germans saw it and then get that package to me. Inside, the government sent escape supplies, like maps, money, radio parts, and civilian clothes. My job in security required me to hide these materials. I'd gone to the University of Alabama, and soon our squad became known as "Alabama and his Forty Thieves."

Now it just so happened that Colonel Goodrich, the senior officer at Stalag Luft III, put me in charge of a building, so my room was at one end of the barracks. Unlike the normal six to eight men sharing a room, I had only one roommate. A few of the boys came in and moved the rear wall in about fifteen or sixteen inches and placed it on hinges. When we pulled our double bunk away from that wall, we could swing it open to a closet space where we hung civilian clothing and secured escape materials.

The Germans conducted regular inspections, but our secret closet went undetected for months. Then one day they ordered us to vacate the barracks. They must have measured my room and the measurement came up short, because they discovered our cache of supplies.

I was sent to the cooler for a couple of weeks for destroying Reich property.

"We didn't destroy Reich property," I argued. "We improved it. We built you a closet."

Our guards didn't share our sense of humor. The cooler was just a long building with cells opening onto a hallway. The cell offered four blank walls, a single bunk and a small barred window near the ceiling. Occasionally, I grabbed the bars and pulled myself up, catching a glimpse of the prison yard.

The worst part about solitary confinement is the way time stands motionless. They fed you twice a day, but that was the extent of human interaction. I generally sat with my back against the wall, replaying scenes from my childhood, and thinking about Esther, wondering what she was doing. I smiled with the memories of our short time together and the little ways she managed to lift my spirits while confined in prison. Mail sent to the prison was strictly regulated. I wear a size 11½ shoe, and a pair of shoes wouldn't fit in the pre-scribed package limitations. Esther sent one shoe in the first package and the second shoe two months later. Little things like that would make me smile.

But still, the long hours alone closed in on me.

The rhythmic bouncing of a ball against the wall in a neighboring cell began to chip away at my patience. He kept it up for hours and finally I couldn't stand it any longer. I banged on my cell door with clenched fists.

"Guard!" I yelled in my newly acquired, fractured German, "Take the ball away from that guy next door. He's driving me crazy!"

Wordlessly, the guard opened my door.

"Come," he said.

I went out in the hall and looked through the space in my neighbor's door. The prisoner, an American lad, sat naked on the floor. Rhythmically, he beat his arms and legs, his hands and feet against the floor. He had simply gone out of his mind and was literally beating himself to death.

Within a couple of days, the bouncing stopped and the Germans carried his body away.

By January 1945, the Russians were pushing the Germans across Poland and back into Germany. We'd built radios with our supplies and kept abreast of Allied victories. When the Russians reached the Oder River, we felt pretty good about the situation. We could hear their artillery and believed our release was days, maybe hours away.

But the Germans made other plans for us. There were probably between 15,000 and 20,000 American and British air officers in Stalag Luft III. Perhaps they felt we could be used as hostages for barter at a future date. On January 27, 1945, Hitler ordered the Allied airmen to Moosburg in Bavaria.

"The Goons have just given us 30 minutes to be at the front gate. Get your stuff together and line up," Col Charles G. Goodrich told us.

Six inches of snow covered the ground, freezing our feet, and falling snow penetrated the layers of inadequate clothing we wore for protection. We stood for hours before setting out around midnight in the pitch dark over icy ground. The wind drove the temperature down to near zero.

I was one of the luckier ones. Having been a prisoner for almost two years, I had the opportunity to collect various items of winter clothing and wore multiple layers. Some of the newer boys had only the uniforms they wore when captured. There were thousands of us on the road. As long as we kept moving, we would build up a little body heat. Once in a while, a column would stop on the ice-slick road, and the men would just flop down and lie there for a half an hour or so. When the columns started to move again, we had to pick up some of the men—they just couldn't get up by themselves. Many of the prisoners suffered from frostbite and exposure. Some collapsed and were later picked up by Germans in trucks. We marched for two days before resting in a warehouse near Muskau on the Neisse River. A couple of days later, our ragged brigade marched to Spremberg. It was quite an ordeal.

Over the next few days, we found ourselves packed 50 or 60 prisoners into boxcars built to carry no more than 40 men. Crammed like sardines, we couldn't sit or stretch out. The best we could do was squat, resting our thighs against our calves. Two small windows near the ceiling at each end of the car provided the only ventilation. The smell of vomit and human excrement clung to the frozen air, permeating our rags and infiltrating our lungs.

It took another three days to reach Stalag Luft VII-A at Moosburg. Originally built to house 14,000 French prisoners, it now held over 130,000 prisoners of war of all nationalities and ranks. Our accommodations were old dilapidated barracks, no more than hollow shells with dirt floors. We slept on stacked bunks, rickety tables and the floor. Food was severely limited and what little cold water available was used for drinking, never for bathing. Hopelessly infested with vermin, we waited out the next four months in squalid conditions and near starvation.

On April 29, 1945, Patton's forces attacked the SS troops guarding Moosburg. There was a firefight around our camp, but only four prisoners were hit. One of them was a friend of mine. He got hit right in the belly, but the bullet had spent most of its velocity so that it mainly knocked the wind out of him. He landed on his back, but it didn't kill him. We never knew if it was friendly or enemy fire.

The next morning, on a hill just to the east of our camp, two tanks and a command car were perched, overlooking the prison camp. Gen George Patton stood tall, big as life, with his ivory-handled pistols strapped to his hips. This was the first we'd seen of the Americans. Boy, were we glad to see them.

Conditions in Moosburg left us filthy and covered with lice. But mostly we found ourselves starving. The Americans told us to stay put, that they'd bring us food, but the promises of the beautiful Bavarian countryside on warm spring days lured us away.

Two buddies and I would stroll away from camp into the surrounding towns, knock on the door of a German home and request food.

"*Essen*," we'd say, our fingertips lightly touching, we would gently tap our lips.

Generally the family would take us into the kitchen and feed us slices of fresh bread and chunks of cheese.

Occasionally the inhabitants would decline.

"*Kein Essen*," they would say. No food.

Smiling, we would lead them into their kitchens and show them where the food was kept.

Then we would walk for another two or three hours, enjoying the warm sunshine and the freedom of wandering, before knocking on another door. At night we returned to the prison camp, our bellies full.

One morning, a fellow prisoner asked to join us. Each of us believing someone else knew him, we agreed to his company. It turned out that none of us knew him very well.

We wandered through the warm spring air, this fellow skillfully guiding us.

"Let's go this way," he'd suggest.

None of us particularly cared where we went; we just enjoyed the beauty of Bavaria and followed his lead.

"Let's go over to this village."

"OK. You want to go there, we'll go there." And we'd wander down the path.

As lunchtime approached, one of us suggested stopping to eat. Our new friend continued to steer our journey.

"I know a good place," he said, indicating a neatly groomed German house. We didn't catch on right away.

The four of us walked up to the door and knocked. A German couple answered.

"Now I've got you!" our new friend said, his .45-caliber

pistol pointed directly at the couple.

"Put that thing away!" we all told him. "There's no need for this!"

It took some convincing, but he finally put the gun back into his jacket. We made our way back to the kitchen, each of us keeping an eye on our new friend.

When we returned to the road, I turned and asked, "Now, what was that all about?"

"Well," he began, "when I came through this place with a line of prisoners, we'd been marching for hours. The column stopped and I was right here, right in front of this house. I was hungry and thirsty and asked for something to drink."

We all knew that prisoners were forbidden to talk to the German citizens, but sometimes a compassionate individual would provide a sip of water or crust of bread.

"The husband caught the guard's attention and told him that I'd asked for water. The guard responded by hitting me with the butt of his rifle. He broke two of my ribs. I swore if I ever got out, I'd pay them back."

We continued our wanderings, but never allowed that character to join us again.

It took a couple of weeks for the Americans to organize our release and transportation home. They lined us up in rows and dumped white powder over our naked bodies to kill the lice. Finally, they moved us to Le Havre, France, where ships took us back to the States.

It was just my luck to catch a transport bound for the West Indies. Some of our troops, having manned an airfield for three years, were due for relief. Our ship carried the men assigned to relieve them, so instead of taking a direct route to New York, we sailed south into the Caribbean. The weather was beautiful and we frequently stretched out under the spring moon and enjoyed the tropical nights; quite a change from the northern route that took us to North Africa three years earlier.

I married Esther when I got home. The Army Air Force wanted to send me back to Germany to work with the State Department. But my orders wouldn't permit Esther to go with me. I didn't want to leave her again.

During my years in prison, I got to know Colonel Goodrich pretty well. He recommended my promotion to major after we were released from Moosburg. In a letter to Headquarters, Army Air Forces, Goodrich wrote:

"This officer was a prisoner of war under my jurisdiction at Stalag Luft III, Germany. While on this status, his performance of duty under adverse conditions was outstanding and warrants his immediate promotion."

I kept his letter along with a letter from Admiral Mitscher congratulating the men who flew on the Tokyo Raid with Jimmy Doolittle. I stayed in touch with the general and the other Raiders. We still get together every year in April. And when asked about the war, most people focus on my role in the Doolittle Raid. But for me, that was just the beginning.

Tom opened an accounting firm in Cincinnati, Ohio. He and Esther were married for 60 years before she passed away in 2005. He is an active member of the Kiwanis Club and a fanatic sports fan. Tom, a Doolittle Raider, makes regular appearances speaking about his war experiences. Tom and Esther have two sons and two grandchildren. He lives in Cincinnati, Ohio.

★ ★ ★ ★

Decorations and Awards: Distinguished Flying Cross; Air Medal with three Oak Leaf Clusters; the Chinese Army, Navy, and Air Corps Medal, Class A, First Grade

MAX FULLMER

—⟨•/•⟩—

ONE OF PATTON'S MEN

We were replacement troops. Retreads. Sent in to fill the vacancies left by soldiers killed in battle. Our "number," like theirs, could be up at any moment. Most of us just recently turned 19.

I carried a little green card that proved I passed the entrance examinations for the Army Air Corps, my ticket into the cockpit of an American plane. Only, I knocked out an expert rifleman score in basic training.

"You really screwed up, buddy," the kid next to me said. "You're never gonna get to fly now."

You see, at this point, they needed more infantrymen carrying rifles than pilots.

I climbed on the USS *West Point*, a luxury liner converted into a troop transport, with several thousand other soldiers. We sailed out of Boston in the winter of 1944, and all I could think about was the sinking of the *Titanic*. There wasn't a tree in sight—just endless miles of cold gray water.

We zigzagged across the Atlantic, eventually landing

near Glasgow. We crossed England in a train that dropped us off in Southampton. The cruise ship, once scuttled by the French to keep it out of German hands, still reeked of mildew, but allowed us to safely negotiate the English Channel. We docked at night in Le Havre and climbed aboard 40 and 8 boxcars.

Ka-chum . . . ka-chum . . . ka-chum . . . all the way to the front line.

Spring stirred in a countryside marred with the first real, visible signs of war. Old blown-up rusty tanks dotted hills scarred by shell craters and deep zigzagging trenches—which looked like they dated back to World War I—left open wounds on the valley floors.

We reached Metz as night fell. The first sergeant threw the boxcar doors open and, as we climbed out, stretching legs cramped from the bumpy ride, called out, "All right, you guys! You're in Patton's Third Army now!"

Rumors abounded about Gen George Patton. His infamous slapping of a soldier made headlines around the world. The thought of serving under him struck both fear and admiration in my heart. I remembered my father's advice:

"Patton is a leader. Don't pay attention to the things you read or hear about him. Pay attention to what he does."

I figured I'd give him a chance. I soon grew to admire him. He was the right man at the right time.

I was assigned to the Second Platoon, G Company, 318th Infantry, Eightieth Division of the Third Army. We picked up our weapon belts, bandoliers and hand grenades, grabbed our M1 semiautomatic rifles, piled into open trucks and bounced along the rutted road to the front. In less than two miles, we saw the flashes of artillery fire. Moments later, we heard the thunder of shells closely followed by concussion waves that shuttered through the thick, smoky air.

They took us new guys and put us on the downside

of the hill, as far away from the battle as possible. We dug in, unrolled our blankets and settled in for the night. Our sleep was interrupted with the intermittent staccato of rifle fire, the periodic blasts from mortar explosions and the deep rumble of tanks.

When daylight broke, I looked up from my makeshift bed.

"Holy mackerel!" An M-4 tank, complete with rocket launchers, idled not 30 feet from my head.

Kaboom! Kaboom!

The very air surrounding our camp vibrated with the concussions of launched rockets.

"Pull out your K-rations," Sergeant Duffy told us. "It may be some time before you have a chance to eat again."

"Uh oh!" I thought. "This is it!"

We pulled out breakfast, each lost in our own thoughts.

"See that little town over there?" Duffy asked.

"Yes."

"Well, we're gonna take it." He turned to me. "I want you to lead this squad. See that?" He pointed to a building.

I nodded my head.

"There are some Germans in that building. Silence that machine gun and don't let them get away."

Our boys had been kicked out of that town a few days earlier, and they were mad. The plan was to kick butt and take names.

We moved forward as a unit, dirt flying up in front of us.

"You're shooting too low!" Duffy yelled.

"They're shooting too low," I yelled back before suddenly realizing, *they're shooting at me.*

I've had pheasants, deer, elk and moose in my crosshairs, but this was the first time I ever had a man on top of that little peg inside the sight.

He came out of the building and looked around. And there he sat, dead center, right on top of the notch. I took aim, pulled the trigger and he was gone. The guy next to me got sick. I could have been sick, too. It went against everything I'd learned as a kid.

We gathered up 14 Germans. They surrendered when we surrounded the building.

"Come on, Max," Sergeant Duffy said. "You got to look at that man."

It didn't sound like such a good idea to me.

"If you don't, you're going to have it on your mind forever."

So I looked at the man. I'd made a good shot. I looked at his uniform and at his helmet. That helmet with the swastika filled me with fear. He was no longer a man. After that he was the enemy.

We lost nine of our men that day. I knew every one of them. We cleared the area, and then went down through Echternach to Trier on the border of Luxembourg. We pushed on, engaging the Germans wherever we found them. Rolling forward like the well-oiled machine of Patton's army.

By the time we got to Weisskirchen, we knew we were in trouble. A real bad firefight broke out behind us.

Boom! Boom! Boom!

We'd penetrated the German line, and our guys were coming to rescue us.

We dug in behind the low rock fence of a cemetery. I found myself tucked between two graves. I looked up and a little white stone cherub floated above my foxhole.

"Now you stay there," I told her, "and I'll stay here."

Boom! Boom! Boom! The fighting drew closer.

We lost our platoon leader in that battle. He was calling in the artillery fire and got a short round. I think it was a

75 that got him. Friendly fire. It happens.

I felt really bad about that. I'd gotten to know him pretty well. He was a good leader.

We were in a pretty bad spot.

"Now you just stay there," I kept telling my little cherub. "Don't you go anywhere."

I looked over that graveyard wall to see if there were any Germans coming. My mouth was dry and the acrid smell of smoke filled my nostrils. I could still hear the firefight, see the shells exploding in the distance. They were getting closer. It was our job to get those buggers before they got into town.

Fatigue from lack of sleep caught up with me. I must have dozed off. The battle had quit some time ago. I awoke to the rumble of tanks.

"Oh man," I said to the little cherub hovering above me, "I don't remember seeing any tanks!"

I sat up, stuck my head out of the foxhole and looked over the fence.

A jeep! A whole column of American jeeps and tanks!

Rumble, rumble, rumble. The Tenth Armor Division rolled past our platoon. They'd broken through.

"They saved our bacon!" I told my angel as I crawled out to join my comrades.

The snow was pretty much gone now, and we could see that whole beautiful brigade going through the town. What a glorious sight they were rolling down the main street.

We started to form up. I stopped and walked back to my little cherub.

"Thanks," I said, touching the top of her head. "Thanks a lot!"

I considered myself lucky to be assigned to what we fondly called the Blue Ridge Division. We were a bunch of rebels and any time we had a break in the action, those boys would gather up their guitars and mandolins and play the most incredible, lively music. One of the guys made a guitar out of an old jerry can. It sounded a bit tinny, but we didn't care. For a few hours, the music transported us home to the lives we hoped still waited for us at the end of the war.

I also felt lucky to be one of Patton's men. My dad was right. Patton brought his troops through some really rough times. He was a real senior guy and we all looked up to him. He instilled a deep respect, edged with disdain, because he never let up. But any less of a leader couldn't have made the Third do what it did.

We drove back through Germany, through St. Wendel—rich with the history of Martin Luther and the Lutheran Church—to Kaiserslautern and on to the Rhine River. The vineyards above the banks of the Rhine were thick with heavily armed German troops.

We piled into Landing Craft Infantry vehicles to cross the river.

"You guys get down!" the little redheaded sailor told us. "Keep down!"

He sat up straight, upright in his little chair, the ting, ting, ting of bullets hitting the sides of the LCI. I swear he was looking at us and thinking, "And you guys are protecting *me*?"

We made it across the Rhine and landed on the shore. I made it into a cement ditch a few yards from the water's edge and dove for cover as the Germans lobbed mortars down on us.

We were pinned down in the ditch, contemplating our potential losses when we assaulted the hill. The prospects were bleak. And then they came. Those beautiful P-47s. Above our heads, they circled in a wheel formation. Burr, burr, burr. One right after the other until all German firing from the vineyard ceased.

Oh man, the carnage left on those hilltops. It was bad. The Germans still used horses to pull their munitions wagons and stuff. There were dead horses and soldiers everywhere. Those P-47s took everything out. When our troops got up to the top, any surviving German readily surrendered.

Without the close air support of the Eighth Air Force, we would have eaten it on the banks of the Rhine. I always believed someone in Patton's Third Army had a buddy in the Eighth. It was years before I learned that Patton and Doolittle shared a close friendship.

It wasn't long after the Rhine crossing that we learned some mistakes were made someplace to the north. We abandoned our drive to Berlin and diverted to Kassel.

That was a real battle. Henschel, the German tank manufacturing plant, was located in Kassel. They were putting out half-tracks, still red with primer, not even in camouflage. They were filled with kids. And those poor kids were just sitting ducks. But we couldn't cut them any slack. Those boys had Mausers and the tanks were fitted with Schmeisser automatic submachine guns. It was real bad because those kids didn't know what they were doing. They were just ordered into battle. We had to take them out because they could shoot—Hitler taught them to shoot and they would.

We were pinned down in a house and those tanks came around the corner. I was the squad leader now, because we'd lost a lot of guys, and the highest-ranking guy left alive moves up. So anyway, I told my men, "You take the first one, you take the second, and you take the third, but don't fire until that third one comes around the corner."

It was an old Indian trick; you shoot the last Cavalry man first. If you hit the first guy, the others will turn and run, but if you get the last guy first, you have a good chance of getting them all.

Well, there only happened to be two tanks in that bunch and we got them both. Two tanks filled with kids.

It was a tough battle at Kassel. We got out of that scrap,

but it was close. They had those 88 millimeters and they beat our 75 millimeters to pieces. The 88 millimeter was a masterful piece of machinery. They had us outgunned until we got the 90 millimeters. Then it was a whole new ball game.

I made mistakes. We captured a lot of equipment and personnel. We set up POW camps.

"Max," my buddy called out to me. "This woman's husband wants to surrender. He's an important man. Now you go with her and bring him in."

There wasn't much question on anyone's part about the eventual outcome of the war.

So I followed her down the road, around the corner and down the street—way too far for a soldier to go alone. We came to a cement abutment where the road goes over the railroad track.

"He's in there," she told me.

There wasn't another American in sight. If that German had a gun or a grenade, I was a dead man.

"Come out without your weapons," I yelled through the door.

Twenty-six German soldiers came out from under that track. I marched them back to my platoon. One little soldier with twenty-six German prisoners.

"How," I wondered, "am I ever going to explain this?"

Our next stop was Hof. This was shortly after the Yalta Conference in February 1945. The Big Three—Roosevelt, Churchill and Stalin—anticipating an Allied victory, divided Germany into zones for the occupation. Part of the agreement was to return citizens of the Soviet Union and Yugoslavia, regardless of their consent, to their respective countries.

Hof was filled with White Russians, "Old Believers" who'd fled Russia after the Revolution and made Germany their home. Our job was to put them on trains and return them to Russia.

We called them DPs, displaced persons. I thought it was great. People should be happy to go home. They didn't want to go.

We got within a couple of blocks of their building and we could hear all this commotion, moaning and wailing.

"Please don't send me back. Shoot me, but don't send me back to Russia!"

"Well, that's your home. Don't you want to go home?"

"Shoot me! Just shoot me!"

I didn't quite get it until somebody threw a baby out of an upper floor window. They didn't want that baby growing up in Russia. Boy, for a 19-year-old, that was sobering. I got the picture real quick that these people really didn't want to go back.

While in Hof, we ran into an old German man and his wife. They spoke perfect English.

"We'll do anything we can for you if you'll take our son with you to Munich."

Why, I sure would've liked to do that. He was a real nice kid, a peach of a guy. But we had our rules.

"We can't take him. If we put him in uniform, he'd be impersonating an American soldier. He'd probably get in all kinds of trouble."

"Please help us," they begged.

You see, the Germans made a big mistake during Operation Barbarossa. A lot of Russians were tired of Stalin, and if they'd treated those people halfway decent, they'd have gone with the Germans. But the German army was atrocious. So all the Russians were getting even with extra measure. Rumors abounded telling stories of all kinds of debauchery and things going on that I don't even like to think about.

Our water tanks were finished on the inside with porcelain. Carried on trailers, they had a big opening at one end. We put the kid in the water tank. He told us the name of the town and we dropped him on the side of the road with a five-kilometer walk. I don't know if he made it, but I like to think he did.

Our next stop was Dachau. The grub wagon rolled out early. About 20 miles out of Dachau, they had the chow line set up for us. After lunch, Counter Intelligence held a meeting for all the troops.

"You'll be seeing things you will never believe," they told us. "Hitler devised a program he called the Final Solution. The concentration camp ahead is part of a network of extermination centers used to purge the country of Jews, gypsies, political prisoners, mentally handicapped individuals, and other so-called 'undesirables.' Conditions are not the best."

The gate was locked when we arrived. So we put a chain behind the jeep and jerked it open. With guns ready, we made our way into the first building on the lookout for German collaborators.

We passed ditches, mass graves with bodies thrown on top of bodies. I'd seen them before, filled with soldiers. I didn't like it, but I could handle it. But those naked bodies, bleached paper-white from the sun, piled on wagons. So many of them. The workers were hauling them down to the graveyard when we got there. They took off and just left the wagons stacked with bodies. I couldn't take that.

We opened the door to that first building. Oh my gosh, the smell! Decay, fecal matter, vomit, sweat, fear, hopelessness, cremated human remains. There were rows, long rows of bunks, and in the bunks were skeletal bodies lying on dirty straw, their hands sticking out, their arms crepe-paper skin draped on bones.

We had to walk down the center, away from the bunks or the people would grab on to our uniforms.

"Thank you. Thank you."

Most of these people were ill from malnutrition. But

I'll never forget how happy they were to see us. Their faces lit up with joy even though their bodies couldn't muster the energy to rise from the straw beds. I felt sympathy for the older people but I couldn't really relate to them. The kids caught my full attention. Children as young as two or three and ranging in age to about twelve or thirteen just barely hanging on to life and so happy to see us. I've been told that 190,591 prisoners died or were exterminated at Dachau. We saved only a handful.

There were political prisoners in Dachau, too. That's what got me about sending the White Russians back. The Russians were supposed to be our allies and I was expected to shut my ears to their pleas and send them home. But we could help these people. Set them free. Ignorance is bliss sometimes. Stalin was waiting. It didn't dawn on us until long after the war ended.

Other troops followed us into Dachau as witnesses of the Holocaust.

We continued to move forward, on to Austria and the infamous Mauthausen concentration camp at the west end of town. Here we found American GIs, airmen who had jumped out of B-17s. They had it all together. I don't know how these guys kept themselves so clean. Their uniforms and coats reflected American pride.

"Thanks for coming when you did," an airman from Dyersburg, Tennessee, said to me that first afternoon, "because I was getting pretty tired of this place!"

Another kid with shaggy hair wanted a haircut.

"I couldn't stand those Krauts cutting my hair."

One of our troops carried clippers. It wasn't the best haircut, but that kid sure was happy to have an American cut his hair.

A medical team, complete with nurses, accompanied us to Mauthausen and you should have seen those GIs. American women talk differently than anybody in Europe and they'd hear that and their whole bodies responded. Those boys just couldn't get enough of those nurses talking!

The war wasn't over, but the end was close. We headed back across the Inn River to Braunau am Inn, Austria, Hitler's birthplace. Hitler committed suicide the day before, but we didn't know that yet. Although there appeared to be a certain animosity toward the Americans, the townspeople seemed relieved that the war was over and they were out from under Hitler's heel.

Ernst Kaltenbrunner, Himmler's number two man, was reported to be in Altaussee. Our squad was assigned to accompany the CIC (Counter Intelligence Corps) on a mission to capture him. We stopped at *Herr* Kaltenbrunner's house.

Reports led us to the salt mines, which dated back to 1213. We opened the door and discovered an American GI sitting in the opening, armed with a .50-caliber machine gun. The mine was filled with row after row of fabulous art, looted treasures from across Europe, all destined for the Great Hitler Museum in Linz.

More intelligence reports came in, revealing that Kaltenbrunner was hidden away at Wildensee Huette atop the Totes Gebirge. We started out around midnight climbing up a wooded mountain path that wound its way up the mountain with snakelike switchbacks and hairpin turns. The snow was thick on the mountainside. We trudged on, our boots breaking through the icy crust and sinking calf-deep into the powder beneath.

We reached the cabin just as dawn began to light the sky. The two-room wooden Alpine hut lay just below the crest. The sheltered porch faced the downslope. Our approach took us directly across an open, snow-covered expanse of land.

Although the cabin appeared deserted, we found four men inside: two SS guards, Arthur Scheidler—the former adjutant to Reinhard Heydrich—and Kaltenbrunner. Although posing as a doctor, Kaltenbrunner was hard to mistake. At six foot two, he was a powerfully built man with dark features and deep scars on his face. The cabin was also filled with loot, including sacks of gold coins and boxes filled with Federal Reserve notes, thousands and thousands of dollars purportedly stolen from the United States Consulate in Hungary.

We hauled sacks of $20 Gold Eagles out of the cabin, two sacks each. We could hear a train off in the distance. It was coming towards us.

"You guys hurry up and get on that train," one of the CIC guys called out. "Enemy planes regularly patrol this area and you don't want to get strafed."

So we dropped the gold and ran for the train. We left those CIC boys to take care of all that loot. I saw one of them in town one day flipping one of those coins.

The war was winding down, but hadn't ended yet. We were poised to take another town when the call came in. I held that big old walkie-talkie when the company commander's voice barked out, "Cease all forward action."

That was it. Cease all forward action, and the war in Europe was over. It was three o'clock in the morning. Pitch dark out. Low and behold, the cat eye lights used under blackout conditions turned off, and the headlights and spotlights turned on.

We partied hard. Someone passed around cigars and we all lit up. I got so sick, I thought I'd die, and then I got so sick I was afraid I wasn't going to die. Some of the guys got so drunk, we had to make sure they didn't shoot themselves when they fired rounds of ammunition into the air.

"Don't kill yourself now!" I told my buddy. "Leave the bullets in the bandoliers."

I didn't have enough points to go home yet, so on May 8, 1945, I officially joined the Army of Occupation. I spent some time at the Nuremberg Trials and covered a lot of ground in Europe, even helped out as a medic for a short time. But I was glad to go home when I finally got out.

My homecoming was a bit anticlimactic. Nobody was there when I walked in the front door. My 15 minutes of fame were over, but I knew in my heart that I'd been a part of something important. I saw those people in Dachau, and I knew that the Final Solution only ended because of Allied blood spilled across the battlefields of Europe. And I knew that only with vigilance would America and her allies remain truly free.

Max earned his bachelor's degree at Rick's College (now BYU Idaho). He taught sixth grade and was a school principal in Idaho Falls. He eventually went to work for the FAA as an air traffic controller until his retirement in 1984. Max volunteers at the Warhawk Air Museum in Nampa, Idaho, working on the restoration of warbirds. He married Darlena Belmap in 1949. They have one son and one granddaughter.

Decorations and Awards: Good Conduct Medal, WWII Victory Medal, ETO, Expert Rifleman Medal, Expert Machine Gun Medal, Army of Occupation Medal

DICK HAMADA

JAPANESE-AMERICAN SOLDIER
FOR THE OFFICE OF
STRATEGIC SERVICES (OSS)

I never considered renouncing my Japanese citizenship until December 7, 1941. However, on December 8, 1941, my brother George and I went down to the Japanese Consulate on Nuuanu Street and did just that.

You see, I am an American by birth because I was born in the territory of Hawaii. But my father, Tokuichi Hamada, immigrated to Kukuihaele, Hawaii, from Hiroshima Ken, Saiki Gun, Jigozen Mura, Japan, on February 3, 1905. My mother, Shige Yoshino, also from Hiroshima, joined him in Hawaii just a few years later. Tokuichi, with the birth of each of his five children, registered us with the Japanese government, automatically giving us dual citizenship

My father's last wish, having been diagnosed with cirrhosis of the liver, was to return to Japan to see his parents before passing. He went home to Hiroshima on December 12, 1939, and was buried there two months later.

But on December 7, 1941, my brother George and I were awakened by thundering explosions from Hickam Field

and Pearl Harbor Naval Base. Accustomed to a military presence that held many military maneuvers, we first thought the
explosions were another ordinary exercise. However, thick
funnel clouds of black smoke caused us much concern.

"Turn on the radio," George called to me as he stuck
his head out the bedroom window.

"PEARL HARBOR IS UNDER ATTACK!" the announcer exclaimed. "THIS IS NOT A MANEUVER. PLEASE TAKE
COVER!"

I reached for my $2.98 mail-order telescope and
scanned the skies above our house. Japanese planes sporting
the red *Hinomaru* flew past our house and on to Pearl Harbor.
The canopy pulled back, I could see the pilot, navigator and
gunner laugh with glee over their sneak attack.

My heart filled with fury as I watched plane after
plane drop bombs on the Pacific Fleet, and I vowed vengeance
against my father's and my ancestors, if given an opportunity.
I had no love for them.

Chaos reigned for the next few days as the proclama-
tion of martial law altered the order of life in the Hawaiian
Islands. Gasoline and food were rationed and strict curfews
enacted. All auto headlights and taillights were masked and
blackout curtains blanked out home and business windows.
Being carpenters, George and I installed black panels to en-
close all internal lights, but heat quickly became a problem,
and fans, at a premium, rapidly sold out. We were lucky to
get one!

By Tuesday, island workers returned to their jobs.
George and I worked for the Pacific Naval Contractors building a barracks at Pearl Harbor. As we approached the main
gate, George grabbed my arm.

"Look," he said, pointing to the knot of men standing
outside the base.

Nisei workers, attempting to report for their shifts

at the shipyard, found themselves detained. Marine guards, armed with rifles, bayonets attached, challenged those with the face of our Japanese enemy. Marines ripped the badges from Nisei shirts and, rounding them up, marched them double time to busses headed for Honolulu. It was obvious that no American of Japanese ancestry would be allowed to enter any military base.

Black smoke rose above the damaged ships framing the drama in front of the gates. Anger pulsed in my veins and perspiration rolled down my forehead.

"*Baka yaro!*" I cursed our Japanese enemy under my breath. "Crazy fools!"

Realizing our impotence and humiliated by the events unfolding before us, George and I decided to return home. Our hearts filled with vengeance, we vowed to protect our American heritage from our Japanese ancestors.

After a week of stalemate, we Nisei were ordered to report to Red Hill to work on the Tripler Hospital. The marines returned our tools, previously locked up at Pearl Harbor, intact.

Life on the islands found its own rhythm, but not without periods of great sadness. Ayako, my older sister, married and living in Sacramento, died suddenly by her own hand. Young and pregnant with her first child, she was detained in a relocation camp far from her husband, where she found the loneliness and stress unbearable. Unable to stand the pain of isolation, she drank iodine to end her life and that of her unborn child. We were pleased to hear that the baby, Ken, survived, but were greatly saddened by our loss of Ayako.

In March 1943, I got my chance to serve my country. With my mother's blessing, I volunteered for the 442nd Regimental Combat Team. Knowing that my mother would display the star banner in her window with honor, I left for boot camp filled with pride. After a short stay in Schofield Barracks, we

prepared for our trip to our new home at Camp Shelby, Missis-
sippi. It was finally the Nisei's turn to show our loyalty.

We set sail on the troop ship *Lurline* in the late spring
of 1943. Our berths were located in the hot and humid bow-
els of the ship, three decks below the main deck. Gambling,
especially dice, ever prevalent on troop ships, occupied sailors
and soldiers alike, and the gamblers appeared immune to the
inhospitable temperature. Large-denomination bills lay on
the floor as we passed through the tight corridors.

The ship was also filled with practical jokers, and life
on board proved interesting. Our latrine was a stainless steel
trough with seats installed every few feet. While making a
nature call one afternoon, I noticed guys to my right jump up
and scream. Laughter broke out around me. It didn't take long
to figure out the problem. A few of the soldiers lit bundled
newspaper and dropped it into the trough of water. As the
ship rolled with the current, the paper slid along the row of
seats. One had to be quick and stand to avoid getting his rear
end sizzled.

Camp Shelby, our new home, was the hellhole of the
South. Our barracks, crude, single-walled bungalows that
housed 30 soldiers each, were heated by coal pots and venti-
lated by glassless hinged flaps that could be propped open to
air out the interior. Chiggers and snakes thrived in the inhospitable climate and created a problem for us during our time
at the bivouac.

Winter encampments during basic training got so cold
that the standard issue of two blankets per soldier proved insufficient. Pup tents, designed for one, housed three, and we
took turns sleeping in the coveted center. Water left in our
helmets for washing and brushing our teeth, froze during the
night, leaving us with useless blocks of ice in the morning.

Many of the soldiers in the 442nd Regimental Combat
Team were mainland-born, and friction developed between

them and our Nisei from Hawaii. Fights broke out between the two groups and the *Kotonks*, named for the sound of a mainlander's head when struck by a Hawaiian, frequently took a beating.

When our HQ Company was scheduled to undergo rifle firing qualification, my first sergeant, Sergeant Kariya, challenged me to a shooting competition. He offered to give me 20 points and said he would still beat me. I accepted the challenge. For five days we fired the M1 rifle. When the scores were posted on the HQ Company bulletin board, I discovered that I could have given him 20 points and still have beaten him.

"Where did you learn to shoot?" Sergeant Kariya asked me.

Embarrassed, I told him that I was on the high school rifle team.

He took the loss well and we became close friends. Shortly after our friendly competition, I was promoted to private first class and assigned as squad leader.

When our basic training drew near the end, a request went out for volunteers who could read, write and speak Japanese. Professor Daniel Buchanan warned that the mission, earmarked a "one-way street," was more hazardous than combat.

"If selected," Buchanan said, "you will be expected to live on the land, many times without help."

Over a hundred men volunteered. Twenty-three were selected.

On December 29, 1943, under a cloak of darkness, those selected for Secret Order #210 left Camp Shelby. We were ordered not to bid any of our friends goodbye. Our mission was so secret that we didn't even know what organization we worked for.

Our training for this assignment was extensive: communications, Morse code, cryptography, survival, Japanese military terms, Japanese geography, interrogation techniques and military intelligence. Nine more volunteers washed out, leaving us with four officers and ten enlisted men. When we finished, each of us was assigned a code name. My name was MAN. We worked for the newly formed OSS—Office of Strategic Services—the United States' first intelligence gathering agency and predecessor to the CIA. My unit, OSS Detachment 101 Burma, after a crash course in the Burmese language, was flown deep into the jungle behind enemy lines. Our mission was to engage in guerilla warfare, interrogate Japanese prisoners, translate captured documents and keep track of enemy troop movement. In other words, we were to keep a very close eye on the Japanese.

Since my face was that of our enemy, the radio operator, Rubio, became my constant companion. As a result, my added duty was to assist him with radio operations. Those duties included sending and receiving coded messages, which included the number of enemies killed and of our losses, which were few. We also sent messages to the Air Force, including map coordinates of heavy enemy concentration and our movements for bombing action.

Our battalion, the Second Battalion under Lt Dan Mudrinich's command, consisted of five Americans, an Anglo-Burmese interpreter and about 500 Kachin Rangers. The Kachin Rangers were natural jungle fighters. Wiry, small in stature, the tallest about 5'6", many of them were just barely teenagers. Dressed in GI issue uniforms with green caps, most found their trousers too large and held their pants up with fabric belts or clip belts, which carried ammunition and grenades. Each and every Kachin Ranger carried a sword called a dha with a square tip in an ornately decorated wooden scabbard. They used their swords like machetes to clear the jungle trails, or to cut up meat for dinner. Or for cutting up the enemy. Most of the Kachins carried a knitted pouch slung across their shoulder for ammunition or food. Generally armed with single-firing American or British 9 mm carbine weapons and tommy guns, they supplemented their arsenal with automatic British Bren guns or American BARs. None of the Kachin Rangers wore steel helmets, for they were heavy and very cumbersome in the jungles.

The Kachins shared a deep-seated hatred for the Japanese, for many of their parents and siblings had been tortured and slaughtered by Japanese soldiers. A wise Japanese soldier feared the Kachin Rangers, for they were small and daring and had no fear.

When I first got to the camp in Burma, our Kachin Rangers had just returned from a scouting patrol where they had run into some action.

"How many enemy soldiers did you kill?" I asked.

"Twenty."

Seeing my doubtful expression, they quickly pulled 20 enemy ears from their knitted pouches. From that day on, I never questioned their claims. A short time later, orders were issued to cease collecting enemy soldiers' ears as souvenirs.

Possessing the face of the enemy put me at a distinct disadvantage with the natives, but being a non-smoker served me well. I shared my ration of cigarettes with the Rangers, and they, in return, always made sure I had fresh water. Sometimes this entailed traveling many miles down the valley to fetch water. Our symbiotic relationship developed from mutual respect and a loving condition.

All our food, ammunition, weapons and cigarettes were air-dropped by parachute. Sugar, rock salt, rice and blankets were on free fall. On a normal approach, the Air Force would buzz the field, warning us that on their next pass they would drop their cargo. One day, the Air Force made a supply drop in the morning, but was unable to complete its mission. They returned several hours later. But this time they failed to follow the established procedure and commenced dropping on their first run. As we observed the plane approaching, I could clearly see that the staples were being dropped, without warning, on the field where our pack horses and mules were grazing. Several Kachin Rangers and I attempted to chase the animals away, without success. As the staples fell, we tried to take cover. It was most frightening to hide behind a large tree while bombs of food shattered against it. Three animals and three Kachin Rangers were killed that afternoon.

Living conditions were tolerable, but uncomfortable, especially during the monsoon season when constant drizzle fell day and night. Our clothing and boots stayed damp, and "jungle foot" caused relentless misery for all of us. Adding to this discomfort, we were continuously attacked by hungry bloodsucking leeches. While walking through the trail, we could see the leeches reach out, stretching on their hind ends and hoping to brush against a victim passing by. Those leeches were about one and a half inches long and would infiltrate our clothing, attacking and sucking until they grew, filled with blood, to about a half inch in diameter.

I was attacked on the side of my head behind my right ear. I couldn't feel the sucking leech, but one of my buddies spotted it. He put a cigarette to its head and got it off, but boy, did I ever bleed.

Frequently, while passing through the jungle, we would visit a village where the *Dua,* the village chief, would invite us to sleep in huts made of bamboo with grass rooftops and siding. As comfortable as it was to have beds for sleep, during the night, pigs, sleeping under the floor, would move about, lifting the flooring and rudely awakening us, not to mention scaring the life out of us. Grunts could be heard throughout the night.

When huts were not available, we slept in lean-to tents, and always with weapons at our sides. But nights were not restful for those of us deep in enemy territory. Kachin Rangers patrolled the perimeter of our camps. During the night, when the Rangers made contact with the enemy, we could hear machine gun and rifle fire. Sometimes the shooting went on for hours, as if the supply of ammunition and enemies was unlimited. In the morning, we would gratefully awake to find the enemy dead while sustaining few losses ourselves. We Americans were relatively safe inside the protected circle of our encampment, but that changed when we went out on patrol with our Kachins.

After many months in Burma, I suffered from malaria and dysentery. The Kachin Rangers rigged up a bamboo stretcher and carried me through the jungle. When I recovered, for my second mission, I requested to jump into the jungle to rejoin my squadron. Colonel Peers approved, and I was one of five Americans to parachute deep behind the enemy line. I landed in a large tree. The impact broke a five-inch limb about ten feet from the ground. I tried to extricate myself, but couldn't. Fortunately, natives near the jump site climbed the tree like monkeys, cut the risers and gently lowered me to the ground. I rewarded my rescuers with the torn chute, which they gladly accepted. I guess bowing in thanks is the universal language of gratitude.

Shortly after rejoining my unit, a Kachin Ranger was injured by the enemy. He sustained a deep wound on his right thigh. While two Rangers and I held the wounded man on a makeshift table, Doc Edwards probed the wound for shrapnel. Blood gushed out like a broken water pipe and the wounded Ranger screamed and squirmed. Since we were out of painkiller, the operation took place without anesthetic. I couldn't stomach the procedure, so I excused myself and threw up. Feeling much better, I returned to assist with the operation. After much searching, Doc Edwards located and removed the projectile and gave it to the wounded soldier, whose screams subsided to mere sobs.

When Lt Ralph Yempuku's First Battalion, situated approximately a full day's walk from our Second Battalion, requested my services, I received permission to help out. Two
squads of Kachin Rangers arrived to escort me. We reached
the First Battalion late in the afternoon. No sooner had I arrived, than Lieutenant Yempuku returned from patrol.

"A large enemy force is gathering," Yempuku reported.
"We need to return immediately to battalion headquarters."

Night soon fell, plunging the jungle into darkness so
complete it was impossible for me to see tree branches, discovering them only when they scraped against my face. We
walked so close together that soft voices easily spanned the
distance between us. My senses, on alert, sought out tigers
and snakes and other inhabitants of the Burmese jungle,
including the enemy who gathered behind us. Our troops
reached headquarters in the early morning, exhausted mentally and dead tired physically.

When headquarters deactivated OSS Detachment 101
Burma, our troops were reassigned to Detachment 202 Kun-
ming, China. Before being deactivated, the president of the
United States presented the Distinguished Unit Citation to
OSS Detachment 101 for their completed missions.

Monsoon season kept the Burma Road wet and unstable with mudslides that almost washed our jeep over the
side of a steep precipice. Our first night on the road, we were
warned not to sleep in our jeeps or on the open ground, for
tigers had been seen lurking near the camp. Just the night
before our arrival, a native, standing near the bamboo bleachers, was snatched during the showing of a movie and dragged
away into the jungle. That night we slept in an overcrowded
Rover-type van.

During the night, long after the camp settled into restless slumber, two shots rang out.

"Did you get him? Did you get him?" A young GI, eyes

round with fear, yelled from the portal of a Rover. A nervous chuckle ran through the ranks. Everyone knew that humans were the best and easiest prey for the big cats, and the memory of the missing native stirred in their thoughts.

Dinner in the camps was served cafeteria style and leftovers were dumped into a 30-gallon garbage pail. After eating my fill, I took my plate to the open area behind the mess tent. Starving Chinese peasants gathered near the garbage pail, empty cans, bowls and buckets clutched in their hands. Every now and again, a daring peasant would dart forward, stick his hand into the tub up to his elbow, seeking a bone with meat attached, and, when successful, devour it hungrily.

When I went to dump my scraps, I noticed a young, pretty Chinese mother with a small baby strapped to her back. As I watched, she peeled a grain of dried rice from the empty gallon pail she carried and fed it to the baby. Seeing this pitiful sight, I called out to her and gave her the remains of my dinner instead of dumping them into the garbage.

Bowing slightly in thanks, she made shy eye contact and smiled. However, within seconds, we were mobbed by hungry Chinese men. Pushing and shoving, they attempted to grab the plate from my hand and the food from the young woman. Pandemonium broke out as the peasants fought for scraps of discarded food.

An American GI, observing this, took out his .45 automatic and fired a shot into the air. Everyone froze; slowly the men backed away.

"You cannot feed them," the soldier said to me, his eyes reflecting the same sympathy for the Chinese people that I felt. The peasants continued to hang around the camps, for it was the only place they could get food to sustain themselves. But I never again reached out to feed them, even though my heart hurt for their plight.

At our new station, we were sent to jump school with

a contingent of Chinese soldiers. Before the completion of training, six of us were ordered to parachute into French Indochina to blow up a bridge heavily used by the Japanese military. The French military attaché's briefing sobered us.

"This mission will be very difficult," he said, looking at each of us, but avoiding direct eye contact. "Even if you successfully destroy the bridge, you will have to cross many rivers that are flooded by the monsoons. In addition, the Japanese camp is situated 20 minutes by truck from the bridge."

Again, he surveyed the group. "And if you are successful evading the Japanese and crossing the swollen rivers, you must be very careful of the Chinese bandits who occupy the surrounding area. They have no love for the Americans."

The night before our scheduled mission, the captain and I flew over the bridge to reconnoiter the area. The French Indochina attaché told the truth: the conditions were not favorable.

On the scheduled day for our jump, August 6, 1945, the first atomic bomb was dropped on Hiroshima, Japan. Three days later, the second bomb was dropped on Nagasaki. Our mission was scrubbed. The war was over. The captain and I were ordered back to Kumming, China, immediately. A new mission awaited us.

OSS Operation Magpie called for seven Americans to parachute into Japanese-occupied Peiping, China, to seek and liberate American and Allied prisoners of war before the Japanese executed them. I had never met the other men assigned to the mission. Only two of us, Lt Fontaine "Doc" Jarman Jr. and I had jumped before.

On August 17, 1945, we departed for Hsian, China. Maj Ray Nichols, Capt Edmund Carpenter II, Lt Fontaine Jarman Jr., Lt Malhon Perkins, T/5 Nester Jacot, Cpl Melvin Richter and I, Sgt Dick Hamada, climbed into a B-24.

Taking off from the Hsian airfield, the B-24 bomber,

fully loaded with bales of blankets, cigarettes and medical supplies, created an unbalanced situation. The seven team members were ordered to stand on the catwalk in the bomb bay area while the jump master stood near the cockpit. The bomb bay doors could not be fully secured. We could see the runway and were buffeted by turbulent winds and showered with pebbles and dust. It was frightening, for we could not shield our faces since we found ourselves hanging on to the frame of the B-24 for dear life. I surmised this situation to being similar to a tornado, only we had a place to hang on.

We reached Peiping around five in the afternoon. Since Lieutenant Jarman and I were the only two with parachute training, we decided that he would jump first, followed by the rest of us. I took up the rear. The jump master released handfuls of leaflets informing the Japanese soldiers and citizens that the Americans parachuting into Peiping were seeking American and Allied prisoners of war. The leaflets fluttered about the plane, hitting us in the face like drunken bats.

When the jump master instructed us to prepare to jump, we secured our harnesses to the aircraft and sat around the opening, where the belly turret gun had been removed for our mission.

"Good luck!" the jump master yelled as Lieutenant Jarman departed the plane. One by one the others followed.

I watched as six chutes blossomed and drifted silently below the opening.

"Happy hunting!" the jump master said, as I dropped through the belly, keeping the others in sight.

It was like watching a movie. Six chutes gracefully drifted on the currents below me. Two Japanese fighters taxied on the runway but did not lift to the sky to challenge us. Soldiers scrambled double time in an attempt to surround our team as each member touched down and, fighting a steady, hot breeze, began gathering his half-bloomed chute.

A shot rang out and we all hit the deck.

Finally, standing up, I looked around. Thankfully, no one had been hit. A truck, carrying a squad of Japanese soldiers and the lieutenant in command, flew a white flag as it approached our team.

"What is going on here?" the lieutenant asked. I translated the Japanese into English.

"The war is over," Major Nichols said, "and we're here to retrieve our prisoners."

"No! The war is *not* over yet!" the lieutenant shouted.

He surveyed the members of our team. Aware of the armed soldiers surrounding us, I stood tall, nervous but hiding my fear, I looked him straight in the eye. As we locked eyes, the bomber continued to drop the parachute cargo and the free-fall blankets. American supplies littered the airfield. After all the supplies were released, the pilot buzzed us and flew home.

"Come with me," the lieutenant ordered, indicating that Major Nichols, Lieutenant Perkins and I should join the squad in the back of the flatbed truck.

"Tell the others to stay here," he said to me.

"You guys wait here," I said to the four members still on the ground.

"Where the hell can we go?" Doc asked, surveying the littered airfield.

In the meantime, speaking out of turn, I asked the lieutenant if his men would assist us in gathering the supplies, which were strung from one end of the airfield to the other.

"Japanese soldiers do not work for the Americans!" he answered, looking me directly in the eyes.

"What about the Chinese workers?" I persisted.

"Hmm," he replied noncommittally.

Nichols, Perkins and I climbed into the back of the truck. As we started out, the tire hit a rut in the road, bouncing us around. A soldier, standing next to Major Nichols, accidentally lost his balance and his bayonet inflicted a small scratch on the major's neck. It started to bleed. The soldier, embarrassed and fearful, offered no apology.

Nichols reached up, touched the wound, and then examined the blood on his fingers.

Realizing that the major did not have a handkerchief with him, I reached in my pocket, pulled out mine and offered it to him. He did not thank me. Instead, he pressed the cloth against the wound.

"Now you've earned your Purple Heart," I said to the major. A chorus of snickers erupted from the soldiers surrounding us. The major's eyes flashed, but he did not reply.

Reaching airport headquarters, the officer of the day, a Japanese major, escorted us into a conference room.

"We have come to secure the release of the American and Allied prisoners," Major Nichols told the major. I translated his words.

"Ah," he replied, "you must speak to General Takahashi. He is on his way over now."

"Major," I said, pulling his attention away from Nichols, "would your men please help us gather and transport our supplies?"

The major turned to the lieutenant who had earlier refused my request. "Have your men gather the American supplies and deliver them to the hotel."

The lieutenant caught my eye. I read the fury and frustration in his features. I knew if looks were deadly, my days would have ended in that room. I broke away and hid my smile. The lieutenant had lost face, but I didn't want to make the situation worse for him.

When the remaining four of our team members joined us, the major offered us tea. The tea did not sit well with us, for we were all perspiring.

General Takahashi's arrival was met with much clicking of heels and saluting. We stood as the general entered and waited to be introduced.

"We have come to secure the release of all American and Allied prisoners of war," Major Nichols told the general.

"I see," the general responded with a slight inclination of his head. "But orders for their release must come from Supreme Headquarters in Nanking."

"I'm sure," he continued, "that they will be released within a day or two. I ask you to be patient."

There was nothing left to do but wait. The general told us of his visit to New York and his favorable impression of the tall buildings, including the Empire State Building. He expressed a desire to return to the States at a future date. But he would do nothing about the release of the prisoners without orders from above. Our business with the general was over for the day.

Our team would be housed in the Wagons-Lits Hotel, our transportation already arranged. As we left the airfield headquarters with the general in the lead, a shot rang out. The general's limousine stopped and he stepped out and scanned the area. Everywhere we looked, soldiers stood at attention facing the general.

The sun had set and the night sky was turning dark. "If you had jumped at this hour," he casually reported to us, "all of you would have been killed." A chill ran down my back. I'm sure every soldier there would have liked to put a bullet in our heads and would have had our timing been just a little off.

We soon arrived at the hotel. I looked around the lobby. It was spacious and clean. A line of civilians formed at the registration counter. I assumed they had been forced to vacate to make room for us and, eventually, the prisoners.

After the others were settled in, Technician 5 Jacot and I still had work to do. Two gendarmes guided us to the ra-

dio shack in a small bungalow across from the hotel. We set up
our radio equipment and sent our message to headquarters.

"We've landed safely and are well treated. But the prisoner release has been put on hold, signed Major Nichols."

Our message sent, Jacot and I returned to our rooms
to wait.

On the morning of August 20, 1945, a Japanese team
consisting of several officers, an interpreter and the Swiss
consul general arrived at Major Nichols's quarters.

Finally, the prisoners would be released. I could feel
the blood pumping in my veins. This was the day I had been
waiting for, since that first day in Hawaii when Japanese
planes flew by my home and let loose their bombs of destruction on Pearl Harbor and I vowed vengeance against our enemy. Today spelled the true end of the war and my heart was
filled with pride as I prepared for the release of our soldiers
and sailors and airmen.

Our team members prepared to go, but as we started
for the vehicles, Major Nichols turned to the enlisted men on
the team.

"You three wait here at the hotel."

Dumbfounded, I stared at him.

"I have ample space in my van," the Swiss consul general told Nichols.

The three officers on our team joined in with pleas of
their own, but Nichols was adamant. We were to wait at the
hotel.

With much cursing and swearing, the three of us
watched the convoy pull out. Were we not part of the team?
Was this not the day we'd been waiting for? I thought of my
comment about the major earning his Purple Heart. Could
the man be that shallow? I'd never find out.

Within a very short time, the group returned with
about 50 American, Australian, British and Canadian prison-

ers. Among them were four of the Doolittle Raiders, Lt Chase Nielsen, Lt George Barr, Cpl Jacob DeShazer and Lt Robert "Bobby" Hite. That evening's message to headquarters included the good news about the discovery and release of the Raiders. Headquarters forwarded the message to Doolittle. I'm sure Doolittle slept well that night.

On the evening before their departure, we gave the prisoners a party. Words of praise and thanks echoed in the banquet hall, followed by handshakes and embraces. I felt good to see the happy faces of the liberated and lucky to be in the right spot at the right time.

The morning after the prisoners were sent home, Major Nichols, standing in the window of his hotel room, barely missed being hit by a sniper's bullet. We could hear the crack of the bullet as it ricocheted off the walls of his hotel room.

"Did you hear that?" the major exclaimed as he burst into our room.

Technician 5 Jacot, Corporal Richter and I just looked at him. Not one of us said a word. After the major left, the three of us had our good laugh.

A day later, Japanese soldiers escorted our team to the prison. We found the cells immaculate with a heavy trace of Lysol, but were shocked to learn that eight-by-eight-foot cells, with nothing more than primitive wood-covered holes cut in the corner for nature calls, housed 10 prisoners each. No running water, no heating during the freezing cold winter months or air conditioning in the summer heat.

On November 8, 1945, Sgt Fumio Kido and I boarded the troop ship USS *General Adolphus Washington Greely*, in Calcutta, India, and, after several stops along the way, we arrived in the port of New York on December 5, 1945. As I gazed upon the Statue of Liberty, I remembered Pearl Harbor and the intervening years of war. I was proud of my American citizenship and of my service to my country. And I still am.

After the war, Dick went to work in the shipyards at Pearl Harbor, first as a fire control mechanic and then working his way up to the planning department, where he was the supervisor of electronic and fire control. He retired in 1978. In 2001, he was reunited with three of the four Doolittle Raiders that he helped rescue from a Japanese prisoner of war camp. He is still in contact with Bobby Hite, the only surviving Raider from that group. Dick and Irene have two children and four grandchildren. Dick and Irene live in Honolulu, Hawaii

Decorations and Awards: Two Bronze Stars; Soldier's Medal; Good Conduct Medal; "Special Breast Order Yun Hui" from the National Republic of China; Combat Infantryman Medal; Two Jump Wings; Marksman, HS Rifle Team; Promarksman, HS Rifle Team; Sharpshooter, HS Rifle Team, NRA, FFA, and 4H Club

NICK MORAMARCO

SHELL SHOCK

B-17s are not supposed to fall from the sky, but mine was hurling toward the earth at a rate that rendered bailout impossible. Lying against the tail wheel, a gaping hole where my guns once sat and a large section of the tail missing, completely blown away by enemy fire, I fought the encroaching mental darkness. A kaleidoscope of recent memory spun out of control along with the plane.

"Fighter at seven o'clock!"

I scanned the sky from behind my .50-caliber machine guns in the tail of the *Lucky Lady*, a lumbering Flying Fortress and real combat veteran of over 70 missions. Fifty or 60 German fighters swarmed like angry hornets from a fiery hive inside the sun and, guns blazing, converged on the squadron.

I fired back, but the enemy was all over the place. One by one, B-17s, engines on fire and trailing smoke, fell from the sky. Everywhere I looked, Germans dominated the horizon. Chaos prevailed.

"Fighter at seven o'clock," I yelled, firing burst after

burst at the encroaching plane, but the bullets seemed to bounce off the German aircraft. I couldn't believe the fighter could take so many hits and remain undamaged. But it continued to come, closer and closer, until I could imagine counting the pilot's teeth in his death grin of triumph beneath his mask.

I pulled the trigger again, shooting a hail of bullets at the oncoming plane, but like projectiles ricocheting off the pages of a Superman comic book, the barrage of bullets bounced off the fighter.

Determined in my defense of the *Lucky Lady*, I gripped and fired, even as I watched a bright flash erupt from the German cannon. I felt the impact. My machine guns exploded in my hands. I came to on my back, lying against the tail wheel. The wind howled as it rushed through the mortally wounded plane.

"Bail out!" My headset inoperable, I could barely hear the pilot's voice over the howl of the wind. "I've lost control of the plane!"

I lay pinned against the tail wheel, my back an inferno of pain, my arms lifeless at my sides. I tried to move, but my body refused to respond. Heart pounding, I waited for someone to crawl to the back of the plane to help me, but no one came. I lay there listening to the rush of wind. With the in-house radio system damaged beyond use, I couldn't call for help nor could I hear anyone who might try to contact me. Without the ability to communicate, there was no way to let my crewmates know that I needed help. No one came back to see if I was okay.

"They must think I'm dead," I thought as I lay motionless, listening to the wind. I remembered the strange feeling I'd had that morning as we taxied down the runway for take-off: a conviction that I would not come back from this mission, that we would not finish this run. Lucky thirteenth mission, on December 31st—the last day of 1944. For some unexplained reason, I believed it would be my last.

The plane began to vibrate and went into a steep spin, diving toward the ground. I could hardly breathe. The plane whirled around and around, the motion making me nauseous and disoriented as it spun out of control, hurling toward the frozen earth beneath me. The flying conditions were miserable and dangerous. The temperature dipped to 60 degrees below zero at 30,000 feet—so cold that the windows froze, making visibility impossible, and a man's sweat inside his heavy clothes could lead to frostbite.

"Goodbye, Mom," I whispered as images from my life flashed before me.

"Goodbye, Marie. I love you," I thought about the woman I wanted to marry.

"God help me," I prayed. Marie was everything I ever wanted in a woman . . . tears froze on my face as I acknowledged the nagging fear that I would never see her again.

The plane kept plunging toward the ground. I began to feel light-headed . . . dizzy. Centrifugal force pinned me to the floor—I couldn't move.

Suddenly, the B-17 began to slow its descent and level out. An intense silence lay beneath the howling wind.

"Nick, if you're going to survive, you'd better get out of this airplane, and you'd better do it now," a silent voice whispered inside my head.

Using every ounce of strength and determination, I scooted, inch by inch, toward my parachute. With my arms still numb, I fumbled, finally snapping the chute onto my chest, and then inched over to the escape hatch. As I kicked it open, pain shot through my damaged arms. With great determination, I stuck my legs through the hatch and bailed out.

Cold air rushed past my body as I fell through the December night. Counting slowly to 10, I reached up and pulled

the ripcord. Nothing happened. I looked at the red handle in
my hand with disbelief. Falling faster and faster, I grabbed
the flap of my chute and ripped it open.

★ ★ ★ ★

I sat bolt upright in bed, sweat pouring down my neck and
chest. The nightmares were just one of the reminders of the
war that kept me company in the wee hours of the morning.
The tips of three fingers and the thumb on my right hand,
blown off when my guns exploded, remained tangible reminders, as were the three missing fingers on my left hand. The 18
pieces of shrapnel I'd unwittingly collected as souvenirs from
the war were still embedded in my arms . . . a painful barom-
eter forecasting changes in the humidity. And my back, broken in four places either during the explosion or bailout—I
wasn't sure which—still caused me intermittent pain, especially when waking up from bad dreams.

As I watched the news reports from the Gulf War, my
nightmares increased in frequency and intensity. An American flyer, CWO Guy L. Hunter, had been shot down and taken
prisoner. I couldn't help but wonder how the young airman
was faring in enemy hands.

I suffered a near meltdown as I watched those reports.
Marie, anxious and concerned, insisted I get treatment. I ended up with a psychiatrist.

"What kind of treatment did you receive when you got
home?" the doctor asked.

"Well, we spent two weeks at the Miramar in Santa
Barbara. It was restful, but that's about all I can say about it,"
I rambled on.

"The lectures we attended were a joke. There were 200
people sitting in an auditorium, and everyone was talking at
once. It took so much time to quiet everyone down that there

wasn't much time left to discuss the problems we were having," I shook my head, remembering how naive we were about that haunting aftermath of the war.

"We didn't really know what was going on. There was no personal counseling, and there was no time for questions. The one thing we did get was plenty of rest."

"What you're experiencing is not uncommon," said the doctor. "Today, we'd call it post-traumatic stress disorder."

"Good old fashioned shell shock," I reported to Marie. Almost 50 years had passed since those traumatic days. Almost 50 years, and the war still hadn't ended for me . . . not yet.

So I followed the doctor's orders and wrote about my experiences.

Proud of my service, I believed in America's role in WWII. God only knew what the world would have been like if we hadn't joined our allies against such overwhelming evil.

But I often wondered how many people died by my hands, how much blood stained these broken fingers. God plucked me from that plunging plane and gave me a second chance at life. I vowed that chance wouldn't be wasted. So I woke from the nightmares and placed one foot in front of the other, every day, asking for nothing more than a good life with Marie and the opportunity to serve my fellow man.

They lost five planes that fateful day . . . all from the 728th Squadron. Eleven men died on that mission to Hamburg. They were all brave men who gave their lives for what they believed to be a just cause.

I struggled with forgiveness.

I struggled to forgive the flight leader in the low squadron of the bomber group Green Low for failing to follow orders. A leader was expected to yield his position to his deputy when his engines failed to perform to specs. That pilot's disregard for military procedure caused my squadron to fall behind and lose their fighter cover. We were sitting ducks for the Luftwaffe.

I struggled to forgive the Germans.

My body still remembered the numbing cold as I stood in stocking feet for six hours in weather that must have been 10 degrees below zero, waiting for a train to transport the American POWs to prison camps deep in German territory.

My captivity turned into a series of moves, just steps ahead of the Allied forces. We moved every time the Allies got close. North to avoid the Americans, south to avoid the British, west to avoid the Russians, back and forth, back and forth.

My most disturbing dreams centered on the cattle cars hauling human cargo. Cold shivers run up my spine when I remembered those Jewish prisoners. Men and women clothed in identical blue and white vertical-striped pajamas constructed from coarse, cheap fabric, much like prison uniforms. Crammed in open boxcars, those emaciated, filthy unfortunates stood in their own waste, like livestock on the way to the slaughterhouse. There was no room to sit or lay down; body pressed against body, they stood immobile. I will never forget that smell. Sweat, urine, feces, fear. Or the people, who stared out at the world sadly, with sunken eyes expecting certain death.

I heard stories about the German persecution of the Jewish people, but to witness it with my own eyes eclipsed any tale I'd ever heard. Those poor souls had been denied sufficient food and water for what must have been weeks. And when the train stopped to disconnect the cattle cars, the site burned into my memory forever. An area surrounded by barbed wire . . . the stench overwhelming. The compound looked like a military camp of some kind, with men and women and children in striped pajama-like prison garb, matching the Jews in the cattle cars at the back of the train. I didn't need the sign that read "DACHAU" to realize that this was one of the infamous Nazi death camps, the Germans' "Final Solution" to the Jewish problem.

The stench of burning bodies filled the air.

"It is a terrible thing they do here!" the German guards said.

Those unfortunate victims of Hitler's ultimate evil looked at the Americans through the prison wire. Their eyes told the whole story of what was taking place in the collection of rough buildings and smokestacks.

The train pulled away slowly, leaving the overstuffed boxcars behind. I watched the people cling to the fence as the train passed by. The look of despair and defeat and great sadness hung on their faces.

I knew the Germans couldn't hold out too much longer when I saw columns of Nazi soldiers in full dress uniforms, the packs on their back so heavy that they leaned forward in an attempt to keep themselves from falling over. They couldn't have been more that 12 years old.

I knew the end of the war was imminent when the fighting drew close to Stalag VI, our prison camp in Bavaria. The guards were uneasy and ordered us inside.

"The Americans are coming," one guard told us that night. "We have orders to shoot you."

"We can't shoot all of you," another guard said, shrugging his shoulders. "We don't have enough bullets."

During the night all but the SS guards at the gate disappeared into the surrounding countryside.

I awoke to the sound of guns; first the rapid fire of machine guns, then the boom of cannons, followed by silence.

Moments later, I heard the rumbling engines of tanks and ran out of the barracks. Two columns of Sherman tanks rolled down the main street of camp. A jeep carrying Gen George S. Patton led the way. What a sight! Three stars on his helmet; two .45-caliber, ivory-handled automatics on his hips; and a smile lighting up his face.

Patton's Fourteenth Division had come to liberate the prisoners and I was going home.

Whenever I think about what went on in the concentration camps, depression closes in on my mind and tears threaten to spill from my eyes. I witnessed something terrible and inhuman, and there was nothing I could do about it. Yes, I tried to forgive the Germans . . . but I will never forget.

Knowing that I had post-traumatic stress disorder didn't change me, just as the war never fully left me. The nightmares continued, but, with help from my doctor, their frequency decreased. On dark days, I wondered about those who fell under my guns. It didn't stop me from loving my family, being a productive member of the community, or giving whatever I could to the nation I loved.

Marie and I got on with our lives. I believed the Lord had put me on this earth for a purpose and I hoped that I was serving Him well.

I received a medal for being a prisoner of war. I received eight commendations for serving this country that I am so proud to have served. They didn't bring back my fingers or make things right, but sometimes they helped. I prayed that my sacrifices would keep future generations from having to witness the horrors and brutalities of this world. I wished that they would never have to know the nightmares of war.

Nick married Marie Santiago, his high school sweetheart, in 1945, just four weeks after returning from prison camp. After a short period of time working for his father on the family farm, Nick went to work for Los Angeles County. He retired after 27 years. Nick volunteered for various organizations, including the Elks Lodge, Native Sons of the Golden West, the local hospital and the Civitan Foundation. Nick passed away on February 11, 2008. He and Marie have one daughter. Marie lives in Temple City, California.

BIBLIOGRAPHY

Baker, Ruth. *Eyewitnesses Speak Out Against Denial*. Germany: Verlag Marg.Wehle, Witterschlick/Bonn, 1996.

Baudot, Marcel, Henri Bernard, Hendrik Brugmans, Michael Foot, R.D., and Hans-Adolph Jacobson. *The Historical Encyclopedia of World War II*. New York: Facts on File, Inc., 1980.

Carruth, Gorton. *The Encyclopedia of American Facts and Dates*. New York: HarperCollins, 1993.

Colman, Penny. *Rosie the Riveter*. New York: Crown Publishers, Inc., 1995.

Cooke, Alistair. *The American Home Front: 1941–1942*. New York: Grove Press, 2006.

Coss, Wes. *Stardust Falling*. Torrance, CA: A-1 Printing & Graphics, Inc., 2007.

Daley-Brusselmans, Yvonne. *Belgium Rendes-Vous 127: Revisited*. Manhattan, KS: Sunflower University Press, 2001.

Doolittle, James H. *I Could Never Be So Lucky Again*. New York: Bantam Books, 1991.

Fessler, Diane Burke. *No Time For Fear*. East Lansing, MI: Michigan State University Press, 1996.

"Freeman Field Mutiny." Wikipedia. http://en.wikipedia.org/
wiki/Freeman Field_Mutiny.

Gawne, Jonathan. *Finding Your Father's War*. Philadelphia:
Casemate, 2006.

Glines, Carroll V. *Four Came Home*. Missoula, MT: Pictorial
Histories Publishing Company, Inc., 1996.

Hoover, R. A. "Bob." *Forever Flying*. New York: Pocket Books,
1996.

Moramarco, Nick. *Missing In Action*. Santa Barbara, CA:
Fithian Press, 1998.

Smith, Jean Reeder, and Lacy Baldwin Smith. *Essentials of
World History*. Woodbury, NY: Barron's Educational Series,
Inc., 1966.

"Stalag Luft 3." Second Generation Research. http://b24.net.

Szurovy, Geza, and Mike Goulian. *Basic Aerobatics*. New York:
McGraw-Hill Tab Books, 1994.

Warren, James C. *The Freeman Field Mutiny*. San Rafael, CA:
Donna Ewald, 1995.

Watson, C. Hoyt. *DeShazer*. Winona Lake, IN: Light and Life
Press, 2002.

Yanak, Ted, and Pam Cornelison. *The Great American History
Fact-Finder*. Boston: Houghton Mifflin, 1993.

INDEX

"A personal account of a very public man."
—*Booklist*

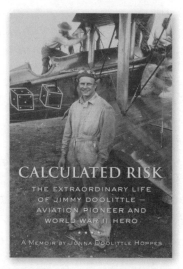

CALCULATED RISK
The Extraordinary Life of Jimmy Doolittle—
Aviation Pioneer and World War II Hero

A Memoir by Jonna Doolittle Hoppes

In 1942, Jimmy Doolittle led the Tokyo Raid ("Thirty Seconds Over Tokyo")—America's first strike against Japan, and the event that changed the course of World War II.

Although best known for the Raid, Doolittle's contributions to aviation had an even greater impact on history. He was a scientist with a doctorate in Aeronautical Engineering from MIT, an aviation pioneer, a barnstormer well known for aerobatics, a popular racing pilot, and a four-star general. The Air and Space Centennial Issue lists Doolittle as number one on the list of the top ten "most important aviators," and a section of the Smithsonian Air and Space Museum is dedicated to him.

Calculated Risk is a firsthand account written by his granddaughter that brings readers inside the public and private world of Jimmy Doolittle and his family and sheds light on the drives and motivation of one of America's greatest heroes. The book also features many never-before-seen photographs from the Doolittle Library archives.